ROUTLEDGE LIBRARY EDITIONS: THE AMERICAN NOVEL

Volume 7

ANNOTATIONS TO WILLIAM FAULKNER'S 'THE HAMLET'

ANNOTATIONS TO WILLIAM FAULKNER'S 'THE HAMLET'

Annotated by
CATHERINE D. HOLMES

LONDON AND NEW YORK

First published in 1996 by Garland Publishing, Inc.

This edition first published in 2018
by Routledge
2 Park Square, Milton Park, Abingdon, Oxon OX14 4RN

and by Routledge
711 Third Avenue, New York, NY 10017

Routledge is an imprint of the Taylor & Francis Group, an informa business

© 1996 Catherine D. Holmes

All rights reserved. No part of this book may be reprinted or reproduced or utilised in any form or by any electronic, mechanical, or other means, now known or hereafter invented, including photocopying and recording, or in any information storage or retrieval system, without permission in writing from the publishers.

Trademark notice: Product or corporate names may be trademarks or registered trademarks, and are used only for identification and explanation without intent to infringe.

British Library Cataloguing in Publication Data
A catalogue record for this book is available from the British Library

ISBN: 978-1-138-09946-3 (Set)
ISBN: 978-1-351-25544-8 (Set) (ebk)
ISBN: 978-1-138-57270-6 (Volume 7) (hbk)
ISBN: 978-1-138-57272-0 (Volume 7) (pbk)
ISBN: 978-0-203-70187-4 (Volume 7) (ebk)

Publisher's Note
The publisher has gone to great lengths to ensure the quality of this reprint but points out that some imperfections in the original copies may be apparent.

Disclaimer
The publisher has made every effort to trace copyright holders and would welcome correspondence from those they have been unable to trace.

Annotations to William Faulkner's
THE HAMLET

Annotated by
Catherine D. Holmes

Garland Publishing, Inc.
New York & London
1996

Copyright © 1996 by Catherine D. Holmes
All rights reserved

Library of Congress Cataloging-in-Publication Data

Holmes, Catherine D.
    Annotations to William Faulkner's The hamlet / Catherine D. Holmes.
    p. cm. — (William Faulkner, annotations to the novels) (Garland reference library of the humanities ; vol. 1966)
    Includes bibliographical references.
    ISBN 0-8153-2277-1 (alk. paper)
    1. Faulkner, William, 1897–1962. Hamlet. I. Title. II. Series. III. Series: Garland reference library of the humanities ; vol. 1966.
PS3511.A86H44   1996
813'.52—dc20   95-41196
                                                                 CIP

Printed on acid-free, 250-year-life paper
Manufactured in the United States of America

Contents

Acknowledgments vii

Abbreviations ix

Preface by Series Editor xiii

Introduction 1

Annotations 7

Works Cited 209

Acknowledgments

I owe debts of gratitude to many people for their direct and indirect help in completing this project. First, I would like to thank Professor James B. Meriwether for his guidance throughout the research and for his friendship. It has been a great source of pride to me to work with Professor Meriwether, who knows more about Faulkner, I am convinced, than anyone on the planet and who has led the field of Faulkner scholarship for nearly forty years. I am particularly grateful for Professor Meriwether's generosity in continuing to direct my dissertation after his retirement. I would also like to thank another great teacher, Dr. Nan Morrison, without whose encouragement and friendship I would never have gone on to graduate work. I continue to be inspired by Dr. Morrison's scholarship, dedication, and enthusiasm. Thanks are also due to Drs. Keen Butterworth, Patrick Scott, and Kevin Lewis for their careful reading of this work.

On a more personal level, I must thank my parents for their love and support and for the greatest gift of all: a happy childhood. To my sister, Mary Pat Walker, thanks for putting up with me as a roommate and for all her other kindnesses over the years. I made the best decision of my life in marrying Allan Holmes and cannot begin to thank him in this context for his many sacrifices, his good cheer, and his love. Perhaps I should thank him most for providing me with Nini and Dada, the best parents-in-law anywhere. Finally, I could not ask for more considerate, fun, and loveable children than Riley and Anna.

Abbreviations

Works by Faulkner

AbAb!	*Absalom, Absalom!*
AILD	*As I Lay Dying*
"Barn"	"Barn Burning"
"Centaur"	"Centaur in Brass"
CS	*Collected Stories*
EPP	*Early Prose and Poetry*
ESPL	*Essays, Speeches, and Public Letters*
Fab	*A Fable*
FA	*Father Abraham*
FU	*Faulkner in The University*
Flags	*Flags in the Dust*
"Fool"	"Fool About a Horse"
GDM	*Go Down, Moses*
GB	*A Green Bough*
Ham	*The Hamlet*
Intruder	*Intruder in the Dust*
KG	*Knight's Gambit*
LA	*Light in August*

LG	Lion in the Garden
"Lizards"	"Lizards in Jamshyd's Courtyard"
Mans	The Mansion
MF	The Marble Faun
Mosq	Mosquitoes
NOS	New Orleans Sketches
Reiv	The Reivers
Req	Requiem For a Nun
Sanc	Sanctuary
Sanc OT	Sanctuary: The Original Text
Sart	Sartoris
SL	Selected Letters
SP	Soldiers' Pay
S&F	The Sound and the Fury
Twn	The Town
US	Uncollected Stories
Unv	The Unvanquished
"Unvanq"	"The Unvanquished"
WP	The Wild Palms

Other Works

AHD	*American Heritage Dictionary of the English Language*
Brewer's	*Brewer's Dictionary of Phrase and Fable*
Brodsky	*A Comprehensive Guide to the Brodsky Collection II*
DARE	*Dictionary of American Regional English*
DNB	*Dictionary of National Biography*
Literary	*The Literary Career of William Faulkner*

Preface by Series Editor

The annotations in the volumes of this series are intended to assist the reader of Faulkner's novels to understand obscure or difficult words and passages, including literary allusions, dialect, and historical events that Faulkner uses or alludes to in the twenty works included. The scope of these annotations varies, necessarily, from volume to volume. But throughout the series the goal has been to provide useful, brief explanations or definitions for what may be puzzling in Faulkner's text.

Obviously what is puzzling to one reader may be clear to another, and these annotations are provided for a varied and changing audience. For many readers today, especially those from the American South, explanations of dialect words and spellings may be unnecessary. The same may be true of many of the historical and geographical annotations. But with the passage of time, a steadily increasing percentage of Faulkner's readers will need help with such points, and what may be foreign today only to Faulkner's readers from other countries, will be increasingly foreign to American readers in the years to come.

Though the annotations have usually been kept brief, each volume is intended to be inclusive, and useful independently of the others. As a rule words that can be found in standard unabridged dictionaries are not annotated, but this rule has not been followed consistently. Usefulness and clarity rather than consistency have been the criteria for this series.

The pioneering work in this field was Calvin Brown's *A Glossary of Faulkner's South* (Yale University Press, 1976). Though our volumes obviously can go into very much greater detail than could Professor Brown's book, almost every volume in this series is indebted to his more substantially than the acknowledgments for individual annotations can show. Even when we have expanded, corrected, or disagreed with him, we have always been conscious of how much this series owes to his knowledge and his labors.

All those involved in this project are fully aware that no such endeavor can ever be complete or definitive. Further close reading of Faulkner's texts and further study of his sources and influences will reveal new allusions. Further linguistic research will provide additional information about his use of dialect. Such progress in the study of Faulkner will be never-ending, with obvious consequences for such reference works as these. Accordingly, in order to correct and update the information provided in these volumes, there will be a regular department in the *Mississippi Quarterly* devoted to notes and queries, addenda and corrigenda, concerning these annotations.

J.B.M.

Introduction

The Hamlet represents Faulkner's genius at its peak: funny, fantastic, passionate, profound, tragic, and true. Faulkner's imagination soars in this great novel like one of his own unreined hobgoblin horses. The vigor and originality come from a mature writer who knows what he can do and who does not stint in doing it. In compiling these annotations, I have been aware of the impossibility of explaining, or reining in, true genius. Faulkner was an omnivorous reader who acknowledged a debt to many of his literary predecessors, but the scope and depth of his achievement cannot be suggested by a compendium of analogues, quotes, and echoes from other works. It is my aim, then, not to reduce Faulkner to the sum of his sources, but through identification of sources, to expand and illuminate understanding of his art.

In an early essay on Eugene O'Neill's drama, Faulkner wrote, "It is not especially difficult--after a man has written and passed on--to trace the threads which were drawn together by him and put on paper in the form of his own work" (*EPP*, "American Drama: Eugene O'Neill" 86-87). Faulkner underestimates the complexity of this kind of endeavor. Regarding his own work, the difficulty of tracing the threads lies not only in their assimilation into the fabric of his narrative but also in their number and variety. Faulkner often insisted that the best way to learn the craft of writing is to study great literature, and his own work certainly bears this out. If a writer will, as he told Jean Stein in the *Paris Review* interview, "rob his mother" (*Lion in the Garden* 239) for art, he will also rob any number of other sources as well to get the story told.

The backbone of Faulkner's literary borrowing comes from the reading he did as a child and as an impressionable young man. His family's library was stocked with the nineteenth-century classics: Balzac, Dickens, Scott. He picked up Dostoyevsky, Tolstoy, Hardy, and Conrad early. *The Hamlet* reflects the social emphasis and the impulse toward inclusivity of these nineteenth-century forebears. In selecting *The Peasants* as the working title of the novel, Faulkner tipped his hat to Balzac, whose novel *Les Paysans* offers a similarly unromantic view of the rural poor. Balzac's novels, like Faulkner's Snopes material, take place in a world where values are often defined and measured economically. Flem Snopes makes his appearance in Faulkner's first attempt to tell the Snopes story, glimpsed "behind the new plate glass window of his recently remodelled bank" (*FA* 13). The language of finance continues to dominate later versions of the story; references to dowries, notes, debts, deals, prices, value, and worth proliferate. Direct borrowings from Dickens are less obvious, but one senses the Dickensian comic spirit and exaggerated characterization in *The Hamlet*. Hardy, like Faulkner, wrote at a time of social upheaval. Both artists register historical changes in their native regions, both present a world that is often at odds with human ambitions and desires, and both locate possibilities for heroism in endurance and acceptance of fate.

The romantic, Victorian, and fin-de-siècle poets were favorite sources of allusion, as were the modernists. When Faulkner sets out to convey the irony and difficulty of love in a sterile environment, for instance, he chooses to chronicle the pursuit of a cow by an idiot in the most lush, overblown, highly allusive language imaginable. Mythological associations with Io and connections to medieval quest narratives, probably as filtered through Weston and Eliot, converge with Keatsian and Swinburnian allusions to celebrate the union. Faulkner dramatizes Eula's allure with the same sort of allusive overlay. A goddess, certainly, she is Venus, Lilith, Brünhilde, and Helen grafted onto such domestic sweethearts as Irving's Katrina von Tassel and G. W. Harris's Sicily Burns.

What is fascinating, and complicating, in an annotative study of *The Hamlet* is Faulkner's dedication to the Snopes material over the span of his career. *The Hamlet* itself was begun in the 1920's. That aborted effort, *Father Abraham*, was not published until James B. Meriwether edited the manuscript in 1983 but was probably written in late 1926 (Meriwether, "Introduction"). The next year, Faulkner abandoned the Snopes book to work on another project, *Flags in the Dust*, which was published in considerably weakened and abridged form as *Sartoris* in 1929. If he laid aside *Father Abraham*, he did not forget the clan he invented there. Flem Snopes, Byron Snopes, and Montgomery Ward Snopes appear in *Sartoris*; I.O. shows up in *The Sound and the Fury*; *As I Lay Dying* mentions Flem's spotted horses; Virgil and Clarence Snopes appear in *Sanctuary*; and Ab plays a role in *The Unvanquished*. Over the years, Faulkner continued to take up and put down again his Snopes book, producing "Spotted Horses," "The Hound," "Lizards in Jamshyd's Courtyard," "Mule in the Yard," "Centaur in Brass," and "Fool About a Horse," all stories which eventually were incorporated into the trilogy.

In January 1934, he insisted that the Snopes material would not "lie quiet" (*SL* 78), only to announce the next month that he was writing instead a novel called *Dark House*, which was to become *Absalom, Absalom!* (*SL* 78). The short story, "Wash," which was originally intended for the Snopes book, went instead into *Absalom, Absalom!*. Finally, in 1938, according to his later recollection, Faulkner set out to write "an induction toward the spotted horse story" (*SL* 197), "Barn Burning," and to expand and structure the existing Snopes stories into a novel. That novel, minus the "Barn Burning" prologue, and augmented by the addition of the Ike Snopes love story and the rivalry between Jack Houston and Mink Snopes, was published as *The Hamlet* in 1940.

The Hamlet benefits from the maturity Faulkner gained between his initial attempt at the material and his completion of the story. While *Father Abraham* is an accomplished piece of work--certainly superior to most apprentice work--it is the product of a young man, and its outstanding asset is a broadly comic rendering of a compelling tale. Faulkner saw both the poor whites of Frenchman's Bend and the Snopeses as types and forces when he began what would become *The Hamlet*. By the time he finished it, his sympathies had deepened so that he could embrace the heroic qualities of a Mink Snopes or understand the grinding hopelessness of a life like Henry Armstid's. The world of *The Hamlet* is considered mean by most standards, yet Faulkner elevates it to mythic stature.

Many of these annotations reflect the reciprocal relationship between *The Hamlet* and other Faulkner works over the length of its composition. Always given to echoings and borrowings of his own work, Faulkner was even more inclined in *The Hamlet* to reflect themes and characters that he took up almost simultaneously. Class permeability--the movement up or down the social ladder--was a favorite subject at this period, from *Flags in the Dust* through *The Sound and the Fury* to *Absalom, Absalom!*. Both Flem Snopes and Thomas Sutpen, for instance, rise out of poverty to positions of prominence, only to be murdered by people they have stepped on along the way. *The Wild Palms*, like *The Hamlet*, considers the possibilities for love in a reduced world and the struggle for, and limits on, individual freedom. *Go Down, Moses*, like *The Hamlet*, takes up the modern exploitive relation to the land. Because it is the first volume of a trilogy and was conceived to be part of a multi-volume work, the most significant connections are with *The Town* (1957) and *The Mansion* (1959), the concluding books in the Snopes narrative. The trilogy begins and ends with books entitled "Flem." The second and third volumes continue the thematic emphasis on love, loyalty, justice, and respectability that Faulkner introduces in *The Hamlet*.

A single further example will illustrate the enriching effect of its long gestation on *The Hamlet*. The novel's concern with waste--the cumulative loss of vitality of an entire culture and the squandering of human and natural resources--operates on three levels. First, when Faulkner began the novel, in the 1920's, he was very much influenced by T. S. Eliot's vision of post-World War I anomie in *The Waste Land*. That poem's equation of the prevailing sexual malaise with the more general erosion of belief and energy in a fragmented world made a profound impression on the young Faulkner. In setting the first edition of *The Hamlet* in the 1890's, Faulkner added a second layer of meaning to the wasteland imagery. Growing up among veterans of the Civil War and listening to their stories, Faulkner saw the post-Civil War South as suffering from the same carnage and devastation that the rest of the world experienced after the Great War. Finally, in the 1930's, with the Depression and the New Deal, and with his own purchase of a farm in 1938, Faulkner became more aware of a different kind of waste: the human toll poverty takes on the lives of the rural poor.

The distance in time and experience between the agrarian world of *The Hamlet* and our increasingly urban world prompts many of these annotations. Most readers will be unfamiliar with vocabulary relating to the sharecropping system, and many will not be familiar with southern colloquial speech. The abundant references to a remarkable variety of both flora and fauna testify to Faulkner's involvement with his environment, but they may present problems to the reader who has not visited the south.

Faulkner's is an art that celebrates his encounters with the world. One need only read his work to know that he observed and loved the physical universe, from the cotton "pickers, arrested in stooping attitudes, ... the long, partly-filled sacks streaming away behind them like rigid frozen flags" (148-9) to the rain that releases the earth from the iron grip of winter: "the belated spring hard on its bright heels and all coming at once, pell mell and disordered, fruit and bloom and leaf, pied meadow and blossoming wood and the long fields shearing dark out of winter's slumber, to the shearing plow" (264-65). Evidence that Faulkner's ear was as much attuned to the world as his eye is especially available in this novel that revels in the vernacular. It is my hope in compiling these annotations to assist the interested reader in appreciating the variety and vividness of Faulkner's created world.

I have chosen to key these annotations to the third edition (1964) of *The Hamlet*, because it is the most readily available. This is the first volume of a uniform edition of the Snopes trilogy, published under the title

Snopes. The first edition (1940) is clearly the purest and represents Faulkner's intentions for the novel. Events in the first edition take place in the last decade of the nineteenth century. For the third edition, Faulkner's editors moved the chronology forward twenty years in order to eliminate inconsistencies with the other two books of the trilogy. Faulkner had expressed his desire in writing more than once to see the earlier volumes of the Snopes trilogy brought into conformation with the final book (see letters to Albert Erskine of 12 March 1959 [*SL* 425-26], 7 April 1959 [*SL* 427], mid-April 1959 [*SL* 429], and 7 May 1959 [*SL* 429-30]). I have noted in these annotations wherever the time frame has been altered to align it with the later chronology.

Annotations

The Hamlet [title]: In his preface to *Mans*, the final volume of the Snopes trilogy, Faulkner calls that work the "final chapter of, and the summation of, a work conceived and begun in 1925" (*Mans* xi). During the long gestation of *Ham*, Faulkner experimented with several titles. The title of his original attempt to tell the Snopes story, *FA*, alludes to the Biblical patriarch's leading his people out of bondage and sets the pattern of progress that carries Flem, and his clan along with him, from tenant farming to bank presidency. This interpretation is reinforced in *Flags*: "With this foothold and like Abraham of old, he led his family piece by piece into town" (154). Kibler suggests that Faulkner may have been thinking not of the Biblical model but of the American Abraham (Kibler 5-6). If his memory is accurate and the Snopes work was incepted in 1925, Faulkner may have been living in New Orleans when he conceived the trilogy. While there, he saw Sherwood Anderson, who was working on a biography of Abraham Lincoln, regularly. Anderson, in the surviving fragment of the biography, refers to Lincoln as "Father Abraham" and stresses his impoverished background as the son of a "no-account" and a "shiftless" father. Dimino mentions Benjamin Franklin's Father Abraham, who, in the preface to *Poor Richard Improved*, tutors the American colonists in strategies for success, in spite of the British tariffs that deplete their profits (noted 164). Dimino sees the allusion as one of a number of references to colonial economies that run through the novel.

The working title of *The Hamlet* during the final composition process was *The Peasants*. In a letter to Robert Haas received 15 December 1938, Faulkner outlined his plans for each volume of the Snopes trilogy and announced his intention to title Book One *The Peasants* (*SL* 107). The title derives from Balzac's *Les Paysans*. During his class sessions at the University of Virginia, Faulkner praised Balzac, along with Dickens, for his "concept of the cosmos in miniature" (*FU* 231-32). Faulkner's own ambitions toward breadth and inclusivity clearly paralleled Balzac's, and the title of this first volume of the Snopes trilogy acknowledges the debt. Stone, in his introduction to *The Marble Faun*, Faulkner's first book, quotes the author as saying, in response to Stone's comment that the trouble with Amy Lowell "and her gang of drum-beaters" was that they had one eye on the ball and the other eye on the grandstand, that he "had one eye on the ball and the other eye on Babe Ruth" (8). As in the case of *The Marble Faun*, Faulkner eyed the masters in the composition of *Ham*. Cohen notes many thematic, structural, and plot analogies between Balzac's study of "rural class warfare" and Faulkner's own treatment of the same ("French Peasants"). Indeed, Balzac's portrayal of the peasants of the title as rapacious, wily hedonists who undermine the aristocratic order and civility of the community is echoed in Faulkner, particularly in his earliest efforts at the Snopes material. Balzac's Fourchon, a peasant who combines "sloth and cunning," is referred to as "Father Fourchon" (*Les Paysans* 28). Although Faulkner's first two Yoknapatawpha novels, *Flags* and *S&F*, both products, like *FA*, of the late twenties, are intimately concerned with the decline of the aristocratic tradition and the displacement of the old families by a new, crasser class of people, he had, by the late thirties, softened his previous harsh attitudes toward the rural poor (Meriwether, "Introduction").

It is not known specifically why Faulkner chose to re-title his novel *The Hamlet*, but the choice, as in all his novel titles, was a superb one. The published title of the novel may owe something to Balzac in its geographical emphasis. Balzac's groupings of the novels in his panoramic *Comédie humaine* center on the physical locus of the action: *Scenes of Private Life*, *Scenes of Provincial Life*, and *Scenes of Paris Life*.

In the early short prose piece, "The Hill," the protagonist ascends a hill and looks down into the valley and the town below: "The hamlet slept, wrapped in peace and quiet beneath the evening sun, as it had slept for a century; waiting, invisibly honey-combed with joys and sorrows, hopes and despairs, for the end of time" (*EPP* 91). The hamlet of that short piece is, like *Ham*, associated with the world of classical mythology; it is a place where "in the dusk, nymphs and fauns might riot to a shrilling of thin pipes" (*EPP* 92).

Dedication: To Phil Stone: Stone, a fellow resident of Oxford, was Faulkner's closest friend and mentor at an important stage early in his career. Professionally a lawyer, Stone was interested in literature, and he introduced Faulkner to many of the modern poets. Stone claimed later, in a 1957 letter to James B. Meriwether, that he had given Faulkner the idea for the Snopes story: "...the real revolution in the south was not the race situation but the rise of the redneck, who did not have any of the scruples of the old aristocracy, to places of power and wealth" (*Brodsky* 207). Although Faulkner dedicated each of the three Snopes volumes to Stone, they had drifted apart by this time. Stone would claim credit in a letter for "giv[ing] him a sense of humor" (*Brodsky* 207) and for inventing "almost all the characters Bill has used" (*Brodsky* 208), but he consistently underrated Faulkner's achievements, as, for example, when, in response to a letter from Meriwether, he predicted that Faulkner's place in history would be that of a "splendid second-rate writer" (*Brodsky* 216).

Meriwether suggests that Faulkner was unable to complete the Snopes work until he had put some distance between himself and Stone's condescending attitudes toward poor white trash (*FA*, "Introduction").

Emily Whitehurst Stone admits to asking Faulkner to honor her husband Phil with a dedication. Snell records the incident in her biography of Stone:

> ...at a cocktail party in 1939 or 1940 she [Mrs. Stone] assayed that reserve, in full knowledge of the risk she ran, because she suspected that her husband's old friend might indeed redeem the self Stone had sacrificed to family honor. She asked Faulkner whether he had decided to whom he would dedicate the first Snopes book. The author "looked away above that lifted neck of his as though to get me out of his world and said in that high-pitched, tentative voice of his, 'No.'" But she had gone too far to retreat. "I wish...you'd think about dedicating it to Phil," she continued, to which Faulkner "did not answer at all" (*Phil Stone of Oxford: A Vicarious Life* 244).

[Manuscript Opening]: Faulkner wrote "Barn," he said in a letter to Malcolm Cowley, as an "induction toward the spotted horse story" (*SL* 197). The first seventeen pages of the manuscript at the Alderman Library of the University of Virginia are headed Book One/Chapter I, as well as indicating the deleted short-story title "Barn Burning." A thirty-two- page typescript version of the story, also housed at the Alderman Library, is headed simply "Chapter One," with no supplementary title. Because thirty-two pages were removed from the typescript setting copy of *The Hamlet*, it is fair to assume that, until a relatively late stage in the revision process, Faulkner intended to open the novel with the story of Sarty Snopes (Millgate 185).

Scholars have questioned Faulkner's decision to eliminate this important material from the published novel. Millgate speculates that Faulkner may have felt that Sarty's poignant story would predispose the reader too favorably toward the Snopes clan and so would not effectively introduce a novel detailing Flem's rise to power (185). Beck suggests that

Sarty's rapid emancipation from his Snopes blood would undermine one of the main tenets of the trilogy: the gradual but implacable rise of Snopesism (*Faulkner* 279). The story nonetheless would have set up several of the themes that run throughout the book and the trilogy. The stress on the kinship bond in the story carries over in Flem's betrayal of Mink, his kinsman, and allows for the revenger's tragedy that dominates *Mans*. "Barn" also establishes the interplay of love and law that is an important factor in the Snopes trilogy. The DeSpain mansion, "big as a courthouse," is a component of an orderly universe and represents the old agrarian ideal of man living in close harmony with nature. The advantage of presenting Sarty's dreaming a dream enforced by the sight of such a mansion and following it with Will Varner's sitting in a chair on the lawn of the Old Frenchman's Place wondering what it would feel like to "need all this" (6) is obvious. Had Faulkner conformed to his original plan, Sarty would have been the first of a parade of dreamers who contrast with Flem, who has no dreams of his own but capitalizes on the dreams of others. Sarty's response to the DeSpain mansion, as the embodiment of a dream in "Barn Burning," would point up the dream's corruption when Flem occupies the same mansion in the third Snopes volume.

Finally, the third-person narration of "Barn" establishes a base from which the reader can appreciate the shaping, creative power of Ratliff's retelling of the same story, which followed in Chapter Two of Book One in the original typescript.

The plot synopsis that Faulkner sent to Robert Haas on 15 December 1938 outlines the expansive role that Faulkner originally envisioned for Sarty:

> This is the plot, if any. Flem gets his wife because she is got with child by a sweetheart who clears out for Texas; for a price he protects her good name. No, before this, his youngest brother tries to keep his father from setting fire to his landlord's barn, believes he has caused the father to be shot, and runs away from home, goes west, has a son which the other Snopes know nothing about.
>
> Flem moves to town with his wife whose child pretty soon sees what a sorry lot Snopes are. She goes to New York (has money from her actual father) and is overseas in the War with the ambulance corps, where she meets the son of the boy who ran away from home, finds him a kinsman, finds how his father has tried to eradicate the Snopes from him. After the war she brings together this Snopes and the daughter of a collateral

Snopes who also looks with horror on Snopes. She and her remote cousin marry, have a son who is the scion of the family.

What this will tell is, that this flower and cream, this youth, whom his mother and father fondly believed would raise the family out of the muck, turns out to have all the vices of all Snopes and none of the virtues--the ruthlessness and firmness--of his banker uncle, the chief of the family. He has not enough courage and honesty to be a successful bootlegger nor enough industry to be the barber for which he is finally trained after Flem has robbed her mother of what money her father and husband left her. He is in bad shape with syphilis and all the little switch-tailed nigger whores call him by his first name in private and he likes it.

By this time Flem has eaten up Jefferson too. There is nothing else he can gain, and worse than this, nothing else he wants. He even has no respect for the people, the town, he has victimised, let alone the parasite kin who batten on him. He reaches the stage where there is just one more joke he can play on his environment, his parasite kin and all. So he leaves all his property to the worthless boy, knowing that no other Snopes has sense enough to hold onto it, and that at least this boy will get rid of it in the way that will make his kinfolk the maddest (*SL* 107-08).

Book One/Flem: Faulkner begins and ends the Snopes trilogy with books entitled "Flem." The final section of *Mans*, consisting of seven chapters, bears the same title as this opening book of the trilogy.

John Cullen remembers a Flem McCain who lived in Dutch Bend. Although he did not resemble Flem Snopes in most aspects, Flem McCain did go to Texas and bring back a string of spotted ponies for auction. Cullen suggests that the model for Flem may have been Lem Prince, whose family were Union supporters during the Civil War. Because the Union army burned their cotton, they were reimbursed handsomely, and Lem became the richest man in the county. His rise out of Dutch Bend to found a bank in Oxford parallels Flem Snopes's similar progress (100). Finally, McHaney advances a model for Flem in Joe Parks, who ousted Faulkner's grandfather from the bank presidency. Parks came from the hamlet of Etta, northeast of Oxford ("Falkners" 257, also noted Cullen 104, but Cullen refers to Parks as Jim Packs).

Kreiswirth proposes another source for the name Flem: the phlegmatic temperament as Faulkner found it defined in a book in his library, D. Starke's *Character and How to Strengthen It*:

Phlegm is a defense against visible emotion. It is not hypocrisy or falsehood, for the phlegmatic utter no sentiment contrary to that which they fill. They are content not to let anything transpire of the cause of their agitation. One may compare a phlegmatic man to a thick veil under which the play of the features, and under this the acts of the mind, are dissembled. Hypocrisy resembles a dead wall covered with lying advertisements.

Phlegm is this dead wall wholly denuded of these. We can conjecture what it conceals, but in no case can we accuse it of saying anything contrary to truth (*The Making of a Novelist* 108-9).

Another possible source for Flem's name was suggested to J. B. Meriwether by Carvel Collins (Meriwether, Interview 5/18/94). A character from Fontaine Fox's comic strip, "Toonerville Trolley," which was widely distributed from 1915-1955, is named Flem Proddy. The local inventor from that strip, Flem Proddy provides an ironic counterpoint to Flem Snopes, who neither invents nor creates. In contrast to Flem Snopes's precision and mechanistic perfection, the wild-eyed, beaming Flem Proddy devotes himself to useless, intermittently successful gadgetry. The sexual connotations of the Toonerville Flem's surname present another area of comment on Flem Snopes's character, as does Flem Proddy's mode of transportation: a hobbyhorse.

The first published reference to Flem is in *Sart*: "Flem, the first Snopes, had appeared unheralded one day behind the counter of a small restaurant on a side street, patronized by country folk. With this foothold and like Abraham of old, he brought his blood and legal kin household by household, individual by individual, into town and established them where they could gain money" (154). The passage then continues to outline Flem's advance from manager of the power and water plant to the vice-presidency of the bank.

3.1-14 Frenchman's Bend...Hill-cradled and remote...jungle... hewed them: Adams suggests that Faulkner borrowed from Conrad a fascination with a remote settlement or trading post situated on a river in the midst of a jungle or wilderness. He finds this setting associated in Conrad with "sexual passion which leads, in obscurely perverse ways, to gestures of ritual impotence" ("Apprenticeship" 21).

3.1 Frenchman's Bend: Faulkner, in the map of Yoknapatawpha County that he included in *AbAb!*, locates Frenchman's Bend about twenty miles southeast of the fictional county seat of Jefferson. Cullen associates Frenchman's Bend with Dutch Bend, a connection that seems to be supported by Faulkner's assertion that to a countryman, every foreigner is a Frenchman, while the same foreigner is a Dutchman to his urban equivalent. Faulkner first introduced the settlement of Frenchman's Bend in *FA*: "Twenty miles southeast of Jefferson, in the hill-cradled cane and cypress jungles of Yocona River lies the settlement of Frenchman's Bend" (14). Around the same period, a passage from *Flags* that was excised from the published *Sart* describes the hamlet in terms that remain fundamentally unchanged throughout his career: "He drove through Frenchman's Bend at two o'clock, without stopping. The village was dark; Varner's store, the blacksmith shop (now a garage too, with a gasoline pump), Mrs. Littlejohn's huge, unpainted boarding house--were without life..." (257).

In "Shall Not Perish," Frenchman's Bend is "that little place that don't even show up on a map" (*CS* 114). It is also featured in "Shingles for the Lord," "Two Soldiers," *KG*, *Twn*, and *Mans*.

3.1-5.3 Frenchman's Bend...after dark: Faulkner echoes the broad historical perspective introduced here in *Req* (101) and in his 1954 essay "Mississippi" (*ESPL* 11-15).

3.5-9 original grant and site...the Old Frenchman's Place: Faulkner first used the Old Frenchman's Place in *Sanc*. Cf. "The house was a gutted ruin rising gaunt and stark out of a grove of unpruned cedar trees. It was a landmark, known as the Old Frenchman place, built before the Civil War; a plantation house set in the middle of a tract of land; of cotton fields and gardens and lawns long since gone back to jungle, which the people of the neighborhood had been pulling down piecemeal for firewood for fifty years or digging with secret and sporadic optimism for the gold which the builder was reputed to have buried somewhere about the place when Grant came through the county on his Vicksburg campaign" (6-7). As the scene of the crimes committed against Temple Drake, the dilapidating mansion is notably open and offers no sanctuary or protection (Watson 155). Polk notes that a mansion or prominent house often represents in Faulkner's work the culmination of a dream, of an ideal that is rarely attained ("Idealism" 110). A ruined mansion, then, suggests the corruption of a dream. The dilapidated Compson house objectifies the life that goes on within it, just as the ruined old Frenchman's Place objectifies the demise of one kind of system and the transferral of power from one element of society to another. A big house figures in Sutpen's "design" (*AbAb!* 14-15), in Colonel John Sartoris's dream (*Unv* 253), and in Flem Snopes's drive toward "respectability and aristocracy" (*Mans* 358-59 as noted in McDaniel 17). Bayard Sartoris returns fractured by his experience in World War I, but he finds his house intact, "the white simplicity of it dreamed unbroken amid its ancient sunshot trees" (*Flags* 10). It is this vision of an intact, ordered world that both Sarty Snopes ("Barn" 10) and V. K. Ratliff respond to (*Ham* 335). Faulkner may also have had in mind the opening of Balzac's *Les Paysans*, which describes Montcornet's mansion, the Aigues, in its glory days, thus setting up a contrast between the past and the degenerate present (3-4).

3.11 Chancery Clerk's office: an office of public records (*OED*), specifically, where land ownership and tax records are kept.

3.13 cane-and-cypress jungle: Cf. "Miss Zilphia Gant," written probably in 1928: "cyprus-and-cane river jungle" (*US* 368). The remote region, though unnamed, from which the Gants depart to start over in town, resembles Frenchman's Bend.

3.13 cane: Brown, in his *Glossary of Faulkner's South*, identifies this cane as "either of two species of reeds with hard, jointed hollow stems, growing along creeks and in river bottoms" (44). Cf. Thomas Bangs Thorpe's "Summer Retreat in Arkansas" for a Mississippi River Valley cane brake: "it is formed by a space of ground where, seemingly from its superiority of soil, more delicate vegetation than that which surrounds it, has usurped the empire. Here the reed...grows into a delicate mast--springing with the prodigality of grass from the rich alluvium that gives it sustenance, and tapering from its roots to the height of 20 or 30 feet, it there mingles in compact and luxuriant confusion its long leaves" (29).

3.13 cypress: Bald cypress (*taxodium distichum*) is a majestic, nonevergreen tall tree of southern swamps that is particularly valued for its durable wood (Petrides 22-3).

3.15-23 He had quite possibly been a foreigner...Dutchman: see 3.1.

3.22 Jefferson: The fictional Jefferson, Mississippi, county seat of Yoknapatawpha County, bears some resemblances to Oxford, Mississippi, county seat of Lafayette County. Faulkner, however, keeps the two distinct in his fiction. Jefferson may have been modelled after Ripley, Mississippi, county seat of Tippah County and birthplace of Faulkner's father and grandfather. Ripley, like Jefferson, Oxford, and most Mississippi county seats, has a courthouse square. McDaniel points out that the distance from Jefferson to Oxford in the fiction is approximately that between Oxford and Ripley (56).

As recounted in *Req*, the town began early in the nineteenth century as a Chickasaw Indian trading post. The original white settlers arrived on horseback together from the Cumberland Gap of Tennessee: Louis Grenier, a Huguenot younger son who brought slaves and established a cotton plantation along the banks of the Yoknapatawpha River, Doctor Samuel Habersham, who brought his eight-year-old son, and Alec Holston, who came with Habersham as a bodyguard cum tutor. Habersham became the first official Chickasaw land agent and gave the town its first name, while Holston opened the first tavern. The settlement of Habersham is eventually renamed for Thomas Jefferson Pettigrew, the federal mail rider (3-29).

3.24 **Will Varner:** Veterinarian and owner of the general store in Frenchman's Bend, Varner figures marginally in many of the stories and novels. In *AILD*, he is one of the mourners of Addie (83), and he sets Cash's broken leg (176). In "Tomorrow," he is the justice of the peace who is awakened at four o'clock in the morning with Bookwright's confession to the murder of Buck Thorpe (*KG* 86). In "By the People," Varner holds the picnic at which political candidates announce for election (*Madamoiselle* 136). Although Varner's character remains consistent over the course of the trilogy, it gets a lighter treatment in this first volume. In *Ham*, he is a usurer and a lecher, but his amorality is presented within a context of comic distancing and hyperbole. He is depicted less sympathetically in *Twn* and *Mans*.

3.24 **who was sixty years old now:** Kibler points out that, if Varner is now sixty, he was thiry-five years old "thirty years ago" (Ed I) when a courier rode down the path to the Frenchman's Place with the news of Sumter, and so could be expected to have known the Frenchman (14-15). The third edition amends the time of the courier's ride to "nearly fifty years ago" (336.26).

3.27-28 **his dream:** With the excision of the "Barn" story, the opening focus of the novel shifts from the progenitor of the Snopes clan to the progenitor of the dream.

3.33-37 the skeleton of a tremendous house which his heirs-at-large had been pulling down and chopping up ...for firewood: Cf. *Les Paysans*: "The Aigues is not to belong to one but to all three of us...the house must be pulled down from top to bottom" (274). Grimwood cites a 1935 article by Richmond Croom Beatty and George Marion O'Donnell, who later wrote the influential essay, "Faulkner's Mythology," in which they envision rednecks taking over a model village and burning the houses for fuel: "What would probably happen to this class, if sent in numbers to the model village..., would be that the homes in such villages would, in many cases be burned piecemeal by the "peasants" themselves for firewood, the rotating gardens by midsummer would be weed-ridden, the radios would be torn to pieces..., the bookcases tobacco-spattered, and the schoolhouse befouled" (80-81, noted Grimwood 162).

4.2 monument: The Frenchman's monument to his own name, unpronounceable to the settlers who come after him, is parodied later in the novel when I. O. and Eck Snopes, at Ratliff's suggestion, buy Ike's cow so that the Snopes name will be kept, as I. O. tells Eck, "pure as a marble monument for your children to grow up under" (204). The Frenchman's monument looks ahead to the opening incident of *The Town*. Flem, who is still feeling his way in Jefferson, makes several miscalculations in this episode, originally published as the short story, "Centaur in Brass," but the town is finally left with a permanent, visible reminder of his presence in the water tank with its polluted water. Charles Mallison, who narrates that section, sees the monument as a measure of Flem's progress: "Except that it was not a monument: it was a footprint. A monument only says *At least I go this far* while a footprint says *This is where I was when I moved again* (29). Later, after Eula's suicide, Flem memorializes her with a stone monument inscribed with the words: "A Virtuous Wife Is a Crown To Her Husband/Her Children Rise and Call Her Blessed" (355). Finally, the Frenchman's wasted monument in the jungle to his own pride recalls Shelley's "Ozymandias," whose pride is also survived by decaying "lifeless things" (7).

4.4 flintlock rifles: Flintlock was a firing mechanism used in firearms from about 1620 to the mid-1800's. When the trigger of a flintlock rifle was pulled, a piece of flint, clamped in the cock, struck a piece of steel on a pivot, creating sparks. The sparks caused a small pan of gunpowder to explode and ignite the main charge in the barrel (Peterson 130-37).

Encyclopedia of Firearms 130-37).

4.9-10 his legend but the stubborn tale of the money he buried somewhere about the place: The legend of the Frenchman's buried treasure prepares the reader for Ratliff's desire to believe that there is something tangible to be gained through ownership of the decaying mansion, thus enabling Flem to dupe him with the salted mine trick in the novel's ultimate episode. The Aigues, Balzac's country estate, is also reputed to be hiding "a hoard of gold" (*Les Paysans* 274). Eugenie Grandet's father is likewise rumored to have squirreled away "a hoard of louis" in a secret hiding place (8).

Stories of the romantic defeat of the South often feature family valuables buried when the Yankees came through. The Sartoris family silver was buried by Joby under the barn floor (34). In "A Return," an old southern woman slips off alone to bury the family silver, falls into the hole she has dug, and eventually dies of the pneumonia she contracts after a night in the rain waiting to be discovered (553-54). "My Grandmother Millard" begins with Granny's weekly, then monthly, rehearsals to collect the silver, store it in a trunk from the attic, and transfer it to an already-dug and waiting hole in the orchard (667-69). In *Unv*, Granny buries the silver, then has it dug up and reburied because she has had a dream that a black man knows about the hiding place (19-21). In "Gold Is Not Always" (227) and in *GDM* (79), Lucas Beauchamp is convinced that there is gold buried on the McCaslin place.

4.11 Grant overran the country on his way to Vicksburg: The Union victory at Vicksburg, captured by U. S. Grant, proved decisive in securing the Mississippi River and the western states for the northern forces. Because the ground to the north of the city was low and marshy, Grant's several attempts to approach Vicksburg from that direction failed. That first, failed, campaign to take Vicksburg ended with a Union defeat in Faulkner's vicinity, at Holly Springs on 20 December 1862. In April 1863, Grant established a base south of the city. His troops then marched along the Mississippi on its western bank, crossed to dry ground south of Vicksburg, and drove toward the city. Vicksburg surrendered finally on July 4, 1863, after a forty-seven-day siege (Foote, *Fredericksburg to Meridian* 379-427, 606-614).

4.12-5.3 The people who inherited from him...pass through it after dark: Cf. "Monk" for a similar description of the same milieu, the "eastern part of our county": "a country which twenty-five years ago... was without roads almost and where even the sheriff of the county did not go--a country impenetrable and almost uncultivated and populated by a clannish people who owned allegiance to no one and no thing and whom outsiders never saw until a few years back when good roads and automobiles penetrated the green fastnesses where the denizens with their corrupt Scotch-Irish names intermarried and made whiskey and shot at all strangers from behind log barns and snake fences" (*KG* 40-41).

4.17-19 Turpin and Haley and Whittington, McCallum and Murray and Leonard and Littlejohn, and other names like Riddup and Armstid and Doshey: Faulkner's roster of the original families of the county includes names that are found elsewhere in the fiction (Turpin, Haley, McCallum, Littlejohn, and Armstid) and others that are mentioned only here (Whittington, Murray, Leonard, Riddup, and Doshey).

4.28 bottom land: low-lying land, a valley, a dell; an alluvial hollow (*OED*).

4.31-34 Federal officers went into the country and vanished...an old man or woman: Because moonshiners do not pay the excise tax on the whiskey they make, federal agents who come to collect it are their sworn enemies (Brown 80). Guerard records Faulkner's telling him a similar story in 1946 about the disappearance of federal officers in a corner of his county (*The Triumph of the Novel* 212). Cf. the description of Sullivan's Hollow in "Mississippi": "vide the legend of the revenue officer hunting illicit whiskey stills, captured and held prisoner in a stable and worked in traces as the pair to a plow mule" (33). Cf. James Street's *Look Away*: "They plowed a revenue officer to death. The folks in Sullivan's Hollow don't like revenue officers and timber detectives" (206).

4.35 in the heel of: in close pursuit of or immediate attendance on.

4.39 Protestants: Protestantism is a world-wide movement that arose from reforms of Western Christianity in the sixteenth century. The first Protestant denominations were formed in reaction to the authoritarian and hierarchal structure of the Roman Catholic church. Most Protestants today consider church authority as secondary to Biblical authority and to the personal experience of faith (Eliade, *Encyclopedia of Religion* 12: 23-38).

5.1 Democrats: During the Reconstruction period, southern Democrats and Whigs formed a coalition party that dominated politically until issues involving integration and economics broke up the "Solid South" after World War II. Since 1876, all of Mississippi's governors have been Democrats.

5.1-3 there was not one Negro landowner in the entire section. Strange Negroes would absolutely refuse to pass through it after dark: Cf. "Mississippi": "No Negro ever let darkness catch him in Sullivan's Hollow. In fact, there were few Negroes in this country at all..." (*ESPL* 33). Moreland notes that, although there are no substantial black characters in *Ham*, blacks are mentioned every few pages in the novel. Whereas, in *AbAb!* and *LA*, the idea of being or becoming black serves as the ultimate horror, in *Ham* blacks are mentioned as analogues for other kinds of alienation or oppression (*Faulkner and Modernism* 133).

5.4-39 Will Varner, the present owner of the Old Frenchman place, was the chief man of the county...within the surrounding ten miles at any time: Varner is strongly reminiscent of Nat Wheeler, the father of Cather's protagonist in *One of Ours*. Wheeler, too, is "rich" (7), averse to work, "active in politics" (6), and "jolly" (8). One of his sons is a "narrow-gauge...prudent young man" (7) who runs a store, where the father enjoys sitting about and joking with the farmers. The novels also share a concern with the waste and sacrifice of young lives and with masculine and feminine modes of living in the world. In *Ham*, men are distinguished by an attraction to games and contests, while, in *One of Ours*, the masculine is signified by machines and war.

5.6 beat: In Alabama and Mississippi, a beat is the principal subdivision of a county, a voting precinct (*OED*).

5.14 Judge Benbow: Although the relationship is not clarified, Judge Benbow is presumably an ancestor of Horace and Narcissa Benbow, who play important roles in *Flags* and *Sanc*. He is the self-appointed executor of Goodhue Coldfield's estate who sustains Rosa Coldfield for the rest of her life (*AbAb!* 211-12). In *Unv*, he makes the arrangements for John Sartoris to buy Redmond's share of the railroad (259).

5.14-15 a milder-mannered man never bled a mule or stuffed a ballot box: Cf. *Don Juan*:

"You're wrong--he was the mildest mannered man
That ever scuttled ship or cut a throat"
(3.41.1-2, noted Brooks, *The Yoknapatawpha Country* 25).

5.17-18 cotton gin: a machine for separating cotton from its seeds (*OED*). In a rural, cotton-producing region, the owner of the cotton gin would have been one of the most prominent citizens.

5.18 grist mill: a mill for grinding grain (*AHD*).

5.23-24 little hard bright innocently blue eyes: Eyes in *Ham* and elsewhere usually reveal something of character. Cf. Sarty Snopes's "eyes gray and wild as storm scud" (*CS*, "Barn" 4), Ab's "cold opaque gray" eyes (8.1), Eula's "eyes like cloudy hothouse grapes" (10.24-25), Jody's "slightly protuberant opaque eyes" (11.22), Ratliff's "shrewd impenetrable eyes" (14.28-29), Flem's eyes "the color of stagnant water" (22.5), I.O.'s "little bright eyes darting" (63.14), Ike's eyes "blasted empty and clean forever of any thought" (85.32), Labove's "quiet pale hard eyes" (105.21), Lump's "bright, alert, amoral eyes of a squirrel or a chipmunk" (144.25-26), the cow's "mild enormous moist and pupilless globes" (182.13), the sheriff's eyes resembling "two bits of black glass pressed into uncooked dough" (255.15), the "periwinkle-eyed" (275.31) Wallstreet Panic, the Texas ponies' "blue-and-brown eyeballs rolling alertly in their gaudy faces" (279.25-26), Henry Armstid, whose mad eyes have "a quality glazed now and even sightless" (293. 25), Mrs. Armstid's "blank eyes" (316.21).

5.24 Methodist Sunday school superintendent: The Methodist religion, founded in the 1720's by John Wesley as a reformist branch of the Church of England, was spread rapidly on the American frontier by itinerant preachers. Wesley published his own succinct definition of Methodism in his 1753 *Complete English Dictionary*: "A Methodist, one that lives according to the method layed down in the Bible" (Eliade, *Encyclopedia of Religion* 9:493-95). Methodists in Mississippi were known for their conservatism and fundamentalism (Ragan, *Annotations* 14). Cf. the Chief Engineer in *Elmer*: "His smooth-shaven face was like a conscientious Sunday school superintendent's" (4). Cf. *WP* in which the judge who sentences Harry Wilbourne is described as having the face of a "Methodist Sunday school superintendent" (317).

5.28 Rabelaisian turn of mind: The writings of the French author,

Francois Rabelais (ca. 1490-1553) are distinguished by extravagant, coarse humor and satire, often of a sexual nature (*OED*).

5.29 (he had fathered sixteen children to his wife): In the overabundant, comically exaggerated world of *Ham*, Varner fathers sixteen children, the ninth of whom is Jody and the last of whom is Eula. The other children are never mentioned, and the family is scaled back to more realistic size in *Twn*. Faulkner was notoriously unconcerned with inconsistencies in his fiction, but he did, according to James B. Meriwether, who helped with the editing, try to eliminate many obvious discrepancies in the Snopes volumes (Interview). He defended what inconsistencies remained in a prefatory note to *Mans*: "This book is the final chapter of, and the summation of, a work conceived and begun in 1925. Since the author likes to believe, hopes that his entire life's work is a part of a living literature, and since "living" is motion, and "motion" is change and alteration and therefore the only alternative to motion is unmotion, stasis, death, there will be found discrepancies and contradictions in the thiry-four-year progress of this particular chronicle; the purpose of this note is simply to inform the reader that the author has already found more discrepancies and contradictions than he hopes the reader will-- contradictions and discrepancies due to the fact that the author has learned, he believes, more about the human heart and its dilemma than he knew thirty-four years ago; and is sure that, having lived with them that long time, he knows the characters in this chronicle better than he did then."

5.32-33 his hair which even at sixty was more red than gray: hair symbolically signifies energy and fertility, while red hair is associated with the Venusian or demoniacal (Cirlot 134-35).

6.2-4 sitting in a home-made chair on the jungle-choked lawn of the Old Frenchman's homesite: By the close of Book One, Flem Snopes has displaced Will Varner on the flour barrel throne (91).

6.8 cob pipe: a pipe made from the cylindrical shoot on which grains of corn grow (*OED*).

6.13-14 an itinerant sewing machine agent named Ratliff: Faulkner told Cynthia Grenier in an interview that his favorite characters were Ratliff and Dilsey (*LG* 224). Gregarious and likeable, Ratliff is, from his inception, the natural antagonist of Flem Snopes. Faulkner stresses their common tenant-farming backgrounds and their common escape through trade out of agriculture. Ratliff is, like the Snopeses, able to cope with change, Faulkner told a class at the University of Virginia, because he "possesses what you might call a moral, spiritual eupepsia" (*FU* 253). Ratliff's practical skill as a trader is balanced by his vulnerability to the dream represented by the Old Frenchman's Place. He can be duped by Flem because Flem has no dreams.

Until he changed the name to Ratliff in the *Ham* manuscript, Faulkner's sewing machine agent was V. K. Suratt (Meriwether, *Literary* 43). Both his mother (Blotner, One vol. ed. 199) and John Cullen (73-74) remember a sewing machine salesman named June Suratt who kept a doghouse painted to look like a sewing machine on the back of his wagon as advertising. Faulkner later said that he changed the name to Ratliff because a Suratt moved to town (Blotner, One vol. ed. 402). Kibler suggests that Faulkner had in mind the Virginia Suratt family, one of whom was hanged in the Lincoln assassination trials (9).

In *FA*, Suratt stays at Mrs. Littlejohn's boarding house while in Frenchman's Bend and recounts the story of his escape out the window in his underwear when a horse invades the room (55). In *Flags*, he gives Bayard a lift to the barn for whiskey (123). In *AILD*, he tries to sell Cash a "talking machine" for eight dollars (181). Suratt gives Flem the bill of sale for his half interest in a Jefferson restaurant in "Centaur" (*CS* 150). He is tricked by Flem into buying a share of the Old Frenchman's Place in "Lizards" (*US* 149). In *Twn*, Ratliff is one of three narrators who try to make sense of Flem's motives. His initials, we learn, stand for Vladimir Kyrilytch, the name of a Russian ancestor who fought as an officer in the American Revolution (322-23). In "A Bear Hunt," he has exchanged his buckboard for a Model T Ford (*Big Woods* 63).

6.21 **get shut of it:** to be rid of (Partridge).

6.23 **wont:** Faulkner, like Shaw, typically eliminates the apostrophe in single syllable contractions.

6.25 **scantling:** a medium-length piece of milled lumber.

6.27-28 **This is the one thing I ever bought in my life I couldn't sell to nobody:** Varner will trade it, along with Eula, for Flem's name on Eula's marriage license (145.22-23).

6.29 **The son, Jody:** Faulkner included Will Varner's son Jody in the Snopes material from its inception. In *FA*, Jody owns the store and is the postmaster as well (16). Prior to *Ham*, Jody was a peripheral character, most often mentioned simply as his father's son. His role in *Ham* is augmented as he takes on the role of protector for his sister Eula and as he gradually relinquishes his position in the family business to Flem.

6.31 **that quality of invincible and inviolable bachelordom:** Faulkner transposes a modern wasteland sensibility, owing much to his familiarity with Eliot's poem, into his turn of the century hamlet. The novel is dominated by sterility, both in the predominance of bachelors and in the failure of love to refresh and renew the parched world. Jody is the "jealous seething eunuch priest" (114.29). Labove is likened to a monk (105.26). Ratliff, the best man in the novel, remains a bachelor. Ike Snopes, *Ham*'s courtly lover, is engaged, in reality, in "stock diddling" (201.28) Three of the novel's males lose their bachelorhood. Houston deserts the prostitute who genuinely loves him to marry Lucy Pate, the respectable girl back home. When she is killed by the stallion, he reverts to a monk-like existence (190). Mink. the cowardly murderer, is the novel's potent man, contrasting extravagantly with all the non-men and sub-men that abound. The ultimate horror of the book is in the marriage of Eula, the fertility goddess, to the sterile, cold, and frog-like Flem.

6.35 **trig:** active, nimble, brisk, sprightly, alert, from the Scottish (*OED*).

6.36-7.1 **He wore, winter and summer...good black broadcloth:** Jody's uniform suggests a priest's cassock. The mechanical regularity of his clothing parallels the same quality in Flem's dress.

7.3-6 **until he sold it to one of the family's Negro retainers...summer roads:** In "Mississippi," Faulkner describes Ned, a family retainer who inherited two trunks' worth of clothes from the Faulkner family and who could startle the author sometimes if he caught a glimpse of him on the road wearing the family's cast-off clothing (*ESPL* 39).

7.11-13 **the perennial and immortal Best Man, the apotheosis of the masculine singular:** see note 6.31.

7.21 **the store:** "Appendix: Compson" describes a farmer's supply store much like the one operated by the Varners: "that gloomy cavern where only men entered--a cavern cluttered and walled stalagmite-hung with plows and discs and loops of tracechain and singletrees and mulecollars and sidemeat and cheap shoes and horse linament and flour and molasses, gloomy because the goods it contained were not shown but hidden rather since those who supplied Mississippi farmers, or at least Negro Mississippi farmers, for a share of the crop did not wish, until that crop was made and its value approximately computable, to show them what they could learn to want, but only to supply them on specific demand with what they could not help but need" (745-46).

7.22 plowline: lengths of cotton rope, usually about twenty feet long, sold in hardware or general merchandise stores. The ropes are attached to a ring on the bit on either side of the animal's head and extend through a ring on the harness (Walton 68).

7.23 bights: the loop of a coiled rope, as distinguished from its ends; the part between the ends (*OED*).

7.24-25 he turned and saw silhouetted by the open door, a man smaller than common: Snyder examines Faulkner's use of the frame motif to suspend action and focus the reader's attention. Ab's initial stance in the doorway, she maintains, underlines the intrusive nature of his entry into a community that was less base before he came (21-23). The progression of doorframe scenes then measures the advance of the Snopeses: Flem is soon sharing the doorway with Jody Varner as they discuss business, and, not long afterward, he possesses the key to the door.

Moreland also focuses on the door and its symbolic role in Ab's initial foray into Frenchman's Bend. He sees Ab's arrival as a re-enactment of the primal scene of southern social exclusion archetypically featuring a poor white, like Sutpen, banging for admittance on the door of the plantation. The store is simply a modern version of the economic power center represented by the antebellum plantation ("Antisemitism, Humor, and Rage in Faulkner's *The Hamlet*" 55).

7.26 frock coat: A "knee-length, double-breasted dress coat" (Brown 86). Ratliff identifies Ab's coat as one that had belonged to Colonel Sartoris and that had been given to him by Rosa Millard thirty years before (33.9-11).

7.32 Snopes: The first printed use of the Snopes name is on page 106 of *Sart* (Meriwether, *Literary* 40). Campbell and Foster comment on the unpleasant connotations suggested by the initial letters of the Snopes name (among them, words like snake, sneer, snarl, snob) (104). Smith speculates that the "opes" sound in the Snopes name is intended as an allusion to the name of John Scopes of the famous monkey trial, with its suggestion of atheistic, anti-traditional forces. Cf. a February 19, 1957 letter from Phil Stone to James B. Meriwether in which Stone says that "the name had no connection to the Scopes trial" (*Brodsky* 266).

8.14-15 Boy and two girls. Wife and her sister: Ab deliberately neglects to mention Colonel Sartoris Snopes, the young boy in "Barn." Ratliff remembers "a little one" when he tells his version of the "Barn Burning" story. See note 13.30-31.

8.20 hands: synecdoche referring to field hands, or manual laborers in the field (Walton 65).

8.30-31 "Third and fourth," Varner said. "Furnish out of the store here. No cash": Walton describes this as a "rather common type of sharecropping, whereby the landowner supplies the tenant with land and one-third of the seed and fertilizer for cotton and one-fourth of the seed and fertilizer for corn and receives in turn one third of the harvested cotton and one-fourth of the harvested corn" (Walton 72). The system, Woodward maintains, was "one of the strangest contractual relationships in the history of finance" (180). A tenant farmer pledged his unmade crop as collateral in order that he might be extended credit on supplies from the store. These supplies he was generally sold at the credit price, which was never less than 30 percent higher than the cash price (Woodward 180). Cf. *GDM*: "When they get done sending you to Parchman you'll have plenty of time between working cotton and corn you aint going to get no third and fourth of even, to study it" (68).

8.32 six-bit dollars: Southern: bits are small silver coins forming a fraction of a Spanish dollar. Now usually applied to a unit of value equivalent to an eighth of a dollar (*OED*). A six-bit dollar, then, is seventy-five cents.

8.36 gallery: porch.

8.37 **squatting**: a characteristic resting posture in the country, with the knees bent and the thighs resting near the heels. When Lucas Beauchamp sees the Memphis divining machine salesman squatting under a tree, he thinks, "*He mought talk like a city man and he mought even think he is one. But I know now where he was born at*" (*GDM* 80). Cf. *Flags*: "They seemed to be able to sit tirelessly and without discomfort on their heels" (126).

8.38 **Varner watched his caller limp stiffly**: see 16.21-23.

9.6-7 **"To hear that ere foot, you'd think he weighed two hundred pounds"**: See 58.11-12.

9.6 **that ere**: that there.

9.11 **sho now**: pshaw, sure (Wentworth, *American Dialect Dictionary*).

9.21 **the breathing archetype and protagonist of all men who marry young and father only daughters and are themselves but the eldest daughters of their own wives**: See 6.31.

9.22 **Tull**: Vernon Tull emerges as one of the voices that tells the story of the Bundrens and their epic adventures en route to bury Addie in *AILD*. Although he won't loan them one of his mules, Tull helps the Bundrens to cross the river (130) and looks for Cash's lost tools (150).

9.25 **cottonhouse**: a small building where cotton is stored after it is picked until there is enough of it to take it to the gin (Walton 63).

9.25 **Ike McCaslin's place**: The McCaslins are listed among Faulkner's aristocrats in Gavin Stevens's 1957 roster of the "proud fading white plantation names" (*Twn* 316). Meriwether points out that the McCaslins were not originally part of the southern aristocracy but were instead yeoman farmers like the McCallums, whom they may have replaced in the fiction. In support of this, he points out that the McCaslin twin who goes to war goes as an enlisted man, while Faulkner's aristocrats enter the service as officers (Interview 5/18/94). Ike is one of the hunters, a good one, who instruct Quentin Compson in the 1935 short story, "Lion" (*US* 186). In "Fool," first published in 1936, he owns the hardware store (121).

When Faulkner incorporated "Lion" into *GDM* (1942) as part of the chapter "The Bear," Ike became the boy who is initiated into the rituals of the wilderness by Sam Fathers. In *Big Woods* (1955), Ike is again one of the hunters, but in most later novels, he is only mentioned in his connection with the hardware store (*Twn* 12, *Mans* 31-32, *Reiv* 14). In *Intruder* (1948), he is still alive at 90 (93).

9.26 **that burnt barn:** see [Manuscript Opening]. The charge of arson was a serious one. Williamson cites Tippah County Courthouse records that have Sam Thompson, editor of the local paper, saying to Faulkner's grandfather, Charlie Butler, "Shoot, you house-burning son-of-a-bitch." Butler, who was a town marshall and was in the process of arresting Thompson for public intoxication and disturbing the peace, did shoot and kill Thompson before a crowd of seventy-five or one hundred witnesses (96). It is not clear why Thompson accused Butler of being a house burner, but arson was considered a cowardly crime, the resort of the low-bred and powerless, and the mere allegation would have been highly insulting (Williamson 108).

9.26 **Harris:** "Our enemy" (*CS* 3) in "Barn," Harris still refuses to question Sarty about his father's part in the barn burning (*CS* 5).

9.35 **leastways:** at least.

10.8 **negligee:** informal or incomplete attire, from the Fr. negleger, to neglect (*AHD*). The word is usually associated with feminine attire.

10.13 **Littlejohn's hotel:** Mrs. Littlejohn's boarding house is first described in *FA* as the place where Suratt rents a room when in Frenchman's Bend (26).

10.15-16 **not only the only Negro servant but the only servant of any sort in the whole district:** Faulkner contradicts this at 214.38-215.1 and at 215.15.

10.19-20 **his mother, a plump cheery bustling woman:** Mrs. Varner's personality alters in *Twn*, where she is "his grim wife herself not church-ridden but herself running the local church she belonged to with the cold high-handedness of a ward boss" (276).

10.23-28 **his sister, a soft ample girl with definite breasts even at thirteen and eyes like cloudy hothouse grapes and a full damp mouth always slightly open...listen:** first description in the novel of Eula Varner, emphasizing her voluptuousness. Cf. "The waiter brings in oranges / Bananas figs and hothouse grapes" from Eliot's "Sweeney Among the Nightingales" (35, noted Adams, "Apprenticeship" 116-17 and McDaniel 92). Cf.*Mosq*: "hothouse face" (16, noted McDaniel 92). Cf. *Flags*: "Belle's eyes were like hothouse grapes and her mouth was redly mobile, rich with discontent" (168, noted McDaniel 92). Cf. Little Belle in *Sanc*: "...darkening into the pale whisper of her white dress, of the delicate and urgent mammalian whisper of that curious small flesh which he had not begot and in which appeared to be vatted delicately some seething sympathy with the blossoming grape" (Corrected Text 175). Cf. *WP* for the tall convict's recollection of a former girlfriend "with ripe breasts and a heavy mouth and dull eyes like ripe muscadines" (338). Eula at sixteen in *FA* is "softly ample" with eyes again "like cloudy hothouse grapes" (16). In *Twn*, her eyes are blue: "not the hard and dusty blue of fall but the blue of spring blooms, all one inextricable mixture of wistaria cornflowers larkspur bluebells weeds" (332). Cf. *Elmer*: "Myrtle's...sweet red mouth half opened to indicate interest, her moving knees he would like to have touched with his if he could only dance, her wide inquiring eyes beneath the pure molasses of her hair when he was at last presented" (21).

10.30 **hadn't aimed to:** hadn't planned to.

10.36-37 **all poste and riposte of humor's light whimsy, tierce, quarto, and prime:** A riposte is a retaliatory action, maneuver, or retort; a quick thrust given after parrying an opponent's lunge in fencing (*AHD*). Poste is presumably the original lunge or the statement that prompts the witty retort. Tierce is the third position from which a parry or thrust can be made in fencing (*AHD*). Prime is the first position of thrust and parry in fencing (*AHD*). Cf. "Riposte in Tertio" (*Unv* 135).

10.37-11.38 **"All I got to do is find out for sho about that barn...He dont dare!":** Jody's plan to cheat Ab initiates the pattern of one-upmanship that runs throughout the novel. Flem does not bring into the hamlet an alien spirit of acquisitiveness and deception; he merely retaliates in kind to what is done to him. See Gold for a discussion of the Snopes-like qualities that prevail in the community (passim). See Hoffman for a discussion of the Yankee motif of the trickster tricked as the model of all the trades and contests in *Ham* (71-72).

11.2 gathering time: harvest time. In this part of Mississippi, the earliest cotton begins to open mid-to-late August, and the job is usually completed by late October. In the Mississippi hills, the corn is not brought in until all the cotton is ginned (Walton 65).

11.10 rents it on shares: In the sharecropping system, the tenant pays a share of the crops raised to the landlord in lieu of rent (*AHD*).

11.16 nohow: in no way.

11.17 outen: out of.

11.31 laying-by: period of rest between cultivating and harvesting the crops (Walton 66).

12.18 buckboard: A four-wheeled open light carriage with the seat or seats attached to flexible planks running between the front and rear axles (*AHD*). Cf. the description of Nat Wheeler in Willa Cather's *One of Ours*: "Half an hour after the wagon left, Nat Wheeler put on an alpaca coat and went off in the rattling buckboard in which, though he kept automobiles, he still drove about the country....He preferred his buckboard to a car because it was light, went easily over heavy or rough roads, and was so rickety that he never felt he had to suggest his wife's accompanying him." Ratliff, too, will sample the automobile (*Twn* 113) and revert to his buckboard.

12.22 dog kennel: see 6.13-14.

12.32 ere: even.

13.9-12 among the women...cabin galleries: Hoffman points out that Ratliff's vocation serves a narrative function because it gives him access to a broad cross-section of people, male and female. In a frontier society, compassion and empathetic response were more often associated with women than with men (79).

13.11 splint chair: chair constructed with thin strips of wood (*OED*).

13.22-18.10 "Just say it was following along...I dont--": Ratliff's version of the "Barn" story differs from the original on several important points. He eliminates Sarty from the retelling and substitutes Flem as the son who accompanies Ab to the De Spain mansion, thus doing away with Sarty's sensation of "peace and joy" ("Barn," *CS* 10) and his warning visit to De Spain (*CS* 23). He invents a conversation between De Spain and Ab (15.14-22), and he fills in the details of what happens after the shots that Sarty hears in "Barn." De Spain rides to the Snopes shack, finds the men gone, and returns to his burning barn where he encounters Flem watching the blaze. The next day, Ab cancels his contract (17.6-18.10).

13.23 druv: drove.

13.30-31 a little one: Sarty. See Manuscript opening. Moreland argues that Faulkner disposes of Sarty and replaces him with Flem in order to present a different type of escape from Ab's repetitive cycle of violence, a "twentieth century capitalist's way out" ("Antisemitism, Humor, and Rage in Faulkner's *The Hamlet*" 56).

13.39 hawgs: hogs.

14.6 chewing sweet gum: "When the sap from the sweet gum tree begins to run in spring and early summer, it can be taken from the tree and chewed like a chewing gum. Too soft, it sticks to one's teeth; too hard, it breaks rather than chews. But at exactly the right stage, it has a satisfactory gum base and tasty flavor" (Walton 71).

14.8 like a pair of heifers: Throughout *Ham.*, Faulkner identifies the bovine with the feminine and the equine with the masculine.

14.11 wore out: worn out.

14.12 snicked: to cut, snip, clip, nick; to strike or hit sharply (*OED*).

14.12 the nigh one: the nearer one (*OED*).

14.13 stern: the buttocks of a person or beast (*OED*).

14.36 wrastling: wrestling.

14.38 **chamber pot:** a portable vessel used especially in a bedroom as a toilet (*AHD*).

15.1 **The nigger said Ab stepped in it on deliberate purpose:** Cf. Balzac's *Gobseck*: "...I went out, leaving traces of my muddy boots on the carpet which covered the paved staircase. I like to leave mud on a rich man's carpet; it is not petty spite; I like to make them feel a touch of the claws of Necessity" (273, noted Cohen, "Balzac and Faulkner" 338).

15.4 **offen:** off of.

15.15 **figger:** figure.

15.22 **tromp:** variation of the verb tramp (*OED*).

15.36 **brickbats:** a piece of brick, usually half a brick, used as a weapon or missile (*AHD*).

15.39 **cussing a blue streak:** a rapid and seemingly interminable stream of words, probably in allusion to a streak of lightning (*AHD*).

16.2 **hames:** curved pieces of wood or metal placed over, fastened to, or forming, the collar of a draught horse (*OED*).

16.3 **choke strops:** a strap which connects the collar with the belly band and keeps the collar in place when the horse backs (*OED*).

16.13-14 **hemming and hawing:** idiomatic: to be hesitant and indecisive; equivocate (*AHD*).

16.19 **Sat-day:** Saturday.

16.21-23 **on that clubfoot where ... the war:** Faulkner details Ab's career as a horse thief in *Unv*. His Civil War injury is first mentioned in "Barn," where he walks "stiffly from where a Confederate provost's man's musket ball had taken him in the heel on a stolen horse thirty years ago" (*CS* 5). Cf. also 29.14-15: "when here comes somebody that never even owned the horses even and shot him in the heel."

16.21 **Uncle Buck McCaslin:** Buck McCaslin is one of the McCaslin brothers who figure in *Unv* and *GDM*. In *Unv* (1938), Colonel Sartoris agrees to allow only one of the McCaslin brothers to enlist in his regiment, and it is Uncle Buddy who wins the card game to determine which one will go (*Unv* 57). Between *Unv* and *GDM*, the roles of the brothers are reversed. In *GDM*, Ike McCaslin recalls that his father, Buck, "was a member of Colonel Sartoris' horse in Forest's command" (234).

16.21-22 Colonel John Sartoris: John Sartoris was modelled after Faulkner's great-grandfather, Colonel William Clark Falkner, who, like Colonel Sartoris, was voted out of his command of the 2nd Mississippi Infantry by his men. Colonel Falkner returned home to organize a volunteer company, the First Mississippi Partisan Rangers, to found a railroad, and eventually to be murdered in the streets of Ripley by a business partner (See McHaney, "The Falkners and the Origins of Yoknapatawpha County: Some Corrections"). Colonel Sartoris first enters Faulkner's fiction as the legendary dreamer in *Flags* (5), great-grandfather of young Bayard. His Civil War career is fleshed out in *Unv*, where he, having been removed from the command by his men, leads a band of marauders against the Yankees. While away from home, he leaves Granny Millard in Ab Snopes' care (136). Ab Snopes expresses his optimism for his younger son's future when he names him Colonel Sartoris Snopes.

16.22 his-self: himself.

16.33-34 Major De Spain's barn taken fire and was a total loss: The loss of a barn and its contents was much more substantial than the loss of a house would have been. De Spain's barn would have housed his stock after dark, feed for the winter, equipment, and all the seeds for next year's crop. Balzac's peasants also pose the threat of arson. Cf. *Les Paysans*: "Here is the harvest beginning! I am not going away until I have lighted my pipe at their ricks" (205).

17.10 cypress-roofed corn crib: a shed, usually close to the barn, built of rough lumber with either a tin or a shingle roof, that stores the corn used to feed farm animals (Walton 63).

17.11 rid: rode.

17.12 towsacks: sacks made of flax, hemp, or jute (*OED*).

17.25 **coal oil:** kerosene (Walton 62).

17.26 **right:** archaic: with intensive force; very (*OED*).

17.26 **smart:** dialectical: considerable in number, amount, extent (*OED*).

17.27 **swinged:** dialectical alteration of singe, scorch (*OED*).

18.34-35 sagging broken-backed cabin set in its inevitable grassless and treeless plot: A broken-backed cabin has a badly sagging roof (Brown 38). For other examples of wasteland imagery, see also 19.38, 21.8-11, 118.5. The ashes, dust, absence of vegetation, and shards of broken pottery all suggest a world that cannot sustain life. See 6.31. While the most obvious source for the wasteland emphasis is Eliot, there is another, more local, source. Howard Odum, chairman of the progressive School of Public Welfare and the Department of Sociology at the University of North Carolina at Chapel Hill, directed his attention to another kind of waste: the "human waste" of poverty and illiteracy in a region of such superabundant natural resources. He writes in the groundbreaking 1936 *Southern Regions of the United States*:

> The measure of human waste will be found in the later inventory of institutions. These are shown in the ranking of the Southeastern States in the lowest quartile of nearly all indices of health and education, of government and public welfare, and of the multiple cultural equipment of the people. Certain aspects of this waste, however, represent such elemental factors in the composite picture as to require cataloguing here. Such is the pathology of submarginal folk, of killings and homicides, of state conflicts and rivalries, of sectarian strife, of race conflict, of lynchings and mobs, of drain and strain in intemperate work and living for men, women, and children (51).

It is realistic to suppose that Faulkner was aware of the UNC-affiliated group of social scientists and historians (See also e.g. Gerald Johnson, *The Wasted Land*, Rupert Vance, *Human Factors in Cotton Culture*, Clarence Cason, *90 in the Shade*, Benjamin Kendrick, *The South Looks at Its Past*, Arthur Raper, *Preface to Peasantry: A Tale of Two Black Belt Communities*). In late 1931, Faulkner visited Milton J. Abernethy, a student at UNC-Chapel Hill and owner of the Intimate Bookshop. While in Chapel Hill, he stayed in a room above the bookshop, was entertained at the home of Phillips Russell, who taught a writing class at the

University, and even met with Russell's writing students (Blotner, One vol. ed. 287). See Grimwood's discussion of the southern intellectual milieu during the period when Faulkner was composing *Ham* (142-167).

18.37 howitzer shell: A howitzer is a relatively short cannon that delivers shells at medium muzzle velocity, usually by a high trajectory (*AHD*).

19.11-37 He saw suddenly in one of the sashless windows...as he rode past: Gresset considers this to be a variation of a typical Faulkner scene, one that recurs with some regularity in his early fiction. In its purest form, a voyeur/intruder comes upon another man, whom he surprises, by a spring. The scene typically occurs at twilight, with the shadows filtering through the trees. The time of the year is invariably springtime, usually April or May, and a bird is always singing. In this scene, for example, although the bird is absent, the "measured plaint" of the well-pulley suggests the "meaningless and profound" noise of the bird in *S&F* (169) and the "monotonous repetition" of the bird in *Sanc* (21). Also figuring in the scene is the act of drinking; Popeye is the only character involved in the analogous scenes who does not share a drink with other characters (*SP* 9,6; *Flags* 2,6; *Sart* 2,6; *Sanc* 1; *Sanc OT* 1, noted Gresset, *Fascination* 184-198). The reversals of the norm are important here: the surpriser suspects that he is himself to be surprised, as if he is approaching an ambush, which figuratively proves to be the case. Instead of the bird notes, as noted, Faulkner substitutes the monotonous plaint of the well pulley and the meaningless drone of the female voices. There is no offer of refreshment in the *Ham* variation.

19.11-15 He saw suddenly in one of the sashless windows...a face...vanished again: first glimpse of Flem in the novel. In *FA*, Flem is first seen "behind the new plate glass window of his recently remodelled bank" (13). Cf. Ratliff's vision of Eula's "calm beautiful mask beneath the Sunday hat once more beyond the moving window" (147.15-16). Cf. also 306.7-9: "They stood, clumped darkly in the silver yard and called up at the blank windows until suddenly someone was standing in one of them. It was Flem Snopes's wife."

19.13-14 the lower jaw moving steadily and rhythmically with a curious sidewise thrust: Constant chewing is also a trademark gesture of Ab's: "He chewed something--tobacco when he could get it, willow bark when he couldn't--all the time" ("Unvanq" 74).

19.18-37 He had already begun to hear the mournful measured plaint of a rusted well-pulley...absolutely static young women beside it...dreamy solidarity of statuary...turning slowly in unison as he rode past: Brooks cites this passage as an example of Faulkner's distancing technique, by which he, while rendering a scene with telescopic clarity, stylizes it so that it is remote from the life of the reader (*Yoknapatawpha Country* 168-69). See also Hönnighausen's study of stylizing features in Faulkner's work, assimilated from fin-de-siècle art nouveau and arts and crafts movements (*Art of Stylization*).

19.22 epicene gallows: Faulkner uses a favorite word, reserved in his earlier fiction for androgynous Flapper girls. Januarius Jones cannot imagine anyone making love to the "epicene" Cecily Saunders (*SP* 249). Cf. also Narcissa Benbow's "epicene unrepose" in the garden (*Flags* 47). The tableau Varner witnesses joins images of life (the well) and death (the gallows), and may even look ahead, with its adjective, to the kind of sexual confusion that is a form of death itself in the world of *Ham*. McDaniel identifies a source for Faulkner's use of the word in Hardy's description of Sue Bridehead in *Jude the Obscure*: "that epicene tenderness of hers was too harrowing" (122, *Annotations* 40) and in Byron's description of Don Juan disguised as Juanna in the sultan's harem (6.58.2, *Annotations* 40). Cf. also "Mr. Eliot's Sunday Morning Service":

> Along the garden wall the bees
> With hairy bellies pass between
> The staminate and pistilate,
> Blest office of the epicene (l.25-28).

19.25-26 "The house aint fitten for hogs": Ab makes this comment in "Barn" (*CS* 9) and in Ratliff's retelling of the same incident (*Ham* 13.37-39).

20.16 writhen: contorted.

21.28 rack: a horse's gait in which the two feet on each side are lifted simultaneously, and all four feet are off the ground together at certain moments (*OED*).

22.4 broad flat face: Faulkner often uses flatness as a sign of inadequacy. Ab in "Barn" is like "something cut ruthlessly from tin, depthless, as though, sidewise to the sun, it would cast no shadow" (*CS*

10). Popeye too has the "depthless quality of stamped tin" (*Sanc* 2). See below 22.15-16 for reinforcement of the impression that Flem is incomplete: "His face was as blank as a pan of uncooked dough."

22.15-16 His face was as blank as a pan of uncooked dough: Cf. the spinster schoolteacher who befriends Elmer Hodge in "Portrait of Elmer": "The teacher had a thick gray face like heavy dough" (*US* 616). The schoolteacher's form of incompleteness does not in any way resemble Flem's: she is sexually unsatisfied.

23.4 Aint no benefit in farming: Flem's contention that there is no benefit in farming indirectly addresses the Agrarian agenda, which was still actively debated in the thirties. What the Agrarians advocated, romantically, as a life on the soil, Flem rejects, realistically, as a life consigned to back-breaking work and poverty.

23.22 chew: chewing tobacco.

23.23 nickel: five cents worth.

23.23 suption: taste, flavor, goodness (Brown 193).

23.38-39 Two miles further on, dusk overtook him, the shortening twilight of late April: Twilight had great significance for Faulkner as a transitional period of time, poised between day and night, between reality and the dream. *FA*, which was probably written in 1926, ends lyrically in the April twilight: "A world of lilac peace, in which Varner's store and the blacksmith shop were like sunken derelicts in the motionless and forgotten caverns of the sea. No sound, no movement; no tide to knock their sleeping bones together. And yet it was not quite night" (71). Cf. "The Hill" (1922): "The sun plunged silently into the liquid green of the west and the valley was abruptly in shadow. And as the sun released him, who lived and labored in the sun, his mind that troubled him for the first time became quieted. Here in the dusk, nymphs and fauns might riot to a shrilling of thin pipes, to a shivering and hissing of cymbals in a sharp volcanic abasement beneath a tall icy star" (*EPP* 92). Cf. *SP* (1926): "Dusk was a dream of arrested time..." (290). *S&F* (1929) was originally to be titled "Twilight."

23.39 late April: Faulkner draws on traditional associations, both literary and religious, of April with the promise of renewal and resurrection. Unlike Chaucer, who finds that the same forces that transform nature are at work in human life (*Canterbury Tales*, General Prologue), Faulkner locates an ironic distance between the burgeoning earth and the sterile relations among humans. He almost certainly has in mind Eliot's "April is the cruelest month" (*The Waste Land* 1). The following April in *Ham*, the men of Frenchman's Bend chase phantom horses in the moonlight while Eula gazes down from a window above, waiting for no one. See note 306. 8-18. Yonce notes the mythic significance of late April. April 30 and May 1 (May Day) were traditionally celebrated with mock marriages between an eligible maiden and a village bachelor (*Annotations* 143). Hönnighausen comments on the large number of poems included in Braithwaite's poetry anthologies that treat April in the style of the late Romantics (*William Faulkner: The Art of Stylization* 83).

23.39-24.2 the blanched dogwoods stood among the darker trees with spread raised palms like praying nuns: The dogwood (*Cornus florida*) ties in with the religious connotations of April. Blooming at Easter time, it has a legend that links it to the Crucifixion. The central bloom, a light green berry, is surrounded by four flat white leaf bracts that resemble flower petals (Petrides 76). Each bract is tipped with a dark brownish spot that suggests the wounds of Christ. The metaphorical association with the palms of praying nuns highlights the religious association. Quentin Compson on the last day of his life thinks: "Roses. Not virgins like dogwood, milkweed" (95). Cf. *The Marble Faun* (1924): "Dogwood stands so cool and still,/ Like hands that, palm up, rigid lie/ In invocation to the sky/ As they spread there, frozen white/ Upon the velvet of the night" (34). Cf. also *SP*: "At the foot of the hill, a dogwood tree spread flat, palm-like branches in invocation among dense green, like a white nun" (158).

24.1-2 darker trees with spread raised palms like praying nuns: Traces of Faulkner's New Orleans encounter with Catholicism occasionally crop up in his later work. Imagery derived from Catholic ritual is common in his early stories and poetry. Cf. "Nympholepsy" (1925): "ring of hammer and anvil like a call to vespers" (*US* 332), "this green cathedral of trees" (*US* 332), "repeating slow orisons in a green nave" (*US* 333), "a priest...reading his soul" (*US* 333, noted Hönnighausen 176). Cf. also "The Priest" (1925): "Evening like a nun shod with silence" (*NOS* 38). Later in the same year that he wrote "Nympholepsy" and "The Priest," Faulkner went to Europe and probably had further encounters with Catholicism.

24.2 **whippoorwills:** an insect-eating nocturnal North American bird (*Caprimulgus vociferus*) of the goatsucker family, having spotted brown feathers that blend in with its natural habitat. Its name is imitative of its call (*AHD*).

Chapter Two

25.2-3 **harrow teeth:** A harrow is a farm implement consisting of a heavy frame with sharp teeth or upright disks, used to break up and even off plowed ground (*AHD*).

25.30-31 **fire insurance policy:** Cf. Michaud's warning in *Les Paysans*: "General, speaking of fire, you ought to insure all your houses and farm buildings" (149).

26.25-28 **There was another boy then...them movings:** see Manuscript opening.

26.33 **dogfennel:** a strong-smelling European weed (*Anthemis cotula*) naturalized in North America (*AHD*). Also known as mayweed, it bears a daisy-like flower (Brown 72).

26.34 **bitterweed:** A North American species of wormwood, bitterweed blooms in late summer and early fall. It is intensely bitter and makes milk taste the same when cows eat it (Brown 31). Malcolm Franklin, Faulkner's stepson, titled his 1977 memoir of Faulkner *Bitterweeds: Life at Rowan Oak with William Faulkner*.

26.36-39 **I growed up next to where he was living...Holland:** Faulkner stresses the common background of Ratliff and Flem.

26.39 **Anse Holland:** In "Smoke," Anse Holland arrives from out of nowhere to marry the daughter of the richest landowner in the county (*KG* 3).

27.25-30 **"Take a man like that," he says, "A man that's independent about protecting his-self...a fellow that independent:** This stated philosophy of self-interest recalls Luzhin's arguments along the same lines in *Crime and Punishment*: "Science now tells us, love yourself above all men, for everything in the world rests on self-interest. You love yourself and manage your own affairs properly and your coat remains whole. Economic truth adds that the better private affairs are organized in society the more whole coats, so to say--the firmer are its foundations and the better is the common welfare organized too. Therefore, in acquiring wealth solely and exclusively for myself, I am acquiring, so to speak, for all, and helping to bring to pass my neighbor's getting a little more than a torn coat; and not from private, personal liberality, but as a consequence of the general advance" (131).

27.28 **just as lief**: readily, willingly (*AHD*).

28.4-9 "...there aint but two men I know can risk fooling with them folks...That aint been proved yet neither," Ratliff said pleasantly: Ratliff refers to himself and Will Varner. See notes 71.8-13, 87.33-39.

28.14 **livery barn**: a stable that boards and cares for horses for a fee (*AHD*).

28.19 **drummers**: traveling salesmen.

28.31-32 **intellect still sound enough to make money mistakes at least in his own favor**: Contrast with Flem, who makes no money mistakes whatsoever. See 56.24-25.

28.35 **blood's thick**: The importance of the kinship bond is introduced in "Barn," when Ab tells Sarty, "You got to learn to stick to your own blood or you ain't going to have any blood to stick to you" (*CS* 8). Flem is finally undone because he neglects tribal loyalty to his kinsman Mink Snopes (*Mans* 416).

29.6 **fireflies**: any of various nocturnal beetles of the family *Lampyridae*, characteristically having luminescent chemicals in the posterior tip of the abdomen that produce a flashing light (*AHD*).

29.10-26 "There was that business during the war...that's just hearsay": See 16.21-23.

29.15 **shot him in the heel**: Thetis, a goddess, bore seven sons by

Peleus, a mortal. She thrust each of the children into a fire to purge them of their mortal inheritance. Peleus, however, snatched the last, Achilles, from the fire when Thetis had burned everything but his ankle bone (Graves 272). An Achilles heel has come to mean a single weak spot, because Achilles was slain by an arrow that pierced his heel (Evans, *Brewer's Dictionary*).

29.32 **Pat Stamper:** legendary horse trader in the tall tale tradition, derived from the shrewd Yankee peddler of downeast humor and the archetypal horse trader of frontier humor (Wheeler 69). Stamper makes his first appearance in "Fool."

29.33 **plumb:** utter, absolute, sheer (*AHD*).

29.33 **curdled:** separated into curds and whey. Brown remarks that, as Ratliff has already declared Ab to be soured, he is now taking the process a step further, since milk curdles only after it has already soured (65).

29.34-47.8 **"You mean he locked horns with Pat Stamper...he says":** The novel version of the "Fool About a Horse" story differs from the short story version, published in the August 1936 number of *Scribner's Magazine*, in a single essential: an unnamed narrator, identified as Suratt in earlier manuscript and typescript versions of the short story, is telling a tale about his own father, while Ratliff, in the novel, is relating a story about himself and Ab Snopes (Meriwether, *Literary* 42). The "Fool" story rehearses in a simpler, comic fashion the "Spotted Horses" story. The matrix of the novel, the economic deal that rises from masculine pride and competitiveness, is here, as in the "Spotted Horses" story, tied up with the surrogate masculinity of a horse. Here, again, it is the women who are practical and sane, and it is the women who lose because of male gamesmanship. Ratliff's telling of the story generates intense sympathy for Ab Snopes without emphasizing the tragic potential embedded in his horse dealings.

"Fool" falls in the tall tale tradition, with its horse swap, its trickster tricked motif, its framing device, its oral delivery in the vernacular idiom, its hyperbolic good spirits, and its ironic view of human behavior (see Roarke, Jacobs, Blair, Hoffman, Wheeler). The immediate source for "Fool" may be Augustus Baldwin Longstreet's "The Horse Swap" in *Georgia Scenes* (noted Jacobs 305) or Twain's "The Celebrated Jumping Frog of Calaveras County" (noted McHaney, "What Faulkner Learned"

122), but Faulkner owes something to George Washington Harris, Johnson Jones Hooper, Joseph Glover Baldwin, Bill Arp, Henry Clay Lewis, and all the oral storytellers who passed on tales of Davy Crocket, Mink Fink, and their ilk. Faulkner himself ventured into the tall tale as a young man when he and Sherwood Anderson exchanged yarns about the web-footed Al Jackson who metamorphoses into half-man, half-sheep (*ESPL* 7, *US* 474-479, *Mosq* 277). He later recalled a dream that Anderson told him about, in which he wandered a country road, trying to exchange a horse for a night's sleep (*ESPL* 3).

29.39 **Stetson:** "a trademark used for a hat having a high crown and a wide brim" (*AHD*).

30.3-4 **for the pleasure of beating a worthy opponent as much as for gain:** Cf. "The Horse Swap": "I'd rather lose ten dollars any time than not make a trade, though I hate to fling away a good hoss" (*Georgia Scenes* 29).

30.5 **hostler:** one who is employed to tend horses, especially at an inn (*AHD*).

30.20 **separator:** a device that separates cream from milk (*AHD*).

30.35 **Whiteleaf Bridge:** According to Brown, the bridge where the road to Frenchman's Bend crosses Whiteleaf Creek, which, if Jefferson is Oxford, would correspond to Yellow Leaf Creek four miles east of Oxford (215).

31.1 **bob-wire:** barbed wire, or "twisted strands of fence wire with barbs at regular intervals" (*AHD*).

31.4 **He was a fool about a horse:** McHaney cites Faulkner's mention of human/animal pairings (Eve and the serpent, Androcles and the lion, Mary and the lamb, Ahab and the whale) as emblems of desire in *Notes on a Horsethief* (19) and *A Fable* (161): "and all the celestial zoology of horse and goat and swan and bull...the firmament of man's history" ("What Faulkner Learned from the Tall Tale" 133).

31.12 **jawing:** to talk vociferously; jabber (*AHD*).

31.14 gumption: boldness of enterprise; initiative or aggressiveness (*AHD*).

31.16 straight stock: a simple tool, composed of two wooden handles, a wooden beam, and a standard to which different metal plows are attached. One end of the beam is attached to the singletree, and the other end is connected to the plowhandles (Walton 71).

31.17 sorghum mill: a mule-operated device for extracting the juice from sorghum, a large tropical grass (*Sorghum vulgare*). The juice is then boiled in shallow vats until it is reduced to sorghum molasses (Brown 183-84).

31.24 far field: the field that is farthest from the house (Walton 64).

31.26 plow stock: the basic frame of a plow (Brown 151).

31.36 sidemeat: salted pork or bacon, typically eaten by the poor (Brown 178).

32.8 passel: considerable number or quantity (Brown 145).

32.9 morning glories: among the most decorative of wildflowers, morning glories (*Ipomoea purpurea* or *Ipomoea pes-caprae*), with their showy purple flowers and broad, thick, shiny leaves, will grow in the most unlikely places (Greene and Blomquist 103).

32.15 drove of a horse: Faulkner hand-wrote a note in the margin of the typescript setting copy regarding its usage: "Please ask the printer to keep his high school proof reader from changing the text such as here for instance. The man never had but *one* horse" (*Manuscripts II* 58).

32.17 Miz Snopes's separator money: looks ahead to Mrs. Armstid's five dollars, "earned weaving by firelight after dark" (292.1). In *GDM*, Lucas Beauchamp swaps Roth Edmonds's $300 mule for a divining machine (83).

32.32 forced draft: This is a steamboating term, derived from the use of fire or artificial means to increase the pressure in a boiler by increasing the heat that impels it. The sense here is that Ratliff and Ab have used artificial means to make the horse go faster.

33.17 **Ab in the traces:** a comic foreshadowing of Henry Armstid's actual manner of plowing with his wife (313.19-21). In the bitter, hardscrabble life of these farmers, humans are in constant danger of being debased to the level of animals. Cf. another comic treatment in "Sut Lovingood's Daddy, Acting Horse": "I'll be hoss now *mysef,* an' pull the plow whilst yu drives me" (*Sut Lovingood: Yarns Spun By a Nat'ral Born Durn'd Fool* 22).

33.24 **Whiteleaf store:** Varner's store in "Fool" (122).

33.25 **double tree:** a cross bar with single-trees at each end, to which each of a pair of mules is attached (Walton 64).

33.32-34 **that horse of Beasley's eyes rolling white as darning eggs and its mane and tale swirling like a grass fire:** Cf. the Pegasus-like horse in the short story, "Carcassonne," which was first published in *These Thirteen* (1931): "A BUCKSKIN PONY *with eyes like blue electricity and a mane like tangled fire*" (*CS* 895). A convention of the horse trading story is the deceptively spry look of the horse. Cf. Bullet's tail, which "made amends for all his defects" with its "festoons" and "curves" (Longstreet, "The Horse Swap" 25). Cf. also Sut Lovingood's horse "spreadin his tail feathers to fly" (*Sut Lovingood: Yarns Spun by a Nat'ral Born Durn'd Fool* 35).

33.33 **darning eggs:** an egg-shaped piece of porcelain which is slipped inside a sock to facilitate darning (Brown 68).

33.34 **I be dog:** exclamatory expression of surprise, derived from "I'll be doggoned," and used in the same way as "I'll be darned."

33.35 **dark blood bay:** a reddish brown horse, having a dark mane and tail (*AHD*)

34.3 **Hugh Mitchell:** Jody Varner in "Fool" (122).

34.13 **nohow:** anyhow.

34.20 **Pat Stamper, a stranger:** Strangers were distrusted in the tight-knit little farming communities of the Mississippi hill country. Jody, for instance, tries to take advantage of Ab Snopes because he is an outsider (7.37).

34.37-39 the entire honor and pride of the science and pride of horse-trading in Yoknapatawpha County depending on him to vindicate it: The two basic themes of the novel, according to Brooks, are love and honor (183). Ab contests with Pat Stamper not for money but for honor. Eula is sacrificed to Flem to save her honor, but her honor is preserved, as Brooks points out, by a commercial transaction (185). The theme of honor gets a humorous treatment when I. O. and Eck buy Ike's cow so that the Snopes name can be kept "pure as a marble monument" for Eck's children "to grow up under" (204.22-23). Neither Jack Houston nor Mink Snopes is willing to compromise his principles to avert the confrontation that results in Houston's murder. For Houston, it would be intolerable to allow Mink Snopes to get something for nothing by pasturing his yearling free for the winter. Houston is further riled by the fact that Mink lives on a piece of what was his own land until Varner foreclosed on it about a year before the quarrel over the yearling. Mink in turn kills Houston to defend his honor and pride (218.27-28). In the ultimate betrayal of honor, Flem refuses to come to Mink's rescue (333.38-39).

35.16 Three Mile Bridge: Brown identifies as the bridge over Four Mile Branch, on Miss. 334, three and a half miles SE of Oxford (199).

35.20-21 a dime's worth of saltpeter and a nickel's worth of tar and a number ten fish hook: Hoffman identifies these as common ruses in the science of horse-trading (85).

35.20 saltpeter: either of two white crystalline compounds, potassium nitrate or sodium nitrate, used in solid rocket propellants, in the manufacture of explosives, and in fertilizer (*AHD*).

35.24 laying into the collar: The horse's posture, leaning into the collar, conveys effort, rather than speed, on the part of a draft animal.

35.30 headstall: the section of a bridle that fits over a horse's head (*AHD*).

35.34 plow point: According to Walton, "big plows (especially middlebusters and turning plows) consist of two main parts--the wing and the point. The metal point is detachable, for sharpening or replacing. A new point is a dull gray. After it is used for plowing, a cast iron point shines like stainless steel" (68).

35.37-38 **get shut of it:** get rid of it.

35.38 **trimmed:** Informal: to thrash or beat soundly; to defeat; to cheat (*AHD*).

36.16 **span of mules:** pair of mules.

37.29 **durn fool:** Cf. *Sut Lovingood: Yarns Spun by a Nat'ral Born Durn'd Fool*.

38.5 **traces:** one of two side straps or chains connecting a harnessed draft animal to a vehicle or whiffletree (*AHD*).

38.23 **tongue:** the harnessing pole attached to the front axle of a horse-drawn vehicle (*AHD*).

38.30 **swurging:** surging (Brown 196).

38.35 **nigh wheel:** the wheel on the left side of an animal or vehicle (*AHD*).

38.36 **holp:** helped.

38.39 **snubbed up close:** secured by turning quickly about a post, so that there is no slack (*AHD*).

39.9 **bed:** the part of a wagon, truck, trailer, or freight car designed to carry loads.

39.21 **bits:** The bit is the metal mouthpiece of a bridle, serving to control, curb, and direct an animal (*AHD*).

40.12 **spraddled:** sprawled, spread apart; straddled (Wentworth, *American Dialect Dictionary*).

40.12-13 **breathing like a sawmill:** It is a sign of exhaustion that the horses are breathing loudly and with great effort and that their heads are down.

41.12 **hackamore:** a rope or rawhide halter with a wide band that can be lowered over a horse's eyes, used in breaking horses to a bridle (*AHD*).

41.35 **blow:** storm.

41.37 **croker sacks:** Lower southern: a large sack made from loosely woven, coarse material, such as burlap. Also called a towsack, gunnysack, or a crocus sack (*AHD*).

42.31-37 **that same air of perpetual bachelorhood which Jody Varner had...a pruner of vines, say:** first of two overt comparisons of Jody Varner and V.K. Ratliff. See also 318.36-319.4.

42.31 **faded clean blue shirt:** worn to match his eyes (*Mans* 168).

43.25-28 **Then there was a sound like a nail jabbed into a bicycle tire...vanished:** Inflation of a horse was not uncommon; the air was pumped into the loose skin under the shoulders. Faulkner exaggerates the effect, but he did not invent the strategy (Hoffman 85).

43.30 **Only it was the same horse we had left home with that morning:** In a collection of horse-trading lore, *Mister You Got Yourself a Horse*, approximately one fourth of the stories center on the back trade (noted Hoffman 84). Cf. *Les Paysans* for Old Fourchon's habit of selling the same otter to every new gentleman that comes through (33). Cf. "I Outwit a Yankee" by Davy Crockett, in which Crockett, running for Congress, trades a Yankee saloon keeper the same coonskin ten times over to slake the local thirst with ten quarts of New England rum (Schmitz 311).

44.19 **clumb:** climbed.

44.23 **et:** ate.

44.34 **middle buster:** a large plow most often used for breaking land in the spring. According to Walton, it "has a heavy metal beam, to which two animals are hitched by means of a doubletree; plow handles; and the major part of the plow, a V-shaped point with big wings on each side. When it is used, it plows a deep furrow--a trench with dirt evenly thrown on either side" (67). Cf. *My Ántonia*: the plough that has been "left

47

standing in the field" and which, "magnified" by the sun, achieves "heroic" dimensions (156) and glorifies the purposeful life worked close to the land.

44.40 **yonder:** Predominately, though not exclusively southern: being at an indicated distance, usually within sight.

45.4-5 **now it looked like all Texas:** hyperbolic referent for anything of enormous size.

45.17 **dicker:** to bargain, barter. Etymologically, the choice is interesting here because its first recorded use, in 1802, is in reference to horse trading (*AHD*).

45.25 **hams:** the thigh of the hind leg of certain animals (*AHD*).

45. 25 **hove:** Nautical: past tense of heave (*AHD*).

46.25-47.8 **I reckon if she wants it to run through more than once, it will run through more than once....It looks like she is fixing to get a heap of pleasure and satisfaction outen it,' he says":** Cf. *One of Ours*, where a separator, bought for Mrs. Wheeler by Claude's machine-mad brother Ralph, is also a symbol of the wasteful expense of energy (18).

Chapter Two, 3: See Chapter Three, 1.

47.14-23 **loud flat sound of two female voices...apparent absence from which of any discernible human speech or language...emitted by two enormous birds; as if the aghast and amazed solitude of some inaccessible and empty marsh or desert were being invaded and steadily violated by the constant bickering of the two last survivors of a lost species that had established residence in it:** The image of two sisters as birds conjures up the story of Procne and Philomela, who were transformed into the nightingale and the swallow. Philomela was raped by her sister's husband, and, although her tongue was cut out so that she could not reveal the crime, she transmitted the story by embroidering it on a piece of material. Eliot used the Philomela legend in *The Waste Land* to suggest both the debased relations among men and women and the failure of language (97-103). By stripping the sisters' speech of any discernible meaning, Faulkner, too, addresses the wasteland breakdown of language. He also presents an alternate vision of the end to the inspiring one of the Nobel Prize acceptance speech. Here, rather than the valiant "puny inexhaustible voice" of the last human (*ESPL* 120), he substitutes the incomprehensible and "bickering" voices of the final survivors of a "lost species."

47.29 bodies of that displacement and that apparently monstrous, that almost oppressive wellness, would need air and lots of it: See similar statements at 9.6-7 and 58.11-12.

47.32 fleeting vision of them as two cows, heifers: Faulkner identifies the feminine and the bovine elsewhere in *Ham*: Cf. Eula's bovine serenity and placidity as she chews on the constant sweet potato (113-15) and Ike's devotion to the apotheosis of the feminine in Jack Houston's cow. See note 165.38. Cf. also *Mosq*: "Jenny's bovine placidity" (58).

48.20 He has done swapped a man for a span of them: Ratliff's comment playfully acknowledges a commercial ethic that will finally allow for the bartering away of Eula Varner to Flem Snopes. He suggests here that Ab has traded Flem for a team of mules.

48.23 yawing: Nautical: To swerve off course momentarily; to move unsteadily or to weave (*AHD*).

48.24 sawed them about: maneuver them by pulling back and forth on the reins (Brown 169).

48.24 with absolutely needless violence: When Ab strikes the mules with a willow branch in "Barn," the narrator interpolates: "it was exactly the same quality that in later years would cause his descendants to overrun the engine before putting a motor car into motion, striking and reining back in the same movement" (*CS* 6).

49.7 McCallum's best: moonshine.

49.10 sup: sip.

49.12-34 The other took the bottle...hid the bottle in the weeds...raised it: Ab's refusal of the hospitality of a convivial drink with an old friend reveals how far he has curdled.

49.21 "How about in the rain?" Ratliff said: On rejected typescript page 80, after Ratliff asks Ab this question, there follows an exchange about Sarty Snopes: "The other didn't answer. He didn't move, no change in the harsh, knotted violent face. "Eight years," Ratliff said. "I heard that little one I saw then wasn't with you. You lost him, I reckon."
"Yes," the other said. He was looking at the bottle in his hand.
"I'm sorry," Ratliff said. The other shook the bottle and raised it, perhaps watching the forming bead" (*Manuscripts II* 672).

49.28 testing the bead: The bead is the small bubbles made by shaking a bottle of whiskey. Their size and duration reveal the quality of the whiskey (Brown 26).

49.30 Then he saw the eyes again, fierce and intractable and cold: When Ratliff sees Mink for the first time, he is reminded of Ab's eyes: "it's the same eyes" (73.12). Cf. also 161.10 for a description of Mink's "intractable face now cold and still with fury behind the single eyebrow."

50.7 "Come up, rabbits," he said. "Let's hit for town": See note 366.14-27.

Chapter Three

Chapter Three, 1: In early stages of composition, Chapter Three, part 1 preceded Chapter Two, part 3. Among miscellaneous typescript pages at the Alderman Library are those numbered 73-81, with the Chapter Three, part 1 material occupying 73-76, and the Chapter Two, part 3 material following on pages 77-81 (Kibler 272, *Manuscripts II* 644-49).

51.1-20 On the Monday morning when Flem Snopes came to clerk in Varner's store, he wore a brand new white shirt...particular soiling groove: Flem's adoption of a uniform suggests connection with two of Balzac's misers. Cf. Rigou in *Les Paysans*: "His dress never varied" (226). Cf. Grandet in *Eugenie Grandet*: "a man of bronze whose dress never varied" (8).

51.16-20 It was as though its wearer, entering though he had into a new life and milieu...established in it even on that first day his own particular soiling groove: Flem, as was common in that time and place, takes a bath once a week.

51.21-52.30 He rode up on a gaunt mule...nickels and dimes and went away: Flem's precipitate appearance behind the counter of Varner's store recalls Elmer Moffat's similar arrival in Apex in Wharton's *Custom of the Country*: "No one in Apex recalled where young Moffat had come from, and he offered no information on the subject. He simply appeared one day behind the counter of Luckaback's Dollar Shoe Store, and drifted thence to the office of Semple and Binch, the coal merchants, reappeared as the stenographer of the Police Court, and finally edged his way into the power-house of the Apex Water-Works" (309, noted McHaney, "Fouqué's *Undine* and Edith Wharton's *Custom of the Country*" 181).

51.21 He rode up on a gaunt mule: Dickerson charts Flem's rise from the gaunt mule on which he rides into town to the Varner team behind which he leaves town (377).

51.25-52.2 He did not speak...clap into the center of the face a frantic and desperate warning: Faulkner's description of Flem is reminiscent of Balzac's physical description of the usurer Gobseck: "Can you grasp a clear notion of that sallow wan face of his? I wish the Academie would give me leave to dub such faces the lunar type. It was like silvergilt with the gilt rubbed off....A pair of little eyes, yellow as a ferret's, and with scarce an eyelash to them, peered out from under the sheltering peek of a shabby old cap, as if they feared the light. He had the thin lips that you see in Rembrandt's or Metsu's portraits of alchemists and shrunken old men, and a nose so sharp at the tip that it put you in mind of a gimlet. His voice was low; he always spoke suavely; he never flew into a passion. His age was a problem; it was hard to say whether he had grown old before his time, or whether by economy of youth he had saved enough to last him his life" (*Gobseck* 268). Balzac emphasizes Gobseck's inhumanity by labeling him "a clockwork man" (268) and a "bill of exchange incarnate" (268).

51.32 tiny predatory nose like the beak of a hawk: Cf. *Mosq*:

"Gordon's hawk's face" (12). Cf. *Flags*: Colonel John Sartoris's "bearded hawklike face and the bold glamor of his dreams" (5) and Bayard Sartoris's face with its "hawklike planes" (38 noted Arnold, *Annotations* 14). Cf. Rigou's nose in *Les Paysans*: "his resemblance to a condor was but the more strikingly complete by reason of a nose of sanguine hue, immensely long, and very sharp at the tip" (noted Cohen, "Balzac and Faulkner: the Influence of *La Comédie humaine* on Faulkner's *Flags in the Dust* and the Snopes Trilogy" 334). Cf. the merchant Ryabin in *Anna Karenina* who buys Stephen Arkadyevitch's forest: "The smile vanished at once from Ryabin's face. A hawk-like, greedy, cruel expression was left upon it" (1:202). Cf. the agent of the Central Station, a "papier-maché Mephistophèles" (97), in *Heart of Darkness*: "his delicate hooked nose set a little askew and his mica eyes glittering without a wink" (100).

51.33 It was as though the original nose had been left off: Cf. *Sanc*: Popeye's incomplete face: "...he had no chin at all. His face just went away, like the face of a wax doll set too near a hot fire and forgotten" (4).

52.8-15 They came not belligerently but completely wary...look at the man whose name a week ago they had never heard...depart as quietly as they had come: Cf. Sutpen's advent in Jefferson: "face and horse that none of them had ever seen before, name that none of them had ever heard, and origin and purpose that some of them were never to learn" (*AbAb!* 32).

52.23-24 If the clerk was eating his lunch, he had hidden to do it: Flem's isolating himself to eat secretly mirrors his father's hiding the gift bottle of McCallum's best away to drink alone. See note 49.12-34.

54.5 plug: a flat cake of pressed or twisted tobacco (*AHD*).

54.8 smoking car story: a dirty joke, typical of those that would have been told in the male-only smoking car of a train.

54.12 chew: piece of tobacco to be held in the mouth and chewed (*AHD*).

54.16 "You aint paid for it," the clerk said: See note 56.24-38 regarding Flem's strict accounting.

55.4-6 He found himself not only on foreign soil but shut away

from his native state by a golden barrier, a wall of neatly accumulating minted coins: Money is for Ratliff a temptation, an impediment that bars him from not only his physical native state but also from his spiritual native state. Greed will be his downfall. See 357.36-37.

55.33-37 he looked about him with something of the happy surmise of the first white hunter...idyllic solitude of a virgin African vale teeming with ivory: first of two explicit analogies to colonial economies (noted Dimino 160). As so often occurs in *Ham*, the first reference is comical and harmless. The second is less so, because it is related to the unnaturalness and to the exploitive nature of Flem's economic operations in Frenchman's Bend. See 60.39-61.2. Faulkner here certainly alludes to one of his favorite books, Conrad's *Heart of Darkness* and to its treatment of the profit-making enterprise of collecting ivory in the Congo. In that context, the comparison of Ratliff to a white hunter is perhaps meant to hint at the corrupting potential of the commercial impulse and may even point toward his temptation and fall in Book Four, Chapter Two.

56.21-22 who answered Yes and No to direct questions: Cf. Balzac's "bill of exchange incarnate," Gobseck: "Indeed, even in transports of joy, his conversation was confined to monosyllables; he wore the same noncommittal countenance" (*Gobseck* 268).

56.24-38 yet who never made mistakes in any matter pertaining to money....But the clerk never made mistakes: Flem's arithmetic reliability, like his machine-made bow tie, reinforces the sense that he is a mechanical man and that he does not share in the general humanity. Jehlen cites Bergson's definition of the comic as it relates to this aspect of Flem: "the attitudes, gestures, and movements of the human body are laughable in exact proportion as that body reminds us of a mere machine" (noted 142). Cf. Balzac's Gobseck, who "went through his days with the regularity of a pendulum, and in some sort was a clockwork man" (268). Balzac's Grandet is renowned for his adherence to the strict letter of the law. Des Grassins says of him: "Grandet...is a man who will never swerve a hair's breadth from the strict course of honor; he will not endure the slightest spot on his name! Money without honor is a disease..." (*Eugenie Grandet* 112). Balzac goes on to say that "in town they all speak of his scrupulous integrity, forgetting the morning's sale of his vintage in disregard of the agreement made among wine growers" (115). Cf. Tolstoy's Karenin, who is "not a man, but a machine" (*Anna Karenina* 1:227).

Moreland argues that Flem's precision highlights the flaws in the economic system itself. For the first time, the people of Frenchman's Bend see the system working exactly as it is supposed to work, without the malfunction of an occasional mistake ("Antisemitism, Humor, and Rage in Faulkner's *The Hamlet*" 60).

57.5 Odum Bookwright: buys the Old Frenchman's Place from Flem along with Ratliff and Armstid, paying his third of the price in cash (354). Bookwright's role in the salted mine scheme is reiterated in *Mans* 127, 137.

57.9 how can you tell?: Bookwright believes, as does Ratliff, that Flem's precision is inhuman. Without human flaws, he asks, how can one tell that Flem is a human being?

57.13 Quick: Lon Quick, operator of the saw mill and first to make an offer on one of the spotted horses. In *AILD*, he owns the spotted horse, a descendent of Flem's Texas horses, that Jewel buys (127). Brown identifies Quick as an old Lafayette County name, there being three artificial ponds seven miles NE of Oxford called Quick's Lakes (158). Boswell notes that the etymological meaning of the surname Quick is "cow farm" (38).

57.19 grumble-gutted white horse: flatulent. See also 157.3-4.

57.32-34 And the next morning he who had never been seen in the village between Saturday night and Monday morning appeared at the church: Flem makes two simultaneous concessions to "civic virtue" (*Twn* 175) and respectability: the first, attendance at church services, like Sutpen's (*AbAb!* 24), and the second, the bow tie that punctuates his shirt front (*Ham* 57.37). The pull of respectability becomes even stronger in *Twn*: "Respectability?"

"That's right," Ratliff said. "When it's jest money and power a man wants, there is usually some place he will stop; there's always one thing at least that ever--every man wont do for jest money. But when it's respectability he finds out he wants and has got to have, there aint nothing he wont do to get it and then keep it" (259).

57.37-58.13 a necktie--a tiny machine-made black bow which snapped together at the back with a metal fastener...that afternoon

in the spring: See note 57.32-34. See also note 56.24-38.

58.11-12 **that quality of outrageous overstatement of physical displacement:** See 9.6-7 and 47.29-31.

58.29-31 **with a good deal of the quality of a spider of that bulbous blond omnivorous though non-poisonous species:** probably the Rabid Wolf Spider (*Lycosa rabida*), a gold-colored spider of the tarantula family, which was common to the area. Though fierce-looking and reputed to be deadly, it is no more dangerous to humans than a bee. Legend had it that the bite of a tarantula induced tarantism, a disease that caused its victims to leap about and make incoherent noises. The cure for the disease was the lively folk dance, the tarantella (*The Audubon Society Field Guide to North American Insects and Spiders* 869).

58.33-34 **The cotton had opened and was just being picked:** "As the cotton balls first open five burrs spread out in a star shape and make way for five fluffy locks of cotton. The cotton picker places a finger on each lock of cotton and picks all five with one pull from the opened boll. The cotton is placed into a sack and later emptied into a wagon or cottonhouse before the trip to the gin" (Walton 63).

58.39 **gin:** a machine that separates the seeds, seed hulls, and other small objects from the fibers of cotton (*AHD*). See 160.11-28 for the following September's activity at the gin.

59.13 **scale beam:** "beam of a platform scale. The wagon-load of cotton is driven onto this scale and weighed. The platform of the scales is under the suction pipe by which the cotton is unloaded. Then the empty wagon is weighed, the difference between the two weights establishing the weight of the load of cotton" (Brown 170).

59.14 **suction pipe:** "a sheet iron pipe which operates like a huge vacuum cleaner to unload cotton from wagons and convey it directly into a cotton gin" (Brown 192).

59.37 **tail gate:** "the removable plank forming the back of a wagon box" (Brown 196).

59.39 **stanchion:** an upright pole, post, or support (*AHD*).

60.7 **snuff:** a preparation of finely pulverized tobacco that can be drawn up into the nostrils by inhaling (*AHD*).

60.34 **nail keg:** "Nails are packaged in 100 pound kegs which, when empty and inverted, make convenient seats" (Brown 135).

60.39-61.2 **Varner and Snopes resembled the white trader and his native parrot-taught headman in an African outpost:** See note 55.33-37.

61.18-19 **the house which he owned and which his widowed sister kept for him:** In *Mans*, Ratliff keeps " the cleanest little house you ever saw" for himself (206).

61.20 **scrub cattle:** mongrel, unpedigreed (Brown 170).

61.28 **Herefords:** breed of cattle developed in England and having a reddish coat with white markings (*AHD*).

61.30 **transmogrified:** a colloquial country expression signifying a major change. Buck Hipps calls his Texas ponies "transmogrified hallucinations of Job and Jezebel" (*Ham* 273.33).

61.38 **son-of-a-gun:** "The familiar designation implying contempt but now used with jocular familiarity derives from the days when women were allowed to live in [British vessels]. The "son of a gun" was one born in the ship, often near the midship gun, behind a canvas screen. If paternity was uncertain, the child was entered in the log as "Son of a gun" (Evans, *Brewer's Dictionary* 495).

62.1-4 **And Snopes said, "They're in Varner's pasture...pasture.":** As in the spotted horse episode, Flem does not acknowledge his involvement.

62.10 **winy air of October noons:** Cf. *LA*: "pinewiney silence of the August afternoon" (8).

62.11 **a man named Houston:** In *AILD*, Houston is mentioned as one of Addie's mourners (83). In "The Hound," Houston is, as in *Ham*, the man who is killed and stuffed in a hollow tree (153-155).

62.12 magnificent grave blue-ticked Walker hound: a Walker hound having small markings of a bluish color (Brown 33).

62.15-17 a stranger--a young, well-made, muscle-bound man who, turning, revealed an open, equable face beginning less than an inch below his hairline: Eck Snopes. In *FA*, Eck and his son Admiral Dewey are involved in the spotted horse auction. Buck Hipps gives him one horse, and he bids two dollars for the next horse (43). He plays the same role in "Spotted Horses" (170) and again in Book Four, Chapter One of *Ham*. At the trial of Armstid v. Snopes, Eck refuses to perjure himself, even to exonerate his kinsman (326), and he tries to repay the Tull family for damages at the trial of Tull v. Eckrum Snopes (330), but the judge rules that ownership of the horse was never legally conveyed. This inherent honesty causes Flem to fire him from his job at the Jefferson restaurant when he asks within hearing of customers if there should not be beef in the hamburgers (*Twn* 33). Stevens removes him from the roster of Snopeses in *Twn*: "except that one who had inherited into the restaurant was not a Snopes; even to impugn him so was indefensible and outrageous and forever beyond all pale of pardon, whose mother, like her incredible sister-by-marriage a generation later, had, must have, as the old bucolic poet said, cast a leglin girth herself before she married whatever Snopes was Eck's titular father" (31). He dies in an explosion at the oil company's storage tank, where he works as night watchman, while trying to locate a lost five year old child (*Twn* 108-09). Montgomery Ward Snopes says of Eck: "I dont count Wallstreet and Admiral Dewey and their father Eck, because they dont belong to us; they are only our shame" (*Mans* 83). Eck's innate good-will and courtesy defy all rigid, narrow, abstract definitions of Snopesism. In Faulkner's early short story, "The Liar," the title character is named Ek. That character, though he bears no resemblance to Eck Snopes, is connected to the spotted horse story in that he recounts a similar tale of a runaway horse that is chased all night and that, in his nocturnal adventures, runs through a house.

62.29 "---t," Houston said: "Shit." Faulkner learned with *WP* that editorial censors would reject such expletives. *WP* was intended to end, as the typescript does, with the tall convict's observation, "Women, shit,". Instead, it reads "Women, ---!" (339). McHaney reports a July 1968 interview with J. B. Meriwether, in which Meriwether remembers Saxe Commins admitting that he had "insisted" on the change and that Faulkner was "powerless but quite angry" (noted Kibler 99). In a July 8, 1938 letter to Robert Haas, Faulkner defended his use of the expletive: "It is only what people see that shocks them, not what they think or hear, and they will recognize these words or not [with the substituted dashes] and no harm done in either case. But these words are exactly the ones that my characters would have used and no other, and there are a few people whom I hope will read the book, among whom the preservation of my integrity as a faithful (even though not always successful) portrayer of living men and women is dear enough for me to wish not to betray it, even in trifles" (*SL* 106). Knowing what his publisher's reaction to the word would be, Faulkner typed "---t" in the final typescript of *Ham*, rather than risk a repetition of *WP*'s inscrutable dash. Mink addresses I.O. with the same epithet at 161.23.

63.8-13 It contained another stranger--a frail man none of whose garments seemed to belong to him, with a talkative weasel's face ... already (or still) talking: I. O. Snopes. In *FA*, it is I. O. who works as a clerk in Varner's store and sells ropes to the men who buy horses (52). In *Flags*, I. O. runs the restaurant in Jefferson and takes in Byron when he leaves Mrs. Beard's boarding house. He is described there as a "nimble, wiry little man with a talkative little face like a nutcracker, and false merry eyes" (217). He is a cotton speculator in *S&F* (271). I. O. is again the clerk in Varner's store in "Spotted Horses" (174). In "Mule," he speculates in mules, buying them in Memphis, selling them in Jefferson, and allowing the surplus to escape to its death at a blind curve of the railroad (252). After his stint at the blacksmith shop, I. O. takes over as schoolmaster in Frenchman's Bend (*Ham* 69.20) until he has to leave town when a wife and child appear (*Ham* 264.15-16). In *Twn*, he is the "blacksmith-cum-schoolmaster-cum-bigamist" (36) who is again mixed up with Mrs. Hait and the mules (232-58). In *Mans*, I. O. is mentioned as the father of Clarence Snopes (83) and as having been sent back to Frenchman's Bend by Flem (152). Faulkner indicates a possible source for I.O.'s name in *Elmer*, where the father of the Hodges, a nomadic family who bear some resemblances to the Snopes tribe, is described as an "inverted Io with hookworm and a passionate ambitious wife for gadfly" (15). While Faulkner makes clear the strong connections between Ike's beloved cow and the mythological Io (see note 165.34), the comparison between Mr. Hodges and Io suggests that Faulkner may have had in mind a male version of the mythological wanderer when naming I. O.

63.15-19 Good, good: save the hoof and save all...love me, love my

horse, beggars cant be choosers, if wishes was horseflesh we'd all own thoroughbreds: I. O.'s malapropisms, axiomatic sayings, and homiletic attitude suggest several Dickensian characters, among them Mrs. Gamp and Mr. Pecksniff of *Martin Chuzzlewit*, as well as their probable ancestor, Sancho Panza. In *Twn*, Ratliff says of I. O. that "you stay so busy trying to unravel just which of two or three proverbs he had jumbled together that you couldn't even tell just exactly what lie he had told you until it was already too late" (242).

63.18 **beggars cant be choosers:** This is listed in the earliest collection of proverbs in English, John Heywood's *A dialogue conteining the number in effect of all the proverbes in the Englishe tongue* (1546): "Nay (quoth I) be they wynners or loosers,/ Folke saie alwai, beggars should by no choosers" (noted *The Macmillan Book of Proverbs, Maxims, and Famous Phrases* 149).

63.18-19 **if wishes was horseflesh we'd all own thoroughbreds:** The most familiar version of this proverb is "If wishes were horses, beggars would ride," cited in James Kelly's 1721 *Complete Collection of Scottish Proverbs* and in H. O. Halliwell's 1844 *Nursery Rhymes of England* (noted *The Macmillan Book of Proverbs, Maxims, and Famous Phrases* 2542).

63.31 **hog piss:** Houston has taken a rusty can of water from I.O. The point is that I.O. believes the can to contain kerosene, and he is so ignorant that he attempts to put out a fire with it.

63.38 **just a new broom in it:** A new broom is said to sweep clean; thus those new in a position are often zealous and are sometimes ruthless in making changes (Evans, *Brewer's Dictionary* 155).

64.25 **touching the animal's quick:** "the living, sensitive inner part of a horse's foot. A shoe is supposed to be nailed to the insensitive wall of the hoof" (Brown 158).

64.27 **shrinkingtub:** "a large tub of water used by blacksmiths in putting tires on wagon and carriage wheels. The tire is a hoop of iron which, when expanded by the heat, will just go over the wooden wheel. It is heated, driven into place, and then contracted in the cold water of the tub so that it makes a very tight fit" (Brown 177).

65.28-29 a wagon with a broken hound: The hound is a reinforcing bar used in the running gear, or chassis (Brown 106).

Book One, Chapter Three, section 2: Faulkner expands an incident which originated in section two of "Lizards in Jamshyd's Courtyard," the second of the Snopes stories to be written and the third to be published. The main difference between the two episodes is that, in *Ham*, Ratliff deliberately conveys information to Flem about the goat trade, while, in "Lizards," he reveals it unwittingly, thus allowing Flem to get the better of him. Faulkner also complicates the novel version of the goat transaction with the addition of Mink Snopes and his cousin Ike. See note Book Four, Chapter two.

67.22 sleeping partner's half interest: partner who invests in a business without actively participating in the everyday operations.

68.1-2 the pleasure of the shrewd dealing which far transcended mere gross profit: Dimino sees Ratliff as a representative of the concrete southern barter economy that was giving way to a more abstract concept of money, signified by Flem's notes and interest payments (161). See note 78.36-80.18.

68.10-15 supremely gutful lassitude of convalescence in which time, hurry, doing, did not exist, the accumulating seconds and minutes and hours ... thrall to time's headlong course: Cf. *Ham*: Mink's impulse "to run, not in panic but to keep ahead of the avalanche of accumulating seconds which was now his enemy" (250.16-17).

68.26 stock whip: short-handled whip with a long lash (Brown 190).

68.33-34 "We all missed him," Bookwright said. "My wife aint mentioned nobody's new sewing machine in almost a year: See note 354.37.

69.4-5 dripping sterns: The rear part dripping urine and excrement.

70.6 hisn: his.

70.8 So Will Varner has caught that bear at last: "caught the proverbial bear by the ears, that is, got hold of something dangerous that one can't get rid of or turn loose" (Brown 48).

70.8-10 Flem has grazed up the store and he has grazed up the blacksmith shop and now he is starting in on the school: Ratliff is referring to the proverbial search for greener pastures (Brown 48). In *Twn*, Ratliff refers to this grazing activity as "Farming Snopeses: the whole rigid hierarchy moving intact upward one step as he vacated ahead of it" (31). The tendency to consume that Faulkner associates with the Snopeses gets a comic treatment in *Twn* when Byron Snopes's four half-Indian children come to town and eat a Pekingese dog (362-64). In a letter to Robert Haas, received 15 December 1938, Faulkner stresses the predatory and destructive nature of Flem's grazing: "as he gradually consumes a small village until there is nothing left for him to eat" (*SL* 107). In *FA*, Snopes spread is destructive to organic matter and is compared to "mold on cheese, steadfast and gradual and implacable" (20). In "Mississippi," the Snopes clan is likened to the boll weevil, because "he too has taken over the southern earth" (14). Cf. Balzac's dedication to *Les Paysans*: "Here you will see this indefatigable sapper at work, nibbling and gnawing the land into little bits, carving an acre into a hundred scraps, to be in turn divided, summoned to the banquet by the bourgeois, who finds in him a victim and ally. Here is a social dissolvant, created by the Revolution, that will end by swallowing up the bourgeoisie, which in its day, devoured the old noblesse."

70.27 fierce dark face: Uncle Dick Bolivar calls Bookwright "that black one." See note 344.27-28.

70.33-36 He lent me five dollars over two years ago and all I does, every Saturday night I goes to the store and pays him a dime. He aint even mentioned that five dollars: Dimino labels the charging of interest "a true perpetual motion machine," foreshadowed by the earlier image of the milk separator (161).

71.8-13 "Aint none of you folks out there done nothing about it?" he said..."I believe I would think of something if I lived there," Ratliff said: Ratliff has already nominated himself as a potential adversary to the unchecked avarice of Flem and his protegees (see 28.3-9 and note 87.33-39). After the debacle of the spotted horse auction, Ratliff voices an attitude that is very much like the hands-off attitude he criticizes here (see note 320.27-321.15). Gold cites Tull's reply to Ratliff in support of his argument that the people of Frenchman's Bend are basically self-interested and unwilling to involve themselves in the affairs of others (318). See note 294.27-28.

71.33 nekkid: naked.

72.17-18 May and June, the summer, the long good days of heat: The recuperative summer that Ratliff envisions counters the long, sterile summer of Book Three: "the summer's rainless heat--the blazing days beneath which even the oak leaves turned brown and died, the nights during which the ordered stars seemed to glare down in cold and lidless amazement at an earth being drowned in dust" (258.35-59.1).

72.22 the Square: A central square, possibly modeled after the Lafayette County courthouse square in Oxford but typical of most courthouse squares in Mississippi courthouse towns, figures prominently in Faulkner's town descriptions. In *Flags*, Faulkner described the Jefferson square thus: "Then the square, with its unbroken low skyline of old weathered brick and fading dead names...and drifting negroes in casual o.d. garments worn by both sexes and country people in occasional khaki too; and their more brisk urban brethren weaving among their placid chewing unhaste and among the sitting groups in chairs before certain stores.

"The courthouse was of brick too, with stone arches rising among elms, and among the trees the monument of the Confederate soldier stood like a white candle. Beneath the porticos of the courthouse and upon benches about the green, the city fathers sat and talked and drowsed, in uniform too, now and then" (149).

72.23 shaded marble gaze of the Confederate soldier: The courthouse that Faulkner places on the Jefferson square is a replica of the one on the square in Oxford, but Faulkner modeled the Jefferson Confederate monument after the one that stands on the grounds of the University of Mississippi, rather than the one by the Oxford courthouse (Meriwether, *Literary* 14). *Req* supplies an additional detail about the Confederate monument: "the marble eyes under the shading marble palm stared not toward the north and the enemy, but toward the south, toward (if anything) his own rear" (206).

72.24 courthouse: The Yoknapatawpha County Courthouse resembles the Lafayette County Courthouse in Oxford, which was destroyed during the

Civil War and rebuilt according to the original design in 1873 (McDaniel, *Annotations* 75). The Ripley courthouse is another possible model for the courthouse in Yoknapatawpha. The courthouse itself accrues symbolic value over the course of Faulkner's fiction. In "Nympholepsy," it is seen from a hill as "a dream dreamed by Thucydides" (*US* 331). In *Req*, Faulkner's creations have invested the courthouse with "all of their hopes and aspirations" (42), making it the "biggest edifice in the country" (42), the "beacon, focus, and lodestar" (192). Polk sees in the courthouse the "symbol of man's ideal state" and of the hope that man is a being capable of recognizing the difference between good and evil and of choosing good ("I Taken an Oath of Office Too" 160).

72.34 **MINKSNOPES**: Mink makes his first appearance in *Ham*, replacing the bachelor Ernest Cotton in the story of Houston's murder. He is, on the one hand, a cowardly murderer, and, on the other hand, a potent man, a man of principle, pride, and integrity presented for our admiration. Flem's refusal to come to Mink's aid results in Mink's being sentenced to a term in Parchman Prison and in his determination to exact revenge for his cousin's neglect. The entire trilogy, then, propels toward the moment in *Mans* when Flem meets his fate at the hands of his cousin (416). Having fulfilled his destiny, Mink returns to his tenant shack and dies, returning to the earth and accepting his place in the universe: "equal to any, good as any, brave as any, being inextricable from, anonymous with all of them: the beautiful, the splendid, the proud and the brave, right on up to the very top itself among the shining phantoms and dreams which are the milestones of the long human recording--Helen and the bishops, the kings and the unhomed angels, the scornful and graceless seraphim" (434-36).

72.38 **a broken-backed cabin**: Cf. Ab Snopes's cabin at 18.34.

73.12-13 **But it's the same eyes, Ratliff thought**: See note 49.30.

73.15-16 **a woman standing on the gallery--a big-boned hard-faced woman with incredible yellow hair**: Mink's marital status adds a dimension to his character that the Ernest Cotton character lacked. In *Mans*, the reader is told that Mrs. Mink Snopes's name is Yettie (10) and that she, returning to her folks while Mink was in prison, died there (93).

74.4-6 **"Not to give away," she said. "Not the man that owns a** hundred head of cattle and a barn and pasture to feed them in his own name": Balzac often treats poor relatives who are tormented in their abject poverty by contemplation of the comforts enjoyed by more prosperous relatives, i. e. Honorine, Cousin Pons, and Cousine Bette in the novels that bear their names (noted Festa-McCormick 108).

74.11-16 He'd let you rot and die right here and glad of it, and you know it! Your own kin...dress like a Snopes too!: Yettie Snopes's accusation foreshadows Flem's failure to come to Mink's aid when he is being tried for the murder of Houston in Book Four. Had Faulkner retained "BB" as the opening chapter, his novel would have begun with an episode that established the importance of the kinship bond in this backwoods society. To follow the code of justice and truth represented to him by the De Spain mansion, Sarty must reject a code that decrees he should "stick to [his] own blood" (8). Cohen notes the dearth of family feeling among members of the Snopes clan and relates it to a similar tendency in the Tonsard family of *Les Paysans*. Lump's exploitation of Ike in the cow show, I. O.'s milking of Eck, and Flem's neglect of Mink in his crisis compare with Tonsard's and his wife's robbing his father of ten francs and with the Tonsards' charging their daughter an extremely high rate for room and board ("French Peasants" 386).

75.2 gathering time: The earliest cotton opens in mid to late August, in this part of Mississippi, and the gathering is completed by late October (Walton 65).

75.11 dispatch box: a metal box for storing important papers (Brown 71).

76.23-26 Say "From one cousin that's still scratching dirt ... To owning cattle and a hay barn": Mink's repetition of the final phrase implies a threat to burn down Flem's hay barn.

77.19 Uncle Ben Quick: In "Tomorrow," one of the stories collected in *KG* (1949), Quick is the owner of the sawmill (93). The stories of *KG* were written between 1931 and 1949. "Tomorrow," which was first published in *The Saturday Evening Post* CCXIII (November 23, 1940), was probably composed in 1937 or 1938. In Martin Ritt's movie version of *Ham*, *The Long Hot Summer*, the Flem Snopes character is named Ben Quick and played by Paul Newman.

77.32 Grenier County: fictional county near the southern edge of Yoknapatawpha County (Brown 95).

77.38 Miss Maggie: "Miss" preceding a woman's given name is a common designation of respect in the south.

78.31 Him or somebody had done sent me a sheep just like He done to save Isaac in the Book: When Abraham is ordered by God to take Isaac, the son of his old age, into the mountains to be sacrificed, he complies with the command. At the last moment, when the baby is on the altar and Isaac has the knife ready, God rescinds the order, and Abraham sacrifices a ram instead that he finds caught in a thicket by his horns (Gen.22:2-13).

78.36-80.18 wouldn't nobody in this country think of it. It would take a Northerner to do that...between Jackson and the Tennessee line apparently: In the postbellum vernacular style of southern nationalism, Ratliff slyly pokes fun at Yankee ingenuity. See, for example, Harris's "A Razor-Grinder in a Thunder-Storm" in which a Yankee merchant gets his comeuppance (*Sut Lovingood: Yarns Spun by a Nat'ral Born Durn'd Fool* 60-65). The southern economy is still based on a concrete barter system, as evidenced in the Pat Stamper horse trading episode, but Flem complicates Ratliff's goat trade gambit with a northern strategy that abstracts cash money into notes and interest (Dimino 161).

78.39 hand grip: small suitcase.

79.2 hill gully: Brown points out that most large gullies are located on the sides of hills (103).

79.3 rabbit grass: Sedge, so called because rabbits hide in it. Any of various species of the genus *Andropogos* grasses, which grow two to four feet high in open spaces on the edges of swamps (Brown 171).

80.15 pro-jeck: project.

80.17 Jackson: state capital of Mississippi.

81.4 Howsomedever: howsoever.

81.11-20 **the figure of a grown man but barefoot and in scant faded overalls...the open drooling mouth encircled by a light fuzz of golden virgin beard:** first glimpse of Ike Snopes. Cf."The Kingdom of God," an early, c.1925, short piece: "The face of the sitting man was vague and dull and loose-lipped, and his eyes were clear and blue as cornflowers, and utterly vacant of thought; he sat a shapeless, dirty lump, a life without mind, an organism without intellect. Yet always in his slobbering, vacuous face were his two eyes of heartshaking blue, and gripped tightly in one fist was a narcissus" (*NOS* 113). Cf. Benjy in *S&F*: "His skin was dead-looking and hairless; dropsical too, he moved with a shambling gait like a trained bear. His hair was pale and fine. It had been brushed smoothly down from his brow like that of children in daguerrotypes. His eyes were clear, of the pale sweet blue of cornflowers, his thick mouth hung open, drooling a little" (342).

81.23 **thick thighs:** See 86.15-17.

81.24-25 **dragging block:** "a clog tied to an animal to impede its movements" (Brown 32).

81.26 **"And yet they tell us we was all made in his image":** Cf. Gen. 1:26: "And God said, Let us make man in our image, after our likeness...." Faulkner makes the same observation in a 1918 letter written to his mother from New Haven: "It's funny to walk the streets and look at these people--Poles, Russians, Italian Communists, all with American flags in their lapels. And yet they say that God made man in his own image" (*Thinking of Home* 54).

81.38 **She can talk to him somehow:** Like Dilsey's ability to read the defective clock in the time-obsessed S&F, Mrs. Littlejohn's ability to communicate with the idiot Ike Snopes in *Ham* distinguishes her from a society in which incoherence dominates.

81.39 **"Maybe she's the one that was then":** i.e. made in his image.

83.27-28 **A man takes your wife and all you got to do to ease your feelings is to shoot him. But your horse:** Faulkner treats the affinity of man for horse comically in the "Fool About a Horse" material, but the preference for the "polygamous and bitless masculinity" (214.30-31) represented by a horse over the love of a wife recurs in succeeding episodes (Jack Houston/Lucy Pate, the spotted horse auction).

83.31 **Yessum:** yes ma'am.

84.14-17 **an instant, a second of a new and completer stillness and immobility touch the blank face...even the jaw had stopped chewing:** The image of Flem, recognizing his first minor defeat, looks ahead to Flem's recognition of his final defeat at the hands of Mink Snopes: "He didn't need to say, 'Look at me, Flem.' His cousin was already doing that, his head turned over his shoulder. Otherwise he hadn't moved, only the jaws ceased chewing in midmotion...Now his cousin, his feet now flat on the floor and the chair almost swiveled to face him, appeared to sit immobile and detached too" (*Mans* 415).

84.29-32 **Ratliff gave him the match and watched him set fire to the note...dust with his toe:** recalls Nastasya Filippovna's disposal of one hundred thousand rubles in the fire in *The Idiot* (noted Weisgerber 270).

85.10-11 **Then something black blew in him, a suffocation, a sickness, a nausea:** Cf. Horace Benbow's premonition of evil in Popeye's presence: "He smells black, Benbow thought; he smells like that black stuff that ran out of Bovary's mouth and down upon her bridal veil when they raised her head" (*Sanc* 6).

85.25-26 **beginning a wet whimpering moaning at once pettish and concerned and terrified and amazed:** Cf. "The Kingdom of God": "The idiot howled unceasingly, filling the street with a dreadful sound" (*NOS* 116). Cf. *S&F*: "For an instant Ben sat in an utter hiatus. Then he bellowed. Bellow on bellow, his voice mounted, with scarce interval for breath. There was more than astonishment in it, it was horror; shock; agony, eyeless, tongueless; just sound" (400). Cf. *AbAb!*: "Jim Bond, the scion, the last of his race, seeing it now too and howling with human reason now since now even he could have known what he was howling about" (376). See also 168.29.

85.28-33 **the mowing and bobbing head, the eyes which at some instant...had opened upon...the Gorgon-face of that primal injustice...blasted empty and clean forever of any thought...soft gold hair:** Adams notes a correspondence with the characterization of Pip in *Moby Dick*: "strange shapes of the unwarped primal world glided to and fro before his passive eyes....He saw God's foot upon the treadle of the loom, and spoke it; and therefore his shipmates called him mad" (noted "Apprenticeship" 35).

85.30 **Gorgon-face:** Gorgo, the once-beautiful daughter of the marine deities Phorcys and Ceto, was transformed into a monster, with snakes replacing hair, a belt of boar teeth, occasionally a beard, wings, and a stare that could turn its object to stone. Perseus killed her, but the dying Gorgo gave birth to Pegasus and Chrysaos (*Oxford Classical Dictionary* 472).

86.2 **cachinnant:** Adjective form of a verb meaning to "laugh hard, loudly, or convulsively" (*AHD*). Faulkner uses a variation of this word to describe the uncontrollable laughing of Ike McCaslin's wife after their final intercourse: "he thought she was crying now at first, into the tossed and wadded pillow, the voice coming from somewhere between the pillow and the cachinnation: 'And that's all. That's all from me. If this dont get you that son you talk about, it wont be mine': lying on her side, her back to the empty rented room, laughing and laughing" (*GDM* 315).

86.5 **cossack holiday:** The cossacks were the Russian cavalry, which operated like military police. A "cossack holiday" carries the implication of pleasure derived from intentionally inflicting physical harm on an innocent and powerless victim. Cf. "The Legend of Sleepy Hollow": "sometimes his crew was heard dashing about farmhouses at midnight, with whoop and halloo, like a troop of Don Cossacks" (32).

86.15-17 **the backlooking face with its hanging mouth and pointed faun's ears, the bursting overalls drawn across the incredible female thighs:** Faulkner returns to a figure from the late Romantic, fin-de-siècle, and Symbolist poetry that fascinated him (see Hönnighausen 88-91, Brooks, *Toward Yoknapatawpha and Beyond* 3, Sensibar, *The Origins of Faulkner's Art* 70-71, Kreiswirth, *William Faulkner: The Making of a Novelist* 14-15). The faun, typically in pursuit of a nymph, embodies a state of permanent desire. Faulkner's first published work, the poem "L'Après-Midi d'un Faune," appeared in *New Republic* (August 6, 1919), and was reprinted in revised form, first in *The Mississippian* and later in *EPP* 39-40. He again turned to the faun persona in his first published book, *The Marble Faun* (1924) and in the sonnet "The Faun," published April 1925 in *The Double Dealer*. The title poem of Faulkner's 1920 poem sequence, *The Lilacs*, features a wounded World War I veteran who chases a "white wanton near a brake" (1.27) in his faun-like "pointed-eared machine" (1.30). In *SP*, Faulkner's first novel, Januarius Jones is a faun/satyr (67, 69 passim). In "Black Music," published in *Doctor Martino* (1934), a mild-mannered draughtsman metamorphoses into a "farn" (805). Finally, both Labove and Ike Snopes have faun characteristics in *Ham*. Ike, especially, picks up the theme of metamorphosis that runs through the novel. He is not only a man verging on the brink of the bestial, but he also straddles sexual categories, with his thick feminine thighs and bulging figure.

87.3-4 Because I missed it, missed it clean: This sentiment is repeated in *Twn*, when Ratliff says of Stevens's belief that Flem is motivated simply by greed: "Because he missed it. He missed it completely" (153).

87.6-7 He could feel what he thought was appetite ebbing with each mouthful becoming heavy and tasteless as dirt: Adams notes that Faulkner often equates eating with the life force (*Myth and Motion* 125). Eula and Lena Grove have hearty appetites, while Joe Christmas refuses food several times (31,145). Mink, realizing that he will have to pay for his crime, "stop[s] being hungry" (226.37). Ratliff's recoil from food perhaps foreshadows his later refusal to interfere in the spotted horse debacle (321.13-15).

87.9-17 counted the five dollars profit he had made...the ultimate pennies: Brooks hired an accountant to make sense of the complicated financial maneuverings of the goat trade. Although Ratliff considers himself to have realized a profit of five dollars, he actually loses money. Because he chooses to burn Ike's note, he must make up the difference himself ($10.00 + $1.80 interest). Thus, he gives Mrs. Littlejohn $16.80 to keep for Ike, and he has the satisfaction of besting Flem morally (*The Yoknapatawpha Country* 402-6). In "Lizards," Ratliff realizes a one dollar profit, which he immediately passes on to two children who happen to be mounting the steps to Varner's store: "'Here children,' he said. 'Here's something Mr. Snopes sent you'" (140).

87.33-39 "I got a message I would like to get to Will Varner....Just tell him Ratliff says it aint been proved yet neither. He'll know what it means": Ratliff has proved himself competitive with Flem commercially and superior to him ethically, but he acknowledges that the battle is ongoing.

88.4 **hickory-tough**: hickory wood is valued for its toughness.

88.4-10 **I just never went far enough...I went as far as one Snopes will set fire to another Snopes's barn and both Snopeses know it...know that too**: Ratliff's plot depends on the assumption that Mink will try to blackmail Flem with the threat of a burnt barn, but his imagination does not extend as far as the Snopes vagaries do. See 351.19-20.

88.11-91.13 **Those who watched the clerk now saw...setting in the flour barrel**: Faulkner concludes Book One with two menacing and portentous occurrences. First, he introduces the conflict between Mink Snopes and Jack Houston over the wintering of Mink's yearling, and, secondly, he promotes Flem to the flour barrel throne, thus reinforcing the sense that an heirship has been usurped.

88.32-33 **jerking his head at the men on the gallery exactly as Will Varner himself would do**: Flem begins by imitating Jody Varner in dress (See 58.8-9), but he graduates to imitating Will Varner in manner. See 144.28-29.

88.36 **bull-goaded**: extremely pestered or irritated, as by a bull goad, which is a stick sharpened at one end and used to prod mules and especially oxen into action (Brown 40, 92).

89.15 **runabout buggy**: small open carriage (*AHD*).

90.1-28 **Houston pulled up, already dismounting...Snopes's yearling in Houston's field**: The end of Book One and the opening chapter of Book Two modify and elaborate the circumstances leading to the murder of Jack Houston. In the *Mans* version, Mink's cow winters on Houston's place. When spring comes, Mink attempts to buy her back from Houston for eight dollars. Houston maintains that the good care and steady diet she has received over the winter have increased her value and that, because his bull, he says, "topped her" the week before, she may have "caught." Professional cattle buyers establish the value of the cow at thirty-seven dollars and fifty cents, and Will Varner arranges with Houston to have Mink dig post holes and string wire for a new fence to make up the eighteen dollars and seventy-five cents that Varner determines he owes. Mink installs the fence, only to be told that he owes an extra one dollar, as a pound fee. When he ambushes Houston and kills him, Mink gives as a reason the unjust addition of the pound fee to a debt he considers himself to have discharged. See note 218.26-29.

90.38 Not that he dont rile easy: In *Twn*, Houston is characterized as "proud to begin with and then unhappy on top of that" (78), a volatile combination.

91.2-4 Only this here seems to be a different kind of Snopes like a cottonmouth is a different kind of moccasin: Cf. *Twn*, where Ratliff pronounces Mink the "only out and out mean Snopes" (79).

91.13 setting in the flour barrel: See note 88.11-91.13.

Book Two

Eula: Faulkner continues in Book Two to set the masculine world of the deal against the feminine realm of love. Eula, who is, in *FA*, "a popular girl" (18) whose "washed and scented flesh" (17) and "rich responsive giggles" (17) attract the local male population, is invested with a rich symbolic association in *Ham*. The rudiments of the story are present as early as the *FA* manuscript: Eula's soft amplitude, her power over men, the male callers who sit each other out on her porch and leave in a body to fight one another before heading home, Eula's pregnancy and abandonment by the baby's father, the hasty marriage to Flem Snopes, and the dowry including the Frenchman's Place (16-19). What changes in the expanded version of Eula's story is not only its meaning for the inhabitants of Frenchman's Bend but its larger import in the context of the novel's emphasis on sterility and waste. The "little lost village" (*Ham* 147.19), unconscious of its blessing, wastes Eula Varner and only realizes too late what it had: "one blind seed of the spendthrift Olympian ejaculation" (147.21).

Eula recalls other earth mother/fertility figures in Faulkner's work, beginning with Juliet Bunden in the short story "Adolescence," and continuing with Emmy of *SP*, Caddy of *S&F*, Dewey Dell of *AILD*, Lena Grove of *LA*, and Laverne Shumann of *Pylon*. Millgate comments that the names of these earth mothers are near anagrams of one another (142). In *AbAb!*, Sutpen's first wife, the only child of the Haitian sugar planter, is named Eulalia (381). Hoffman proposes that Eula's name recalls both Poe's Eulalie and his Ulalume (90). Pruvot points out the homophonic relationship between Eula's name and that of Beulah, the cow saved by the character Faulkner in "Afternoon of a Cow" ("Le Sacre de la Vache" 109). Faulkner explicitly evokes comparisons with mythological characters: the goddesses in Homer and Thucydides (113.16), Venus (114.35, 118.37), Semiramis *(Twn* 30, 44, 50, 133), Brunhilde (306.16). Her modern literary antecedents are too numerous to list exhaustively: among them are Eugenie Grandet (Balzac, *Eugenie Grandet*), Emma Bovary (Flaubert, *Madame Bovary*), Nana (Zola, *Nana*, noted Heck), Eustacia Vye (Hardy, *Return of the Native*, noted Jarrett), and Sicily Burns (Harris, *Sut Lovingood: Yarns Spun by a Nat'ral Born Durn'd Fool*, noted Inge 95).

95.2 **last of the sixteen**: See note 5.29.

95.5-6 **she was already bigger than most grown women**: Cf. Faulkner's 1957 statement at Virginia: "No, you're quite right, she was larger than life. That she was an anachronism, she had no place there, that that little hamlet couldn't have held her, and when she moved on to Jefferson, that couldn't hold her either....You're quite right, she was larger than life. She was too big for this world" *(FU* 31). Cf. also Caldwell's description of Darling Jill in the 1933 novel, *God's Little Acre*: "It's a pity God can't make a woman like Darling Jill and then leave off before he goes too far. That's what he did to her. He didn't know when he had made enough of a good thing. He just kept on and on--and now look at her!" (24).

95.8-11 **her entire appearance suggested some symbology out of the old Dionysic times--honey in sunlight and bursting grape, the writhen bleeding of the crushed fecundated vine beneath the hard rapacious trampling goat-hoof**: Dionysis was a vegetation god best known as "the personification of the vine and of the exhilaration produced by the juice of the grape. His ecstatic worship, characterized by wild dances, thrilling music, and tipsy excess, appears to have originated among the rude tribes of Thrace, who were notoriously addicted to drunkenness" (Frazer 386). The myth of the death and resurrection of Dionysis exists in many different forms. In one version, he is the horned infant, son of Zeus, who visited Persephone in the form of a serpent. He ascends his father's throne, where he is attacked by the Titans as he is looking at himself in the mirror. He assumes various shapes to stave off the attack but is finally, in the form of a bull, cut to pieces. In the Cretan version, his sister Minerva saves his heart and gives it to his father. In some versions, Zeus then eats the heart and bears him again by Semele. In others, his severed parts are pieced together again by his mother. One story has Zeus disguising him as a goat to escape Hera's wrath. Early on, goats were featured in the worship of Dionysis. Worshippers devoured a live goat, believing they were eating the body and blood of the god. Later, goats were sacrificed to the god as punishment for the harm they did to the grape vine (Frazer 388-391).

Faulkner associates Eula with the grape (see 10.25) and Flem with the rapacious goat that will squash its fecundity. Cf. *Mosq*: "You knew that she lived, that her clear delicate being was nourished by sunlight and honey until even digestion was a beautiful function" (80).

Cf. the chorus to the Chief Huntsman's Song in Swinburne's "Atalanta in Calydon": "And the hooped heel of a satyr crushes/The chestnut husk at the chestnut root" (151).

Jarrett links Eula with Hardy's Eustacia Vye of *The Return of the Native*, whose character is delineated on a similarly epic scale: "Eustacia Vye was the raw material of divinity. On Olympus she would have done well with a little preparation. She had the passions and instincts which make a model goddess, that is, those which make not quite a model woman" (noted 166).

95.12-13 She seemed to be not a living integer of her contemporary scene, but rather to exist in a teeming vacuum: Cf. Jude's comments to Sue Bridehead: "Is a woman a thinking unit at all, or a fraction always wanting its integer?" (*Jude the Obscure* 278).

95.13 teeming vacuum: Contrast with Ike's immersion in the "teeming minute life" at creekside. See note 165.27.

95.15-17 she seemed to listen in sullen bemusement, with a weary wisdom heired of all mammalian maturity, to the enlarging of her own organs: Cf. *WP*: "the complete immobile abstraction from which even pain and terror are absent, in which a living creature seems to listen to and even watch some one of its own flagging organs, the heart, say, the secret irreparable seeping of blood" (5).

95.20-22 She simply did not move at all of her own volition, save to and from the table and to and from bed: Herman Basket's sister in "A Courtship" shares Eula's magnetism and indolence: "Because she walked in beauty. Or she sat in it, that is, because she did not walk at all unless she had to" (*CS* 362). Eustacia Vye is "listless, void, quiet" (*Return of the Native* 61). Wittenberg notes the "placid animal poise" and complete indolence of one of the characters in Margaret Kennedy's *The Constant Nymph* (noted "Faulkner and Women Writers" 275) as well as Eula's resemblance to the "indolent and sensual" Lena Linguard in Cather's *My Ántonia* (noted "Faulkner and Women Writers" 291).

95.25 dog-cart: "a light, two-wheeled carriage with back-to-back seats (and originally a compartment for carrying hunting dogs)" (Brown 72).

96.3-4 like a bizarre and chaperoned Sabine rape: According to legend, Romulus, when founding Rome, could not procure wives for his men. He therefore invited the native Sabine men to a festival. While the men were attending Romulus's party, their wives were carried away by his men (Evans, *Brewer's* 948).

96.21 break cover: a term borrowed from hunting, meaning to come out in the open (Brown 37).

96.21-23 At her mother's insistence, Varner continued to have the blacksmith make miniatures of housekeeping implements--little brooms and mops, a small actual stove: Miss Zilphia Gant's mother also tries to tempt her with surrogate household items, including a "miniature cook stove" (372).

96.31-36 It was as if only half of her had been born...itself not accompanied by, but rather pregnant with, the other: See note 100.8-17.

97.19-20 festooned smoke-house rafters: a building, vented at the top, in which meat was aged and cured with woodsmoke. The meat was hung from the rafters, so the rafters would have been festooned with hams (Brown 181).

97.25-26 she saw no need for literacy in women: After the Civil War, the South lagged behind other regions in instituting educational reforms for women. The rate of illiteracy among adult white women was, at the turn of the century, and continues to be, consistently higher in the South (*Encyclopedia of Southern Culture* 1536-38). As late as 1930, Mississippi ranked fourth among the states in illiteracy for women, with 15.6% of women over twenty-one illiterate (Odum 104).

97.32-98.2 It was her brother, Jody, who emerged almost violently in her eighth summer as erudition's champion...just running water through it: The brother/sister configuration here is a common one in Faulkner's work. Elmer Hodge sleeps with his sister Jo, "with whom he [doesn't] mind being naked" (*Elmer* 6). Horace Benbow loves his sister Narcissa reverently, so much so that when he finally constructs the perfect glass vase, "clear amber, larger, more richly and chastely serene" (*Flags* 162), he sets it on the night stand and calls it by his sister's name. Quentin Compson thinks incessantly about his would-be incestuous love for his sister Caddy on the last day of his life. Darl Bundren intuits his sister Dewey Dell's pregnancy. Much of the Sutpen tragedy stems from Henry's determination to protect his sister from unwittingly committing incest and miscegenation.

Ohashi argues convincingly that Faulkner in *Ham* parodied the pattern of *S&F* ("Creation Through Repetition or Self-Parody" 15-27). The plots and characters are similar: the sisters, Caddy and Eula, both associated with nature, become pregnant out of wedlock, and the brothers, Quentin and Jody, who have jealously guarded and coveted them, react hysterically. See 101.2-6.

98.11-18 she emanated an outrageous and immune perversity like a blooded and contrary filly too young yet to be particularly valuable...its raging and harried owner does not dare whip it: This metaphor brings together the theme of metamorphosis and the equation of love and money, particularly as they pertain to the female. Cf. Elmer's sister Jo: "When he thought of her it was to see her starkly poised as a young ugly tree, sniffing that conflagration, that very sound of chaos in a mad unwaked dream, into her flared nostrils mobile as the nostrils of a fierce young mare" (*Elmer* 6). Cf. also a similar passage in "Portrait of Elmer" (615). Cf. Charles Bon's octoroon: "creatures taken at childhood, culled and chosen and raised more carefully than any white girl, any nun, than any blooded mare even" (*AbAb!* 117). Cf. Charlotte Rittenmeyer: "that broad, simple, profoundly delicate and feminine articulation of Arabian mares" (*WP* 38).

98.26-27 me and you will go to the world's fair they are talking about having in St. Louis: The St. Louis World's Fair did not take place until 1904, which could be construed as inconsistent with the 1891 setting of the first edition (see Kibler 14). Quentin remembers in 1910 that Mr. Compson went to the St. Louis World's Fair and brought back a watch charm for Jason (*S&F* 99). The only World's Fair held in the 1890's was the World's Columbian Exposition staged in 1893 Chicago.

98.30-31 sitting supine and soft and immovable: Eula is "richly supine in the porch" in *FA* (17).

98.33-37 So at last the Negro man who used to carry her when her mother went visiting would bring up the family surrey...when school dismissed: Cf. Flaubert's *The Temptation of St. Anthony* when St. Anthony, excited by the scent of a woman's hair, remembers: "That is the way by which they come, rocked in their litters by the black arms of the eunuchs" (26).

98.39-99.1 too wasteful, like firing up a twenty-gallon pot to make a bowl of soup would be wasteful: See *Ham* 159.34-160.1 for Ratliff's meditation on waste. As is often the case in *Ham*, Faulkner introduces a motif in innocuous or comic form only to take it up later in its full tragic implications.

99.8-9 the cheap oilcloth book satchel they had bought her: recalls Caddy Compson's book satchel swinging behind her as she runs to meet Benjy at the Compson gate (noted Ohashi 16).

99.24-26 She's just like a dog! Soon as she passes anything in long pants she begins to give off something. You can smell it! You can smell it ten feet away!: Cf. Elmer's sister Jo: "a bird dog eager to be off" (*Elmer* 13). Cf. Linda Snopes in *Twn*: "just walking on past us just like a pointer dog walks just before it freezes onto the birds" (131). Cf. Zola's *Nana* who gives off similar signals: "The lust that emanated from her, as from an animal in heat, had spread until it filled the house" (25, noted Heck 296). She is also "the Golden Beast, unconscious of her power, corrupting the world by her odor alone" (186, noted Heck 300). Hardy's Arabella Donn also attracts through her animal magnetism: "She had a round and prominent bosom, full lips, perfect teeth, and the rich complexion of a Cochin hen's egg. She was a complete and substantial female animal--no more, no less; and Jude was almost certain that to her was attributable the enterprise of attracting his attention from dreams of the humaner letters to what was simmering in the minds around him" (*Jude the Obscure* 33).

99.29 eight other daughters: See note 5.29.

100.8-17 the inhabitant of that meat seemed to lead two separate and distinct lives...the rent paid up: Faulkner employs the motif of doubling often and in a variety of ways: by splitting a single character, as in this citation; by pairing characters within a book, i.e. Flem/Ratliff, Mink/Houston, etc.; and by duplicating the relationships and incidents of one novel in a succeeding novel, as in the parodic similarities between *S&F* and *Ham* that Ohashi studies ("Creation Through Repetition or Self-Parody"). Faulkner may have borrowed the doubling technique from Dostoyevsky as Weisgerber suggests (122), but there are numerous other potential sources, among them Poe's double stories, Mark Twain's *Pudd'nhead Wilson*, James's "The Jolly Corner," and Jeffers's "Tamar" (noted Irwin 11-20). Cf. Joanna Burden in *LA*: "the two creatures that struggled in one body like two moongleamed shapes struggling drowning in alternate throes upon the surface of a black thick pool beneath the last moon" (246). Cf. Quentin's double nature: "Then hearing would reconcile and he would seem to listen to two separate Quentins now--the Quentin Compson preparing for Harvard in the South, the deep South dead since 1865 and peopled with garrulous outraged baffled ghosts, listening, having to listen, to one of the ghosts which had refused to lie still even longer than most had, telling him about old ghost times; and the Quentin Compson who was still too young to deserve yet to be a ghost, but nevertheless having to be one for all that, since he was born and bred in the deep South the same as she was--the two separate Quentins now talking to one another in the long silence of notpeople, in notlanguage..." (*AbAb!* 9). Cf. Anna Karenina's duality: "It was as though there was something in this which she could not or would not face, as though directly she began to speak of this, she, the real Anna, retreated somehow into herself, and another strange and unaccountable woman came out..." (1:226).

100.15-17 as you are in a house which you did not design but where the furniture is all settled and the rent paid up: Commenting on her inaccessibility to her husband, Tolstoy figures Anna Karenina's body as house: "Now he experienced a feeling such as a man might have, returning home and finding his own house locked up" (1:175).

100.22-26 **He had a vision of himself transporting...across the embracing proscenium of the entire inhabited world like the sun itself, a kaleidoscopic convolution of mammalian ellipses:** reference to the chariot of the sun (noted Adams, "The European Roots" 31). Cf. *AILD*: Dewey Dell's breasts achieve similar cosmic status: "mammalian ludicrosities which are the horizons and valleys of the earth" (156).

100.35 **coarse calico:** brightly colored cloth (*AHD*).

101.2-6 **and speculate with raging impotence whether to call the school-teacher...was convinced must occur:** See note 97.32-98.2.

101.31 **rich mind- and will-sapping fluid softness:** Trouard's Irigarian reading of *Ham* stresses Eula's embodiment of Irigary's "economy of fluids" as opposed to the masculine "economy of solids" that relies on logic, control, and containment ("Eula's Plot: An Irigarian Reading of Faulkner's Snopes Trilogy" 281).

102.4-5 **his meager and monklike personal effects:** Labove's monklike asceticism binds him to the other priests and monks of *Ham*: Jody Varner, V.K. Ratliff, and Jack Houston, and distinguishes him from the novel's lovers, Eula Varner, Ike Snopes, and Mink Snopes. Brooks considers Labove's story as another study in Southern Puritanism, like those of Doc Hines, Gail Hightower, Calvin and Joanna Burden, and Simon McEachern. A feature of this brand of Calvinism is a distrust of and revulsion against the female principle (*The Yoknapatawpha Country* 175, 65). In *Ham*'s immediate predecessor, *WP*, the twenty-seven-year-old virgin, Harry Wilbourne, leads a life that is also described as "monastic" (32). See note 111.7-9.

102.5 **lean-to:** a shelter or shed having a roof with a single slope or pitch (*AHD*). See note 111.7-9.

102.7 **His name was Labove:** Brown remembers a contemporary of Faulkner's in Oxford who had this given name, pronounced to rhyme with stove (115), while Blotner cites Possum McDaniel, Faulkner's high school team mate who played football at Ole Miss as a possible model for Labove

(406). The Labove story was not included in *Ham* until the final writing and pulling-together process, begun in late 1938.

102.17 **Roman holiday:** enjoyment or satisfaction derived from watching the suffering of others, derived from the gladiatorial contests staged as entertainment for the ancient Romans (*AHD*). Also, an allusion to Byron's *Childe Harolde's Pilgrimage*, IV, cxli, in which a gladiator's death in the arena is cast as entertainment for the masses: "Butchered to make a Roman holiday" (noted Evans, *Brewer's* 929).

102.29 **puncheon-floored:** broad, heavy, roughly-dressed timber, with one side finished flat (*AHD*).

102.37 **gingham:** a yarn-dyed cotton fabric woven in checks, stripes, plaids, or solid colors (*AHD*).

103.8-9 **normal term:** school that trains teachers, chiefly for elementary school instruction (*AHD*).

105.19-33 **a man who was not thin so much as gaunt... unappeasable natural appetites:** Cf. "The Legend of Sleepy Hollow" for physical resemblance to Ichabod Crane: "He was tall, but exceedingly lank, with narrow shoulders, long arms and legs, hands that dangled a mile out of his sleeves, feet that might have served for shovels, and his whole frame most loosely hung together. His head was small, and flat at the top, with huge ears, large green glassy eyes, and a long snipe nose, so that it looked like a weather cock, perched upon his spindle neck, to tell which way the wind blew" (23-34).

105.23-24 **the thin lips of secret and ruthless ambition:** recalls Flem's "tight seam of a mouth" (51.29).

105.24 **forensic face:** Jay Watson sees Labove as a forerunner of the Gavin Stevens of *Twn* and *Mans*. He, like Stevens, read law, ambitiously pursued his course of study, and succumbed to the allure of Eula Varner. Labove's flight from Frenchman's Bend anticipates Gavin's flight from Jefferson to Heidelburg after he loses a suit against Manfred de Spain (noted *Forensic Fictions* 224-25).

105.24-26 **invincible conviction in the power of words as a principle**

worth dying for if necessary: The primary conflict of the novel, in Greet's reading, is the conflict between reason and emotion (304). Labove fails Eula because he places his faith in the intellect, the word, rather than in the heart. When Eula's courtship has played itself out tragically, the people of Frenchman's Bend are left with only "the word, the dream and wish of all males under the sun capable of harm" (147.37-38).

105.27-33 militant fanatic who would have turned his uncompromising back upon the world with actual joy and gone to a desert and passed the rest of his days and nights...battling...his own fierce and unappeasable natural appetites: This is the situation of Flaubert's St. Anthony, who retreats to the desert only to be tormented by temptations of the flesh: a sumptuous feast, infinite wealth, and the Queen of Sheba (*The Temptation of St. Anthony*). Hardy's Jude also suffers conflict between his cerebral interests and his sensuous appetites, which seem to compel him against his will: "In short, as if materially, a compelling arm of extraordinary muscular power seized control of him-- something which had nothing in common with the spirits and influences that had moved him hitherto. This seemed to care little for his reason and his will, nothing for his so-called elevated intentions, and moved him along, as a violent schoolmaster a schoolboy he has seized by the collar, in a direction which tended towards the embrace of a woman for whom he had no respect, and whose life had nothing in common with his own except locality" (37).

106.4-19 Because the school here dont need to open until the first of November....Then you can close the school here in March: The exigencies of the agrarian timetable took precedence over formal education in the years before the public school calendar became regulated by the state. Because many school-age youngsters were needed by their families to help out with the crops, rural schools did not generally hold classes during the months between laying in and gathering of crops.

106.34-36 the gaunt body not shaped by the impact of its environment but as though shrunken and leaned by what was within it, like a furnace: Cf. "Miss Zilphia Gant": "She seemed to have shrunk into herself, collapsing from inside, to have lost height, become awkward" (377).

107.14-109.21 It began just before the end of the summer term a

year ago....Labove could have answered: Labove flashes back to his initiation in the game of football, where he discovers, like Flem and Ratliff, that there is greater benefit outside farming. Ross identifies in this passage a blurring of the distinction between thought and word. Faulkner makes a point of stressing that Labove "didn't tell this" (108.31), but Varner replies as if he has eavesdropped on Labove's thoughts (130-31).

109.29-31 **I tried to get the coach to say what a pair was worth. To the University. What a touchdown was worth:** Labove's attempt to decipher the economic value of his football career foreshadows his economic prediction for Eula Varner: that she will be possessed by the "dead power of money" (118.39) in a world where values are skewed and there is no adequate correlation between inherent worth and societal value.

110.9 **a Coke:** Sir Edward Coke, English jurist (1552-1634) who as Chief Justice of the Court of Common Pleas ruled that Common law supersedes Crown law. As a prosecutor, he handled the cases against the Earls of Essex and Southampton, Sir Walter Raleigh, and the gunpowder plotters. His two great legal works are *Coke's Reports*, published in eleven volumes during his lifetime, and *The Institutes*, published in four parts. Labove would own the first part, *Coke upon Littleton*, the work for which Coke is best known, and which he intended to be a law student's first book. Littleton's work, which Coke chose as his text, is a treatise in Norman French, and the law on which it is based was one hundred fifty years old and already growing obsolete when Coke selected it (*DNB* 685-700). Labove's legal textbook is, then, though standard, doubly atavistic.

110.9 **a Blackstone:** Sir William Blackstone (1723-1780), English jurist who was author of the influential compendium of British law, *Blackstone's Commentaries on the Laws of England*, which became the basis of legal education in both Britain and the United States (*DNB* 595-602). It was probably more influential in the American South than in England, and was the standard for the South's lawyers until Chancellor James Kent's *Commentaries on American Law* (1826-1830) replaced it (*Encyclopedia of Southern Culture* 803).

110. 9-10 **a volume of Mississippi reports:** the published opinions of the Supreme Court of the State of Mississippi, which were compiled under that title from 1850-1966.

110.10 **an original Horace:** Quintus Horatius Flaccus (65 B.C.-8 B.C.), the Roman lyric poet. Horace was urbane, witty, and, above all, philosophically moderate. His work is cast deliberately in a minor key, with its conversational tone and everyday diction. He is best remembered for his *Odes* and for the *Ars Poetica*, which was adopted as a handbook of style by the English neoclassical writers of the eighteenth century (*Oxford Companion to Classical Literature* 287, *Benet's Reader's Encyclopedia* 460).

110.10 **a Thucydides:** Greek historian and author of the incomplete eleven-volume *History of the Peloponnesian War between Athens and Sparta* (431-404 B.C.). Thucydides' work is characterized by its highly serious tone and by its effort at accuracy and objectivity, although Thucydides spent most of the war in exile and so cannot deliver an eyewitness record of the events he records. Neither the romantic nor the supernatural has a place in Thucydides' account; history for him was governed by humans without divine intervention and could be explained on a purely rational level (*Oxford Companion to Classical Literature*). This evocation of the Peloponnesian War may obliquely suggest Aristophanes' version of that war's end in *Lysistrata*. In that play, the women, tired of war, withhold sexual favors from their husbands and capture the state treasury, prefiguring both the distinction between masculine and feminine worlds crucial to *Ham* and the conflation of love and money.

110.12-13 **the brightest lamp the village had ever seen:** the lamp is associated with the Roman goddess Vesta, the most chaste of all the goddesses, whose sacred fire was attended by six virgins, called Vestals (Bullfinch, *Age of Fable* 40).

110.20 **Voltaire:** pen name of François Marie Arouet (1694-1778), French philosophe, dramatist, satirist, and historian. Voltaire's name is now synonymous with intellectual opposition to all sorts of fanaticism but especially to that fostered by organized religion and, more particularly, the Catholic Church. His most enduring works are *Lettres philosophiques* and *Candide* (*Oxford Companion to French Literature*).

110.24-25 **had had to meet with his fists to establish his professorship:** Ichabod Crane also establishes his authority through corporal punishment: "Truth to say, he was a conscientious man and bore in mind the golden maxim, 'Spare the rod and spoil the child.' Ichabod

Crane's scholars certainly were not spoiled" ("The Legend of Sleepy Hollow" 24). See note 122.4-5.

111.7-9 measuring the turned pages against the fleeing seconds of irrevocable time like the implacable inching of a leaf worm: recalls Harry Wilbourne's balancing "his dwindling bank account against the turned pages of his textbooks" (*WP* 32) and "matching in inverse ratio the accumulating days" against "the row of cans on a shelf" (*WP* 112). Labove is linked to Wilbourne not only by his monasticism and his failure as a romantic lover but also by the similarly false connections he makes among time, money, and love (or sex). See note 102.4-5. Sutpen also is driven by a sense of "time fleeing beneath him" (*AbAb!* 34).

111.9 leaf worm: measuring worm, looper (Brown 117).

111.11 hammer-headed horse: "a horse with a bony ridge between the ears and, supposedly, a low mentality" (Brown 98). Ichabod Crane rides a broken-down plow horse, "gaunt and shagged, with a ewe neck and a head like a hammer" ("The Legend of Sleepy Hollow" 36). See note 122.4-5.

111.18 two state colleges: Ole Miss in Oxford and Mississippi State, formerly the Agricultural and Mechanical College, in Starkville.

111.25-28 They had accepted him...a woman's distinction, functioning actually in a woman's world like the title of reverend: Around the turn of the century, teaching came to be designated as woman's work. Young, unmarried women were considered to be desirable both because of their superior virtue and because of their low wage expectations (*Encyclopedia of Southern Culture* 266). Irving also pairs the schoolmaster and the parson and stresses their common affiliation with the feminine: "The schoolmaster is generally a man of some importance in the female circle of a rural neighborhood, being considered a kind of idle gentlemanlike personage of vastly superior taste and accomplishments to the rough country swains, and indeed, inferior in learning only to the parson" ("The Legend of Sleepy Hollow" 26). See note 122.4-5.

112.3-7 At the end of the next year the team had beaten every team they could find to play against...overalls and barefoot, they won a Mississippi Valley tournament against all comers: Cf. James

Street's *Look Away!* (1936): "There are four or five towns in Sullivan's Hollow. Mize once had a basketball team that went to Chicago for the high school national championship match. The Sullivan's Hollow boys were a little embarrassed. They never had played indoors or worn shoes while playing, and they didn't even have uniforms. But they were persuaded to play anyway, so they played bare-footed and in overalls" (205).

112.12 an Alma-Tadema picture: Sir Lawrence Alma-Tadema, Dutch-born British painter known for his romantic works of classical Greek and Roman and ancient Egyptian scenes (*AHD*).

113.13-14 sitting with veiled eyes against the sun like a cat on the schoolhouse steps: In answer to a question at the 1955 Nagano seminar, Faulkner, explaining his preference for suggestive description, reminds participants that the only specific trait Tolstoy gives Anna Karenina are eyes like a cat's (*LG* 128). I did not find this description of Anna Karenina's eyes in the Constance Garnett translation.

113.15-18 postulated that ungirdled quality of the very goddesses in his Homer and Thucydides: of being at once corrupt and immaculate, at once virgins and the mothers of warriors and of grown men: Eula's unconscious, innocent sexuality derives from her persona as a fertility goddess in a wasteland world. Cf. Hardy's Eustacia Vye as "Queen of the Night" (*Return of the Native* 58). See note 95.8-11.

113.32 motion, progress: Faulkner often comments on the inevitability of motion and equates it with a progressive state. The aim of the artist, conversely, is to arrest motion: "You write a story to tell about people, man in his constant struggle with his own heart, with the hearts of others, or with his environment. It's man in the ageless, eternal struggles which we inherit and we go through as though they'd never happened before, shown for a moment in a dramatic instant of the furious motion of being alive, that's all my story is. You catch the fluidity which is human life and you focus a light on it and you stop it long enough for people to be able to see it" (*FU* 239). Gidley cites Henry Adams's *The Education of Henry Adams* as a possible influence: "What he valued was Motion, and...what attracted his mind was change" (noted 65).

113.39-114.2 a moist blast of spring's liquorish corruption, a pagan triumphal prostration before the supreme primal uterus: Labove likens Eula's advent to the agricultural myth of Persephone's seasonal return from her exile as Pluto's consort in the underworld. His worship of her abstract power as genetrix suggests the cult of Diana at Nemi, familiar to Faulkner in Frazer's opening chapter. Diana was associated with fertility in general and childbirth in particular (*Golden Bough* 8). Faulkner owned a copy of the 1938 Modern Library edition of *Henry Esmond*, in which he would have found a model of a tutor's obsession with a pupil who is endowed with goddess-like attributes: "...Esmond found his little friend and pupil Beatrix grown to be taller than her mother, a slim and lovely young girl, with cheeks mantling with health and roses: with eyes like stars shining out of azure, with waving bronze hair clustered about the fairest young forehead ever seen: and a mien and shape haughty and beautiful, such as that of the famous antique statue of the huntress Diana....Henry watched and wondered at this young creature, and likened her in his mind to Artemis...at another time she was coy and melting as Luna shining tenderly on Endymion. This fair creature, this lustrous Pheobe, was only young yet, nor had nearly reached her full splendor: but crescent and brilliant, our young gentleman of the University, his head full of poetical fancies, his heart perhaps throbbing with desires undefined, admired this rising young divinity" (117-18). Henry Esmond's vacillation between love of the daughter, Beatrix, and love of her mother, Lady Castlewood, may have provided a model for Gavin Stevens's similar fascination with both Eula and her daughter, Linda, in *Twn*. Cf. the heath dance in Chapter IV of *Return of the Native*: "paganism was revived in their hearts" (noted Jarrett 167-68). Cf. also Jude's reaction to Arabella Donn: "He had just inhaled a single breath from a new atmosphere, which had evidently been hanging round him everywhere he went, for he knew not how long, but had somehow been divided from his actual breathing as by a sheet of glass" (*Jude the Obscure* 35). Cf. Angel Clare's impression that Tess "was no longer a milkmaid, but a visionary essence of a woman-- a whole sex condensed into one typical form. He called her Artemis, Demeter, and other fanciful names half teasingly..." (*Tess of the D'Urbervilles* 107).

114.15-18 that quality of static waiting... until whatever man it was to be whose name and face she probably had neither seen nor heard yet, would break into and disperse it: See 128.21-25.

114.22-23 hands lying motionless for hours on her lap like two separate slumbering bodies: Cf. Patricia's hand in *Mosq*: "Her hand, as if it were a separate organism, reached out slowly" (14).

114.29 jealous seething eunuch priest: See note 6.31.

114.31 baked sweet potatoes: Lind remarks on the similarity in shape between the sweet potato and the uterus. The pumpkins of "The Legend of Sleepy Hollow," "turning up their fair round bellies to the sun," also suggest female fertility (36). To attest to the abundance of sweet potatoes in the region, Owsley cites John F. H. Claiborne, a Natchez traveller to the piney woods of Mississippi who "recounted with gusto one occasion on which his kindly hostess surpassed the usual hospitality in dispensing sweet potatoes. He ate sweet potatoes with wild turkey and various other meats, had a potato pie for desert and roasted potatoes offered to him as a side dish, drank sweet potato coffee and sweet potato home brew, had his horse fed on sweet potatoes and sweet-potato vines, and when he retired he slept on a mattress stuffed with sweet-potato vines and dreamed that he was a sweet potato that someone was digging up" (38).

114.32-115.1 By merely walking down the aisle between them she would transform the very wooden desks and benches themselves into a grove of Venus...for precedence in immolation: Venus was originally an Italian fertility goddess who presided over vegetable gardens. Because she was the mother of Aeneas, the Julian family of Roman emperors, beginning with Julius Caesar and ending with Nero, considered themselves to be directly descended from her. In 46 B.C., Julius Caesar dedicated a temple to Venus Genetrix, the Universal Mother. Venus was eventually assimilated into the Greek goddess of love, Aphrodite. There are two stories of her birth. In one, she is the daughter of Zeus and Dione; in the other version, she emerged from the sea when Uranus's sexual organs, cut off by Cronos, were thrown in the ocean. Jupiter gave her in marriage to Hephaestes (Vulcan), the lame blacksmith who kept workshops in volcanoes, in gratitude for his forging of thunderbolts, although she loved Ares (Mars), the god of war, and, later, Adonis, among others (*Oxford Companion to Classical Literature* 592, Bullfinch 36, Grimal 47-48). In Cyprus, all women were required to prostitute themselves to a stranger at least once before marriage at the sanctuary of the goddess and in her honor (Frazer 330). See note 118.36-37. Zola's Nana makes her first appearance in the novel, performing in the role of Venus, "surrounded by Vulcan and other gods and goddesses" (noted Heck 294). Hardy's Sue

Bridehead is "the girl who brought the Pagan deities into this most Christian city.... Where are dear Apollo, and dear Venus now!" (*Jude the Obscure* 279). Gidley notes Henry Adams's description of the virgin's power, which, he says, derives from Venus, who "was reproduction--the greatest and most mysterious of all energies; all she needed was to be fecund" (*The Education of Henry Adams*, noted Gidley 65).

115.17-24 she would never be at either end of anything in which blood ran. It would have but one point, like a swarm of bees, and she would be that point...the queen, the matrix: See note 128.14-15.

116.27-30 the landlady came in and said, "I have a treat for you...a single baked sweet potato....Why Mr. Labove you are sick: See 87.6-8. Labove's nausea at this reminder of Eula specifically, and the feminine generally, recalls Joe Christmas's revulsion from the female. When he vomits as a five-year-old ward at the orphanage because he has eaten toothpaste, the scolding he gets, and the hush money, are tied in with sex, although he is too young to realize it (*LA* 112-16). He also vomits later when Bobbie tells him she is menstruating (*LA* 178).

117.20-21 the white magic of Latin degrees: Hardy's aspiring stonemason Jude Rawley also believes in the magical properties of education, in the "charm" (*Jude the Obscure* 27) of Latin and Greek. Like Labove, Jude is also waylaid on the path toward his goal by his inability to resist the attractions of a sensuous woman.

118.6 his Gethsemane: garden, traditionally thought to be located on the Mount of Olives, where Jesus suffered his final agony and betrayal on the night before he was crucified.

118.7 his Golgotha: the spot outside Jerusalem where Jesus was crucified.

118.7 virile anchorite of old time: See note 105.27-33.

118.11-12 legs haired over like those of a faun: See note 86.15-17.

118.13-14 eat the food which he would not even taste: See note 87.6-7.

118.22-24 **he just wanted her one time as a man with a gangrened hand or foot thirsts after the axe stroke which will leave him comparatively whole again:** See note 120.4-7.

118.31-119.6 **He could almost see the husband which she would someday have...the crippled Vulcan to that Venus, who would not possess her but merely own her...as he might own a picture, statue: a field, say...to gather and save:** Labove accurately predicts the relationship between Flem and Eula, one of ownership and exploitation that he relates to defacement of the land, a growing concern of Faulkner's and one that occupies an even more prominent place in *GDM*. In most classical cosmogonies, the earth itself is figured as a woman, Gaia, who emerged out of the primordial Chaos, immaculately conceived and bore Uranus, the sky, and mated with him to become the mother of the Titans (Grimal 157-58). The Demeter/Persephone myth emphasizes the intimate connections between the feminine and the land. Demeter, the Olympian Earth Mother goddess responsible for agricultural fertility, lost her only child Persephone when she was abducted by her uncle Hades and secreted to his underworld realm. Demeter then wandered the world searching for her daughter and neglected her duties, so that the earth became sterile. As a compromise, Zeus arranged to have Persephone spend a portion of the year with Hades and a portion with Demeter, thus insuring the seasonal renewal of the earth each spring (Grimal 122-24). When Flem, who is associated with the devil in Ratliff's reverie, removes Eula to Texas, he initiates the long dry spell that finally ends when she returns. A contemporary source for Faulkner's earth mothers may have been Willa Cather, whose Alexandra Bergson and Ántonia Shimerda are linked to the fertility of the soil. See 181.9-11 for an explicit equation of the feminine and the earth: "his the victor's drowsing rapport with all anonymous faceless female flesh capable of love walking the female earth."

118.36-37 **crippled Vulcan to that Venus:** See note 114.32-115.1. The supreme irony is that the most beautiful and desirable of the goddesses was married off in violation of her will to the least attractive of the gods in payment for services rendered.

119.14-19 **There would be times now when he did not even want to make love to her but wanted to hurt her...to leave some indelible mark of himself on it and then watch it even cease to be a face:** Cf. Addie's recollection of switching her students: "I would look forward to the times when they faulted, so I could whip them. When the switch fell I could feel it upon my flesh; when it welted and ridged it was my blood that ran, and I would think with each blow of the switch: Now you are aware of me! Now I am something in your secret and selfish life, who have marked your blood with my own for ever and ever" (*AILD* 162). Cf. *WP*: "'I haven't hurt her.' Then he said, 'Yes I have. If I hadn't marked her by now, I would--'" (101).

119.22-25 that face which...postulated a weary knowledge which he would never attain, a surfeit, a glut of all perverse experience: See Gresset for a treatment of experience as the antonym of innocence. Faulkner, he argues, is not interested in either innocence or experience *per se*, but in the "dramatic confrontation of innocence and experience" (*Fascination* 234). Gresset goes on to identify Faulkner's "favorite topic" as the "*failure* of the capacity to pass smoothly from one to the other" (234). Cf. "A Portrait of Elmer": "But who wants experience, when he can get any kind of substitute? To hell with experience, Elmer thinks, since all reality is unbearable" (*US* 612, noted Gresset 233). Cf. *Mosq*: "Experience: why should we be expected to learn wisdom from experience?" (233, noted Gresset 233).

119.33-34 He knew that sooner or later something was going to happen: Joe Christmas thinks "Something is going to happen to me" (*LA* 97,110). Cf. "Miss Zilphia Gant": "Something is about to happen to me" (380). On his first hunt, Ike experiences something similar: "Because he was just twelve then, and that morning something had happened to him: in less than a second he had ceased to be the child he was yesterday" (181). In a 1953 interview, Faulkner himself is recorded as saying, "Ah have a feeling of doom hanging over me today....Ah wish mah doom would lift or come on....Somethin' is happenin'....Ah can feel it" (*LG* 76).

119.35 he would be the vanquished: For another martial metaphor, see 121.20-27.

120.4-122.5 Then one afternoon he found his axe...Ichabod Crane: Eula's encounter with and escape from Labove in the empty schoolroom recalls Dounia's encounter with and escape from Svidrigailov in his empty flat (*Crime and Punishment* 419-429, noted Weisgerber 268).

**120.4-7 Then one afternoon he found his axe. He continued to hack in almost an orgasm of joy at the dangling nerves and tendons of the gangrened member long after the first bungling blow: Cf: St. Anthony lashing himself in *The Temptation of St. Anthony*: "Oh! oh! oh! each lash tears my skin, rends my limbs! It burns me horribly! ...I would that my blood would spurt to the stars!--let my bones crack!--let my tendons be laid bare!...But how strange a titillation thrills me! What punishment! what pleasure! I feel as though receiving invisible kisses; the very marrow of my bones seems to melt. I die..." (42-43).

120.34-36 He had taught her something else, though he was not to find it out for a minute or so yet: See note 122.4-5.

121.20-27 "That's it," he said. "Fight it. Fight it. That's what it is: a man and a woman fighting each other. The hating...he or she is dead": Polk relates this analogy of sex and war to the old marshall's linkage of sex and war in *Fab*: "and then will have to surrender because the phenomenon of war is its hermaphroditism: the principles of victory and defeat inhabit the same body and the necessary opponent, enemy, is merely the bed they self-exhaust each other on: a vice only the more terrible and fatal because there is no intervening breast or division between to frustrate them into health by simple normal distance and lack of opportunity for the copulation from which even orgasm cannot free them" (344, noted "Women and the Feminine in *A Fable*" 183).

121.24-27 Not even to lie quiet dead because forever afterward there will have to be two in that grave and those two can never again lie quiet anywhere together and neither can ever lie anywhere alone and be quiet until he or she is dead: Faulkner also images Mink as twinned with Houston in a kind of living death. See 217.28-30.

122.4-5 "Stop pawing me," she said. "You old headless horseman Ichabod Crane": There are numerous parallels, as Eby notes, between the Labove/Eula/ Hoake McCarron triangle and the Ichabod Crane/Katrina Van Tassel/Brom Von Blunt triangle. Each features a stereotypical schoolmaster figure and a frontiersman in contest for the hand of a ripe nature goddess figure. Each is set in a xenophobic backwater, and in each the outsider is successfully repulsed (465-69).

123.11-12 sunwise slope of Olympus: the highest mountain in Greece, it is the home of the twelve Olympian gods in Greek mythology. There, Hephaestus constructed houses for the immortals, with the house of Zeus occupying the summit (*The Oxford Companion to Classical Literature* 394).

123.23-27 from that first day...who would make one too many forever after in any room she ever entered and remained in long enough to expel breath: Cf. the schoolmaster Phillotson's thoughts on Sue Bridehead in *Jude the Obscure*: "She's one too many for me!" (182).

123.35-37 That will be proof, he cried silently. Proof in the eyes and beliefs of living men that that happened which did not: Two of Eula's suitors follow McCarron to Texas on the same premise: they want to create suspicion that that happened which did not. See 139.38-140.5.

123.37-38 Which will be better than nothing: Labove's desire to accept any alternative to nothing recalls Harry Wilbourne's final comment: "Yes, he thought, between grief and nothing I will take grief" (*WP* 324). Cf. also McCaslin's advice to Ike in *GDM*: "For grieving and suffering too, of course, but still getting something out of it for all that, getting a lot out of it, because after all you dont have to continue to bear what you believe is suffering; you can always choose to stop that, put an end to that. And even suffering and grieving is better than nothing..." (186).

124.16-19 the stove...masculine, almost monastic--a winter's concentration of unwomaned and deliberate tobacco spittle annealing into the iron flanks: Faulkner again links male congregation, for whatever the reason, to the sterile and monastic wasteland, "out of life" (124.21).

125.1-23 He heard a man cursing....I awready been shot: See note 5.1-3.

126.8 window sash: a frame in which the panes of a window or door are set (*AHD*).

126.30-33 The house...when he passed: Labove, like Ichabod Crane, vacates the country without clearing his room or taking his possessions with him ("The Legend of Sleepy Hollow" 48). Among the effects of both men are two shirts and a razor (*Ham* 110.7-13, "The Legend of Sleepy Hollow" 48).

91

Chapter Two

127.4-5 swarmed like wasps about the ripe peach which her full damp mouth resembled: Cf. Velma, the girl with whom Elmer has his first sexual experience: "He had seen her at school, but from a distance, always, for she was in the eighth grade and was usually surrounded by a crowd of noisy strained-looking boys like wasps, answering some old yet dim compulsion" (*Elmer* 34). Rosa Coldfield talks about the "male predacious wasps and bees of later lusts" (*AbAb!* 144). Mink Snopes's virility is compared to the sting of a wasp (*Ham* 238.34-35). Katrina Von Tassel is described as being "ripe and melting and rosy cheeked as one of her father's peaches" ("The Legend of Sleepy Hollow" 28).

127.24-25 twosing games: Brown has never heard the term, but he assumes it to apply to the party games in which boys and girls pair off to an accompanying song and which often involve kissing (205). Elmer's girlfriend, Velma, is "always organising twosing games" (*Elmer* 34).

127.26 masonic lodge: meeting place for the Freemasons, an international fraternal and charitable organization with secret rites and signs (*AHD*).

128.1 first-Sunday all-day singings: "a summer church festival devoted largely to hymn and gospel singing, with the congregation bringing lunch, which is eaten picnic-style in the churchyard" (Brown 20).

128.1 baptisings: refers to the Baptist, total-immersion ritual, which took place at a creek or lake and was the occasion for a social gathering as well (Brown 25).

128.14-15 the nucleus, the center, the centrice: Heck relates this description of Eula's pivotal position to Nana's racetrack scene, when she is encircled by a "single dense crowd around her landau" (309-10, noted 128).

128.21-25 It was as if she already knew what instant, moment, she was reserved for, even if not his name and face, and was waiting...seemed to be: See 114.15-18.

130.3 corsets: a close-fitting undergarment, often reinforced by stays, worn to support and shape the waistline, hips, and breasts (*AHD*).

130.24-35 a leashed turmoil of lust like so many lowering dogs after a scarce-fledged and apparently unawares bitch: See 99.20-26. Cf. *FA*: "So they sit leashed and savage and loud" (17).

130.29-131.23 After supper the brother would be gone, courting himself....riders sat on the veranda doggedly and vainly sitting each other out...beneath the cold moon, across the planted land: This scene is virtually the same as that included in *FA*: the Sunday suitors sitting each other out, Eula's indifference, the lengthening shadows of evening, the cold leftovers, the friendly departure, and the cathartic fight by the creek (17). Cf. the contest for Katrina Von Tassel's affection in "The Legend of Sleepy Hollow": "and he had to encounter a host of fearful adversaries of real flesh and blood, the numerous rustic admirers, who beset every portal of her heart; keeping a watchful and angry eye upon each other, but ready to fly out in the common cause against any new competitor" (31).

130.31 trace-galled: "a sore place or callus on the flanks of a horse or mule, made by the traces. Trace galls come from hard work like plowing and they are much more likely to be caused by trace chains than by leather traces" (Brown 202).

132.21-22 he not only wore a necktie: the third necktie in Frenchman's Bend, the others being worn by Will Varner and Flem Snopes.

132.37-38 last summer's foreclosed bankrupts: Faulkner's insistence on economic metaphors for love and loss prefigures the actual economic transaction that secures Flem as Eula's husband and the baby's father.

133.25-27 exactly as he would have felt the back of a new horse for old saddle sores, grimly explore with his hard heavy hand to see if she had the corset on or not: See 98.11-18 for a comparable demotion of Eula Varner to the sub-human stratum. Jody's proprietary interest in Eula does not rest on the hope that he will realize a profit if he maintains the exchange value but rather on the kind of obsessive concern that brothers elsewhere in Faulkner's work invest in their sisters' virginity.

133.36 **tack rooms:** rooms in a stable in which the harnesses, bridles, and saddles are stored (*AHD*).

134.2-5 **he had that about him which loved the night...the bright hysteric glitter-glare which made them, the perversity of unsleeping:** Cather's Ántonia, who is like Eula represented as an earth goddess, also attracts her antithesis in a mate. Her husband is a city man, unaccustomed to farming: "He liked theatres and lighted streets and music and a game of dominoes after the day's work was over" (*My Ántonia* 235).

134.11-12 **old Hoake had sat for ten days now with a loaded shotgun across his lap:** Mrs. Gant also waits for Zilphia after her marriage with a shotgun ("Miss Zilphia Gant," *US* 377).

134.16 **overseer:** manager of a plantation.

135.8-10 **his father's assurance in his face which was bold and handsome too...not vain so much as intolerant:** Hoake evokes Brom Von Brunt in "The Legend of Sleepy Hollow," the "broad-shouldered, double-jointed" (31) hero whose "mingled air of fun and arrogance" (31) Katrina Van Tassel finds irresistible.

135.15-17 **He grew up with a Negro lad for his sole companion. They slept in the same room, the Negro on a pallet on the floor, until he was ten years old:** It was a common practice in the antebellum South to pair a white child with a black playmate who would evolve into a personal servant as the two grew older. John Faulkner says of his grandmother, "Damuddy had her own private Negro, like all children did then" (*My Brother Bill* 123). Faulkner's fictional black/white pairs include Ringo and Bayard in *Unv* and Henry and Roth in *GDM*. Hoake McCarron's Negro companion marks him as being from a different social class than the Varners or anyone else in Frenchman's Bend.

136.3-4 **that in which they and the brother had no belief:** Eula's honor, her virginity.

137.38-138.3 **one of them told it was the girl who had wielded it, springing from the buggy with the reversed whip beating three of them back...the other two:** Cf. *Unv*: "Granny standing up in the wagon and beating the five men about their heads and shoulders with the umbrella while they unfastened the traces and cut the harness off the mules with pocket knives" (66).

138.28-29 a piece of scantling: a small timber used in construction (*AHD*).

138.32-33 I reckon a man aint so different from a mule: McCarron's offhand comment is more perceptive and applicable to the men of *Ham* than he intends. The mule is a sterile hybrid of the donkey and the mare (Brown 25), called a "barren clown" in *AbAb!* (200).

139.38-140.5 They and the men who drove them were gone, vanished overnight...travelling fast: See note 123.35-37.

140.18-21 So when the word went quietly from house to house about the country that McCarron and the two others had vanished and that Eula Varner was in...trouble: Eula is among several unwed and abandoned mothers in Faulkner's fiction, including Caddy Compson, Dewey Dell Bundren, and Lena Grove.

140.22-26 this man who cheerfully and robustly and undeviatingly declined to accept any such theory as female chastity...the efficacy of prayer: Faulkner revisits in less gloomy fashion Mr. Compson's fatalistic perspective on female chastity: "Because it means less to women, Father said. He said it was men invented virginity not women. Father said it's like death: only a state in which the others are left and I said, But to believe it doesn't matter and he said, That's what's so sad about anything, not only virginity, and I said, Why couldn't it have been me and not her who is unvirgin and he said, That's why that's sad too; nothing is even worth the changing of it" (*S&F* 96). Cf. also Harry's similar comments on virginity in *WP*: "It was like the instant of virginity, it was the instant of virginity: that condition, fact, that does not exist except during the instant you know you are losing it" (137).

140.28-30 who at the present moment was engaged in a liaison with the middle-fortyish wife of one of his own tenants: Cf. Ratliff's rumors of Varner's "mulatto concubines" in *Twn* (276). Cf. Rigou's method of staying mortgages in *Les Paysans*: "he made a harem of the whole valley" (228).

140.34-35 **sylvan Pan-hallowed retreat:** Pan was a Roman god of shepherds and flocks who had a human torso and head and a goat's legs, horns, and ears. He lived in Arcadia, where he was attracted to streams and shady glens. Pan was renowned for his sexual appetite, which he directed both at Nymphs, whom he spied upon while hiding in the bushes, and young boys (Grimal 324-25).

140.35-36 **the fourteen-year-old boy whose habit it was to spy on them:** See note 196.14-16.

140.36 **Varner would not even remove his hat:** Varner debases the owner/tenant relationship by taking advantage of the wives of his sharecroppers. Faulkner further condemns him with the addition of this detail. Varner's cavalier attitude toward sex fits into the pattern of perversion of healthy male/female relations that runs through the novel. The man who will not remove his hat during intercourse, when he thinks no one is watching, is the same man that has just sacrificed his daughter for appearances' sake. Ratliff will later imagine Flem engaging in the same type of activity with the wife of a tenant farmer. See note 162.19-164.30. Cf. Miss Reba's description of Popeye "hanging over the foot of the bed without even his hat took off" (*Sanc* 311-12).

141.2 **wrapper:** a loose dressing gown or negligee (*AHD*).

141.2-3 **lace boudoir cap:** "a woman's cap adorned with lace and ribbons, worn over curlers" (Brown 36).

141.38-38 **he jerked one hand upward in a gesture of furious repudiation:** Jody's comic and impotent gesture looks ahead to the motion of "supreme repudiation" when Ike throws Houston's fifty-cent piece off the bridge (177.37-38).

142.14-17 **scrabbling a pistol from among the jumble... contained:** Cf. Gavin Stevens's recapitulation of Eula's marriage in *Twn*: "he --old Will--would have done that himself with his pistol, either in his hand or in that of his oafish troglodyte son Jody, if he had ever caught McCarron" (273). Quentin Compson remembers threatening to kill Dalton Ames (*S&F* 187).

142.33-35 **"I'll fix him. I'll fix both of them. Turning up pregnant** and yelling and cursing here in the house when I am trying to take a nap!": Ohashi cites this speech as a parody of Caroline Compson's selfishness and hypochondria (17).

143.6-8 "Maybe you dont give a damn about your name, but I do. I got to hold my head up before folks, even if you aint": The concern for respectability that drives Flem to attend church and wear a tie compels Varner finally to save face by marrying the pregnant Eula off to Flem Snopes. Faulkner parodies the drive toward respectability and conformity when the Snopeses collect money to purchase Ike's cow and end the "stock-diddling," so that the Snopes name can remain "pure as a marble monument for your children to grow up under" (see 204.20-23). The concern for name intensifies in *Twn*. Ratliff wonders why Wallstreet Panic's wife "aint never changed their name" (149). Gavin considers "the very words reputation and good name" (202) as they apply to the teenage Linda Snopes in her association with him. In Gavin's summary of events of *Ham*, Flem marries Eula to supply a name for her baby, disreputable as the Snopes name is (271). When Eula entreats Gavin to marry Linda, he interprets her request as a plea to "change her name by marriage" (332). Ratliff's inherited family name, he tells Eula, "is their luck" (323). In a comic comment on good name, even the massacred Pekingese wears a "gold name-plate" (362). Cf. also *S&F*: "will you even let me try to find out who he is it's not for myself I couldn't bear to see him it's for your sake to protect you but who can fight against bad blood you wont let me try we are to sit back with our hands folded while she not only drags your name in the dirt but corrupts the very air your children breathe" (128). Cf. old Grandet's determination to save the family name from dishonor, because he needs some outlet for his malicious energy: "As a matter of fact, the honor of the family name counted for very little with him in this matter; he looked at it from the purely personal view of the gambler, who likes to see a game well-played although it is no affair of his" (99).

143.17 **diddling:** having sexual intercourse with, but can also imply cheating and swindling (Brown 70). In American colloquial parlance, diddling almost always denotes cheating, as in the Poe story, "Diddling as an Exact Science," while British usage carries the sexual connotation. Ike's affair with the cow is referred to as "stock diddling" (201.26-28).

143.31-32 **lathering horsemeat:** "riding or driving a horse so hard that it gets into a lather" (Brown 116).

143.35-36 **Make Sam dig you some worms and go fishing:** Ohashi sees a parallel in Mr. Compson's suggestion that Quentin take a holiday in the Maine woods to forget about Caddy (noted 17).

143.39 **foxed:** "to trick, deceive, or outwit. To fox oneself is to outsmart oneself" (Brown 85).

144.1-2 **running water through it:** urinating.

144.12-26 **They saw that the clerk was heeled as by a dog by a man a little smaller than himself...bright alert amoral eyes of a squirrel or chipmunk:** Introduction of Lump, née Lancelot Snopes. In early drafts, Lancelot is Mordred, nicknamed Maud (*Manuscripts*).

144.13 **heeled:** followed closely at the heels, usually by a dog (*AHD*).

144.28-29 **Snopes jerked his head at them exactly as Will Varner himself did it, chewing:** See note 88.32-33.

144.34 **battered telescope bag:** "a suitcase made of two separate parts, the top sliding down over the bottom so that the total height is adjustable" (Brown 197).

145.26-28 **The bride and groom left for Texas right after the ceremony...that makes five:** The druggist to whom Dewey Dell Bundren applies for help with her "female trouble" (190) suggests that the baby's father is probably "halfway to Texas by now" (*AILD* 192).

146.13 **mute hissing of tennis shoes:** Mrs. Armstid mounts the steps to the store, hoping to recover her weaving money, her "stained tennis shoes hissing faintly on the boards" (315.20).

146.16 **the man:** Cf. *FA*: "He chews tobacco constantly and steadily, and no one ever saw his eyelids closed. He blinks them of course, like everyone else, but no one ever saw him do it. This is the man" (14).

146.38-147.3 **And so one day they clapped her into her Sunday clothes and put the rest of her things--the tawdry mail order negligees and nightgowns, the big flimsy shoes and what toilet things she had...and married her to him:** The failure of love, the supreme tragedy of *Ham*, is analogous to the marriage of Venus to Vulcan that Labove has predicted (118.27). Wagner's *Ring* tetralogy introduces a sex/love/money nexus that parallels *Ham*'s. Given the choice between love and money, the males of Wagner's opera successively elect the money: first, the dwarf Alberic forswears sex and the Rhine maidens, because they have foresworn him, to possess the Rhine gold instead; next the giants trade Freia for money; and, finally, in *Die Walküre*, Wotan's ambition comes to a tragic conclusion when he must deprive Brünhilde, the dearest and most capable of his children, of her immortality and sacrifice her to the first man that encounters her sleeping on her rock (Shaw, *The Perfect Wagnerite*). Cf. also the story of the fifteen-year-old Indian girl, Litka, daughter of the wealthiest Indian landowner in *Simon Suggs*. Litka, with her "Grecian face," is the "handsomest girl on the ground." When other Indians are forced out, Litka's father takes advantage of her beauty and sacrifices her to a white man so they can retain their land. Litka's husband then persuades her to certify the land to him, which she does, and he then deserts her when she is pregnant (70ff.). Eula's wedding to Flem also recalls Caddy Compson's wedding to Herbert Head in *S&F*.

147.15-17 the calm beautiful mask beneath the Sunday hat once more beyond a moving window, looking at nothing, and that was all: Eula's passing face staring into the void evokes other masks, i.e. Zilphia Gant's "small tragic mask of a face" (372).

147.31-32 the froglike creature: The fairy tale of the frog-prince hinges on a trade: a beautiful princess promises to sleep with a repugnant amphibian in exchange for his return of a golden ball that has fallen into a deep spring. As in many medieval folk tales, the marriage bed has magically transforming properties, and the frog metamorphoses into a handsome prince after three nights with the princess (Opie, *The Classic Fairy Tales* 238-244). The juxtaposition of the two unions points up the ironic contrast between the happily-ever-after ending of the fairy tale and the grim future for Eula Varner Snopes as Flem's bride.

147.33-148.11 a word, a single will to believe born of envy and old deathless regret...the need to flee that word and dream, for past: The "word" seems, literally, to be the news of Eula's pregnancy as it is passed around town. However, the "word" transcends its immediate relevance to suggest the primal logos and may, given the imagined descent into hell that follows, allude to Goethe's *Faust* and his struggles with the ambiguity of the "word" (I.3). Cf. "A Courtship": "And Ikkemotubbe and David Hogganbeck saw Herman Basket's sister. As who did not, sooner or later, young men and old men too, bachelors and widowers too, and some who were not even widowers yet, who for more than one reason within the hut had no business looking anywhere else, though who is to say what age a man must reach or just how unfortunate he must have been in his youthful compliance, when he shall no longer look at the Herman Basket's sisters of the world and chew his bitter thumbs too, aihee" (*CS* 362).

148.11-149.7 Even one of the actual buggies remained...still seeing them--the bank, the courthouse, the station; the calm beautiful mask seen once more beyond a moving pane of glass, then gone: Ratliff's reverie moves from the "word," the initial impulse toward hope and satisfaction of desire, to the yellow-wheeled buggies, and finally, to the travesty of hope and desire represented by the fleetingly glimpsed face of Eula as she passes on a train bound for Texas. The buggies play an intermediary role in this progression. Hitched to the Varner fence, they express eloquently the dream of Eula's current suitors, but they are also part of a chain of obsolescence. At their most glittering, the buggies and the young squires who drive them are watched by the "outgrown and discarded" (131.26) youths whom they have displaced. When Eula is married off to Flem, it is the young squires who are now redundant. The remaining buggy, once a material projection of the dream, is re-introduced to the mundane world and becomes subject to time. Without its driver, and without a horse (so strongly associated with the male principle in this novel) the buggy becomes a reminder of what the young men flee to avoid becoming part of: "the flotsam of a vain dead yesterday of passionate and eternal regret and grief" (140.11-12). The buggies are also reminders of the wrongheaded concern with appearances that ultimately leads to Eula's marriage. The buggies vanish because the young men want it to be believed that something happened which did not; but the young men also want to escape the social consequences of seducing and impregnating Eula. When Ratliff returns to Frenchman's Bend in September, he still sees the buggies, but they are now linked in his mind with another recollection, that of Eula Varner Snopes's departing face. See 159.7-8.

149.9-13 But that was all right, it was just meat, just gal-meat...not wasted on Snopes but on all of them, himself included: Within the context of Ratliff's meditations on waste and respectability, it is obvious that Ratliff does not consider it to be all right that Eula and the dream associated with her should be gone forever, wasted on the men of *Ham*. Cf. *WP* for conjunction of meat, waste, and memory: *It cant be. The waste. Not of meat, there is always plenty of meat....But memory. Surely memory exists independent of the flesh* (316).

149.20-21 another mortal natural enemy of the masculine race: This statement reflects Ratliff's bitterness at the waste represented by Eula's marriage to Flem, but it does not seem to express a deeply felt attitude toward women. Ratliff momentarily abandons his customary idealism and lapses into Varnerian cynicism. See note 157.34-158.2. Cf. also Charlotte Rittenmeyer's anger in *WP*: "not at the race of mankind but at the race of man, the masculine" (11).

149.28-153.16 ***Until at last, baffled, they come to the Prince hisself...clawing and scrabbling at that locked door, screaming***: Flem's descent into hell, the subject of Ratliff's reverie, one of the most effective set-pieces in American literature, has a long literary pedigree, which Faulkner parodies in the extreme for comic effect. The literal or symbolic journey to the underworld, undertaken to accomplish a goal or to secure knowledge, runs through mythology and fictive literature, from Dionysus's dive under the lake to rescue his mother from Hades to Don Juan's debates with the devil in Shaw's *Man and Superman*. Aeneas in *The Odyssey* journeys to the underworld, accompanied by a sybil, to learn his destiny. Dante, in his *Inferno*, descends to the nine circles of hell, accompanied by Vergil. Goethe's Faust, in Part Two, leaves Mephistopheles to descend to "the mothers," the shades of the eternal feminine. Dostoyevsky depicts a different kind of hell in his subterranean novel, *Notes from Underground*; existence and the mind itself constitute hell for the narrator of that novel (*Dictionary of Literary Themes and Motifs* 363). Cabell's Jurgen is despatched [sic] by the Philistines to the Hell of his fathers two days before Christmas. Ironically, all those who are born with a conscience go to hell, because they believe their crimes "to be of sufficient importance to merit punishment" (*Jurgen* 250-95). The pact with the devil central to Marlowe's *Doctor Faustus* and Goethe's *Faust* gets a light, folk-humor treatment in Benet's "The Devil and Daniel Webster." Blotner finds echoes of *Paradise Lost, The Temptation of St. Anthony*, the Temptation on the Mount, *The Mysterious Stranger*, and the Faust legend (*Faulkner*, One Vol. ed. 407).

101

149.32 *now he has come to redeem it*: his soul.

149.35-36 *We sealed it up in a asbestos matchbox*: Scratch, as the devil is called in "The Devil and Daniel Webster," also stores souls in small, specially designed boxes (35).

150.21 *He's got the law*: Faulkner takes up the theme of justice that he introduced first in "Barn Burning." Here, as in the trials of Book Four, it is strict adherence to the law itself that allows the corrupt to prosper. Shaw's devil lists justice among the "deadly virtues" of hell along with honor and duty (*Man and Superman* 604).

151.1 *Chinees*: Chinese.

151.1 *Dagoes*: disparaging term for a Spaniard, an Italian, or a Portuguese (*AHD*).

151.1 *Polynesians*: natives of the South Pacific islands, Polynesia.

151.5-6 *Your father made, unreproved, a greater failure. Though maybe a greater man tempted a greater man*: alludes to Christ's temptation by the devil in the wilderness (Matthew 4:1-11, Luke 4:1-13). The Prince is admitting that Satan was a greater tempter than he is, while Christ was a greater man than Flem Snopes.

151.10 *BB size lava and brimstone*: the small pellets of a BB gun.

151.15-30 *What did you offer him?...He wants hell:* In a parodic reversal of the "Don Juan in Hell" sequence of *Man and Superman*, Flem is not vulnerable to temptation, because he has no desires or passions. Don Juan, a "libertine," all desire, rejects hell because it is incompatible with the Life Force within him (647).

152.8 *"So they tell me," the Prince says, "but you have no soul"*: The devil says to Don Juan: "You have no soul; and you are unconscious of all that you lose" (Shaw, *Man and Superman* 612-13).

152.16-21 *Then the Prince said, "Look yonder...the last imaginable one:* recalls the parade of visions that visits St. Anthony in Flaubert's *The*

Temptation of St. Anthony.

153.10 "*Who are you?*" *he says:* Cf. the Grand Inquisitor's question of Christ in *The Brothers Karamazov*: "Is it Thou? Thou?" (296, noted Weisgerber 270).

153.11-12 *setting there with that straw suitcase on the Throne among the bright, crown-shaped flames:* Cf. Madame Tonsard's accusation to Rigou in *Les Paysans*: "You are the devil himself....People say that you have signed a compact with him (290).

Book Three: The Long Summer

157.4 the rich sonorous organ-tone of its entrails: flatulence. See 57.19.

157.10 that patented necktie: synecdoche for the automaton-like sensibility associated with Flem's little "machine-made black bow" (57.38).

157.15-25 He was not even thinking of Varner's daughter's shame or of his daughter at all. He meant the land...it was too valuable to sell: This passage elliptically treats the core tragedy of *Ham*, that a woman, in Eula's case, a fertility goddess, should be marketed as a commodity and pawned off in trade for something considered by the owner, wrongly, to be of no inherent value. Eula's own position is analogous to that of the old Frenchman's Place, the precinct of the dream, dishonored by those who inherit it. See note 6.27-28.

157.34-158.2 He sat the old horse and looked down at Ratliff...the man who was a good deal nearer his son in spirit and intellect and physical appearance than any of his own get: Faulkner takes some pains at this critical juncture in the novel to make a connection between Ratliff and Varner that extends beyond their earlier identification as shrewd traders, mutually capable, in their own opinion, of defeating Flem (see 28.3-9). Varner, who has so recently sacrificed Eula for the sake of respectability, is now more strongly associated with his limitations as a father than with his strengths as a businessman. In making Ratliff the metaphorical son of Varner, at this point in the novel, Faulkner may be suggesting that Ratliff participates in these limitations. The limitations are two-fold, having to do, first, with women and respectability, and, second, with the land. Given the symbolic and mythical connection of the earth with the feminine, both are part of a network of inter-related associations.

Ratliff is impractically idealistic about women most of the time, while Varner is nothing if not practical and opportunistic. Ratliff casts his "tomcatting's heyday" into the past, while Varner is still sexually active. Ratliff is a bachelor who lives with his widowed sister, while Varner is the married father of sixteen. Yet, at some level, they share common assumptions about women. Ratliff, on the next page, will imply that he and Varner speak the same language in sexual matters by referring to "what he and Varner both would have called his tomcatting's heyday" (159.25-26): this, after Varner has been shown to care very much about the appearance of decency in sexual matters involving his daughter, while at the same time conducting himself much less scrupulously when he believes he is removed from the public eye. Ratliff will make a similar distinction in Book Three, when he closes down the Ike/cow peep show, not because it exists, but because it exists in the open, as Mrs Littlejohn points out at 198.7-11. Secondly, Varner has surrendered title to the Old Frenchman's Place because he cannot comprehend its value. In Book Four, Ratliff will similarly miscalculate the value of the land. See note 157.15-25.

158.2-3 "So you think pure liver aint going to choke that cat," he said: This is a variant of a folk saying implying that the metaphorical cat, unused to rich foods, or the best provisions, will be unable to stomach them. In most versions, the cat chokes on cream or butter (*The Macmillan Book of Proverbs, Maxims, and Famous Phrases* 297).

158.4-5 "Maybe with that ere little piece of knotted-up string in it?" Ratliff said: the foetus. See note 159.37.

158.9 mosey down: Informal: to move in an easy, relaxed way; saunter (*AHD*).

158.12-14 "I got that damn trial this morning. That damn Houston and that What's-his-name. Mink. About that durn confounded scrub yearling": Faulkner picks up the thread that he left hanging at the end of Book One. Cf. the Tonsard habit of pasturing their cows on the grounds of Montcornet's estate: "At first the youngest girl took the two cows to graze by the side of the road; though the animals for the most part, broke through the hedges into the fields of the Aigues....The keepers of the Aigues and the rural policeman scarcely ever caught them in the act" (*Les Paysans* 45-46). There is a minor incident in *O Pioneers* involving some hogs that get loose in Frank Shabata's wheat. Frank is, like Houston, a "rash and violent man" (82) who threatens to "take dat old woman to de court if she ain't careful" (82). Opie notes a folk belief that trespassing cows are a bad omen and a sign of death to come (*Dictionary of Superstitions* 103).

158.20 **beef it:** to slaughter for beef (Brown 28).

158.35 **benzine:** a colorless, flammable, liquid mixture of hydrocarbons obtained in distilling petroleum, used in cleaning and dyeing and as a motor fuel (*AHD*).

158.35-36 **rich preliminary internal chord:** again, flatulence. See 157.4 and 57.19.

159.3 **yellow-wheeled buggies:** "sporty buggies and carriages often had the wheels and other running gear painted bright red, yellow, or green" (Brown 221). Rousselle mentions the use of the color yellow to connote both sexual and physical corruption in *LA* and cites several yellow vehicles: Popeye's yellow car in "The Big Shot" (552), Matt Levitt's "yellow cut-down racer" in *Twn* (183-191), and Gatsby's yellow Rolls Royce (*The Great Gatsby* 64, noted *Annotations* 5).

159.5 **two-legged feice:** a fice is a small, mongrel dog, and a two-legged fice is a human of the same variety.

159.14-18 **so why should not that body at the last have been the unscalable sierra, the rosy virginal mother of barricades...hurled back and down:** This passage links with Labove's equation of the land with the female body, not as an arable plot to be plowed but as a summit to be conquered.

159.18 **leaving no scar, no mark of himself:** See note 119.14-19.

159.25-26 **what he and Varner would have called his tomcatting's**

105

heyday: Tomcatting's heyday refers to that time in a male's life when he is most likely to be sexually active with more than one partner. See note 157.34-158.2.

159.27-30 **It would have been like giving me a pipe organ...swapped a mailbox for, he thought:** See Mrs. Varner's similar thoughts on waste at 98.39-99.1. Ratliff here laments his own inadequacy as a sexual partner for Eula, who has been too much woman for any man in *Ham* since she was old enough to listen to the "enlarging of her own organs." Cf. 95.15-17. Now, Faulkner, punning on the meaning of organ, draws the traditional metaphorical connection between music and sex.

159.31 **cold and frog-like victor:** See note 147.31-32.

159.34-160.1 **What he felt was outrage at the waste, the useless squandering...dung heap, breeding pismires:** Ratliff voices the novel's strongest statement of loss, regret, and condemnation. Cf. Gavin Stevens's similar lament after Eula's suicide in *Twn*: "Why? Why did she have to? Why did she? The waste. The terrible waste. To waste all that, when it was not hers to waste, not hers to destroy because it is too valuable, belonged to too many, too little of it to waste, destroy, throw away and be no more" (358). Eustacia Vye, the goddess of Hardy's *Return of the Native*, is also described as being wasted on the local population: "But celestial imperiousness, love, wrath, and fervor had proved to be somewhat thrown away on netherward Egdon" (59). See also note 162.11-13.

159.36 **a log dead-fall:** "a trap made with a log between two rows of stakes. One end of the log is raised and supported by a device triggered to drop the log on an animal when he pulls at the bait tied underneath it" (Brown 69).

159.37 **freshened heifer:** a pregnant young cow. This passage refers back to the previous one in which Ratliff likens Flem to a cat who will choke on the rich diet of the pregnant Eula Varner, who is compared to a piece of liver with a piece of string knotted up in it (158.4-5). By comparing Eula here to a pregnant cow used as bait to catch a rat, Faulkner extends the metaphor into the next episode, which will also involve, literally, sacrifice of a cow.

160.1 **pismires:** ants (*AHD*).

160.5 **Not to mention the poorhouse:** This remark remains cryptic. Ratliff is referring to the lane that leads to the Old Frenchman's Place. He may be semi-consciously acknowledging a truth that will be borne out in Book Four, Chapter Two.

160.17 **lint:** the mass of soft fibers surrounding the seeds of unginned cotton (*AHD*).

160.19 **gouts:** blobs or clots (*AHD*).

160.26-27 **as if they had both been cut with the same die, but in inverse order of appearance, the last first:** Cf. Faulkner's description of Ab in "Barn": "a shape black, flat, and bloodless as though cut from tin in the iron folds of the frockcoat which had not been made for him, the voice harsh like tin and without heat like tin" (8), and again: "...now, against the serene columned backdrop, had more than ever that impervious quality of something cut ruthlessly from tin, depthless, as though, sidewise to the sun, it would cast no shadow" (10). Popeye also has "that vicious depthless quality of stamped tin" (*Sanc* 2). Cf. also *The Nigger of the "Narcissus"*: "A hum of voices was heard there, while port and starboard, in the illuminated doorways, silhouettes of moving men appeared for a moment very black, without relief, like figures cut out of sheet tin" (23).

160.26 **die:** a device used for cutting out, forming, or stamping material, especially tin (*AHD*).

160.29 **kitten's button:** A newborn kitten has a bright pink button nose.

160.35 **broadcloth:** a densely textured woolen cloth with a plain or twill weave and a lustrous finish (*AHD*).

161.11-12 **the rodent's face of the teacher:** Cf. the "rat-faced youth" in "Sut Lovingood's Daddy, Acting Horse" (*Sut Lovingood: Yarns Spun by a Nat'ral Born Durn'd Fool* 21).

161.17 **Caesar never built Rome in one day:** A variation of this is recorded in Tobler's 1190 *Li Proverbe au Vilain*: "Rome was not made all in one day, so say the vulgar." Heywood also cites it in his 1546 compendium of English proverbs (*The Macmillan Book of Proverbs,*

Maxims, and Famous Phrases 2004-05).

161.17-18 **patience is the horse that runs steadiest:** Several proverbial sayings connect patience and horses or asses. The proverb that matches I.O.'s most closely is: "Patience is a good nag, but she'll bolt" (*The Macmillan Book of Proverbs, Maxims, and Famous Phrases* 1754). Cf. also: "Patience is the virtue of asses" and "The horses of hope gallop, but the asses of experience go slowly" (*Prentice-Hall Encyclopedia of World Proverbs* 363, 238). Cf. also "Patience perforce is medicine for a mad horse" (*The Macmillan Book of Proverbs, Maxims, and Famous Phrases* 1755).

161.20-21 **"When Snopes pays Houston three dollars pasturage, he can get his bull," Quick said:** In *Mans*, Mink calculates that it will cost him even more than the fine imposed in *Ham*. In a more complicated transaction involving the cow, Mink alleges that he had sold the cow for eight dollars but that the cow had immediately escaped from its new owner and made its way into Houston's pasture. The new owner demands to be reimbursed for the cow, and is, but Houston then rejects the eight dollars that Mink is willing to pay for pasturage, maintaining that the fattened cow is worth at least thirty-five dollars. Mink then appeals to Varner, who refuses to serve Houston with papers and instead solicits the advice of two cattle experts who determine that the cow is worth thirty-seven and a half and that Mink fairly owes half that, or eighteen dollars and seventy-five cents. Because Mink can't raise that much money, Houston arranges to pay him fifty cents a day to dig post holes for a new fence he wants to install, which Mink does. When the judgment is finally satisfied by Mink's calculations, he goes to retrieve his cow, only to find that he owes Houston a one dollar pound fee. He works the two extra days to earn the dollar pound fee and then ambushes Houston and kills him, not for the thirty-seven and a half days of work, but for the dollar pound fee (7-39).

161.23 **"---t!":** See note 62.29.

162.5 **jobbing:** working at odd jobs; working by the piece (*AHD*).

162.5-6 **it's the same old stern getting reamed out:** The image of the stern getting reamed out is a vulgarism that refers literally to anal intercourse. Used in common parlance such as this, it does not carry a sexual meaning but implies instead debasement or humiliation by one who exerts power.

162.7-8 "If you would stand closer to the door, he could hear you a heap better," he said: Cf. Bookwright's warning to Ratliff that he should be more discreet about the goat deal at 79.9-11: "Besides," Bookwright said, suddenly and harshly, "if you want to tell them folks at the blacksmith shop about it too, why dont we all just move over there."

162.9 Big ears have little pitchers: Ratliff inverts the common proverbial saying, noted in Heywood's 1546 collection of proverbs: "Auoyd your children: small pitchers have wide eares" (*Proverbs* Pt. ii, ch. 5, noted *The Macmillan Book of Proverbs, Maxims, and Famous Phrases* 1800).

162.9-10 The world beats a track to the rich man's hog pen: This is Ratliff's version of the maxim that the world beats a path to the rich man's door.

162.11-13 Waste not, want not, except that a full waist dont need no prophet to prophesy a profit and just whose: *The Macmillan Book of Proverbs, Maxims, and Famous Phrases* cites the first use of this phrase in Maria Edgeworth's *The Parent's Assistant* (1800): "The following words were written...over the mantelpiece in his uncle's spacious kitchen, 'Waste not, want not'" (232, noted 2457). Ratliff here picks up the previous chapter's meditations on waste and adds a sardonic twist by punning on the homophones waste/waist and prophet/profit. While Eula is wasted on Flem, who cannot possibly want her, her enlarging waist will allow him to realize a profit.

162.19-164.30 "Why, nothing," Ratliff said...whut you ax fer dem sardines?": Ratliff imagines Flem as sexually exploiting a Negro woman whom he furnishes with provisions. The business-like intercourse that he envisions not only recalls Will Varner's quick encounters with these same wives but also highlights the male tendency to commodify women. By juxtaposing this reverie with the furtive movements of the men as they retreat to watch the Ike and cow peep show, Faulkner comments on the state of and possibility for love in the modern world. See note 140.36. Perhaps Faulkner means to conflate the images of Flem and Lump, since the new clerk, Lump, replaces the old clerk, Flem, behind the counter at this time.

162.33 **eave cat:** a stray cat that lives under the eaves.

162.33-36 **A little boy of eight or ten came up trotting...eyes as blue and innocent as periwinkles and trotted intently into the store:** Wallstreet Panic Snopes.

164.20-21 **little tight cans with fishes and devils on them:** Cf. the opening scene of "Barn," in which Sarty too stares at the "ranked shelves close-packed with the solid, squat, dynamic shapes of tin cans whose labels his stomach read not from the lettering but from the scarlet devils and the silver curve of fish" (*CS* 3).

Chapter One, 2: Faulkner composed the idyll of idiot and cow during the period when he was assembling the Snopes material into *Ham*. Among the various love affairs chronicled in the novel, it is at once the least natural and the most celebratory. Faulkner invests this incident of "stock diddling" with the most poetic, lush narration in the novel. In the tension between subject and style, he signals a complex and ironic attitude toward the possibilities for love. On the one hand, Ike exhibits the positive values of unselfish love and devotion in a world that desperately needs them, but, ironically, the loved object is, after all, a cow.

For this incident, Faulkner returned to images and themes from his earliest work, especially from two related short prose pieces, "The Hill" and "Nympholepsy." "The Hill," published in the March 10, 1922 number of *The Mississippian*, features a "tieless casual" (*EPP* 92) who mounts a hill after work, accompanied by his shadow. At the top, he surveys the valley below at sunset and the narrator observes that "here in the dark nymphs and fauns might riot to a shrilling of thin pipes, to a shivering and hissing of symbols in a sharp volcanic abasement beneath a tall icy star" (192). The nymphs and fauns who exist in potentiality in "The Hill" materialize in "Nympholepsy," which Meriwether dates from early 1925. In that story, the day laborer falls into a stream and encounters there "a startled thigh" and the "point of a breast" (335). He pursues the nymph in the moonlight but finally gives up the chase and descends the hill.

The concept of nympholepsy and the word itself were available to Faulkner in several sources with which he would have been familiar. Hönnighausen mentions Swinburne's "A Nympholept," Browning's "Nympholeptos," and a comment made by George Moore: "You ask me why I like the landscape? Because it carries me back into the past time when men believed in nymphs and satyrs. I always thought it must be a wonderful thing to believe in the dryad. Do you know that men wandering in the woods sometimes used to catch sight of white breast between the leaves, and henceforth they could love no mortal woman. The beautiful name of their malady was nympholepsy. A disease that everyone would like to catch" (174). Sensibar adds Conrad Aiken to the list of possible influences. In his introduction to *The Charnel Rose*, Aiken defines nympholepsy as "that impulse which sends man from one dream, or ideal, to another, always disillusioned and therefore always inventing new fictions" (*The Origins of Faulkner's Art* (118).

Snell writes that Phil Stone believed himself to have contributed the story of Ike and the cow while Faulkner was pulling together *Ham*. Emily Whitehurst Stone had heard the story of "the only son of the WIDOW SOMEBODY who had...'taken up with a cow.'" When she told Phil, he pronounced the story "made to order for Bill" and passed it along (243-44).

164.31-165.35 As winter became spring and the spring itself advanced...mist loud with its hymeneal choristers: Adams notes a resemblance to the imagery of dawn, springtime and singing birds that the Provençal troubadour poets often employed in their love songs. The love object of those lyrics was most often admired from afar and was not easily won. The emotion of love itself was linked to the life force, which was thought to run harmoniously through both physical nature and human nature ("The European Roots" 33).

165.1 **April:** See note 23.39. Keats' "Endymion" also begins with the dawn of an April morning, when Endymion beseeches the muse to let a drop of "ethereal dew" anoint his head and "unmew" his soul (I.131-32).

165.2 **false dawn:** In tropical climates, actual dawn is preceded by a lightening of the sky that appears very like the real thing. Fitzgerald's "Rubaiyat of Omar Kyayyam" also begins with "False morning" (4th ed. 2.1). As in Ike's idyll, the progress of the sun across the sky is meant to suggest the human progress through the day and through life. Fitzgerald annotates the reference: "*False Dawn*...a transient Light on the Horizon about an hour before the...True Dawn" (4th ed. 168).

165.3-5 he could already see and know himself to be an entity solid and cohered in visibility instead of the uncohered all-sentience of fluid: Images of birth, or rebirth, such as this description of Ike's emergence into solidity and sentience from the fluid world, are prominent in the episode of idiot and cow. See 178.14 and note 184.27-38.

165.6 **primal sightless inimicality:** See note 85.28-33.

165.14-16 **to let himself downward into the creekside mist and lie in the drenched myriad waking life of grasses and listen for her approach:** Ike's immersion in the natural, and especially, the moist world of the misty creekside sets him apart from the mechanical and infertile men of the novel. Cf. *S&F*: "The grass was ankle-deep, myriad" (149).

165.21 **serene:** The adjective connects Ike with the serene heroines of Faulkner's fiction, among them Eula Varner Snopes and Narcissa Benbow and points up Ike's androgyny. Benjy Compson's eyes are described as "empty and blue and serene" (401).

165.24 **barrel:** rib cage.

165.27 **earth's teeming minute life:** The abundant life and fertility of this section contrast with the "teeming vacuum" in which Eula Varner passes her days, "as though behind sound-proof glass" (see note 95.13-15).

165.30-31 **the marching drops held in minute magnification the dawn's rosy miniatures:** Pruvot suggests that this mirroring represents not narcissism but an analogical relationship between the macrocosm and the microcosm ("Le Sacre de la Vache" 108). Cf. Faulkner's 1955 essay, "Kentucky: May: Saturday": "It rained last night; the gray air is still moist and filled with a kind of luminousness, lambence, as if each droplet held in airy suspension still its molecule of light..." (*ESPL* 56).

165.32 **the flowing immemorial female:** Faulkner's celebration of the regenerative powers of the feminine is juxtaposed with Houston's flight from the "immemorial trap" (205.22) in the following chapter. Cf. also *WP*: "Yet out of the terror in which you surrender volition, hope, all--the darkness, the falling, the thunder of solitude, the shock, the death, the moment when, stopped physically by the ponderable clay, you yet feel all your life rush out of you into the pervading immemorial blind matrix, the hot fluid blind foundation--grave-womb or womb-grave, it's all one" (138).

165.34 **hoof:** It is not clear to the reader that the beloved is a cow until this mention of her cloven hoof. In *GDM*, the novel that follows *Ham*, and on which Faulkner worked concurrently, one of the successful love relationships is also between man and animal. Boon Hogganbeck, who has the "mind almost of a child" (*GDM* 220), loves the dog Lion as if he "were a woman" (*GDM* 220) and sleeps with him for two years (noted Dunn 421).

A cow is often associated with the feminine principle in ancient mythology. Isis, the Eqyptian fertility goddess and consort of Osiris, was regularly depicted with the horns of a cow on her head. When Osiris descended to the underworld, mourners carried a gilded wooden cow with a golden sun between its horns to represent the grieving Isis searching for her beloved (Frazer 373). Isis's story was assimilated with the story of Io, who ended her wanderings in Egypt. Io was the daughter of the river god Inachus and was a priestess of Juno. Jupiter carried on a flirtation with her until, aware that his wife was suspicious, he transformed her into a white heifer. Because Juno suspected the truth, she begged to be given the beautiful animal as a present. Jupiter agreed, and Juno immediately set the hundred-eyed Argus to guard Io. Mercury charmed Argus to sleep with a blend of pipe-playing and story-telling and then cut off his head. Juno put the eyes of Argus on the tail of the peacock and sent a gadfly to torment Io, who traveled the earth attempting to escape its torture (Bullfinch 60-63). Graves notes that Io was associated with the moon in her power as rain-giver. Priestesses of Io at Argives danced a heifer dance in which they pretended to be tortured by gadflies. Men, dressed as woodpeckers, at the same time tapped on doors attempting to solicit rain to relieve her (Graves 192).

165.35 **hymeneal choristers:** Birds of dawn sing Ike's wedding song.

165.36 **bright thin horns of morning:** Cf. Faulkner's poem "The Flowers that Died": "The flowers that died last year again are growing,/ And faint horns of the morning, faintly blowing,/ Lighten the bannered path for dawn to stray" (*Contempo* 3:1). While both descriptions of dawn make use of the blowing horns, *Ham*'s appropriation of the metaphor is enriched by the irony that the "horns" are also those belonging to the cow and coming into full view as the mist clears (noted Millum 34).

165.38 **blond:** Pitavy points out that the relation between Ike and Jack Houston's cow is one of identity, a communion of self with self ("Idiocy and Idealism" 104). Her blonde coat recalls his "soft gold hair" (85.33).

165.38 **dew-pearled**: Cf. Browning's "Pippa Passes":
*The year's at the spring
And day's at the morn;
Morning's at seven;
The hillside's dew-pearled;
The lark's on the wing;
The snail's on the thorn:
God's in his heaven--
All's right with the world!* (133).

165.38 **standing in the parted water of the ford**: Flem's sisters are likened to "two cows, heifers standing knee-deep in air as in a stream, a pond, nuzzling into it, the level of the pond fleeing violently and silently to one inhalation, exposing in astounded momentary amaze the teeming lesser subaerial life about the planted feet" (*Ham* 47. 32-36). Caddy Compson is also associated with a creek; she gets her drawers muddy "playing in the branch" (*S&F* 19). The motif of a nymph who is spied while she bathes in a stream dates from Faulkner's earliest work. Cf. *MF*:
While I lie in the leafy shade
Until the nymphs troop down the glade.

To comb and braid their short brown hair
Before they slip into the pool--
Warm gold in silver liquid cool (p. 26, noted Arnold, *Annotations* 143).

Cf. the scene in *Mayday* when Galwyn comes upon Iseult in a stream bathing (pp. 20-24, noted Arnold, *Annotations* 143). Cf. *Mosq*: "You'd like to watch her from a distance ... in a pool where there were lots of poplar trees" (328, noted Arnold, *Annotations* 143). According to Bullfinch, when Juno first spied Io, she was by the banks of a river with Jupiter (60).

166.3-5 **Because he cannot make one with her through the day's morning and noon and evening**: In the courtly love tradition, Ike's beloved is inaccessible to him and more desirable for that reason.

166.7-12 **yesterday was not, tomorrow is not, today is merely placid and virginal astonishment...irkless**: Like Benjy Compson of *S&F*, Ike Snopes inhabits a timeless present.

166.20-21 **She raised her head and looked at him and scampered**

up the further bank, out of the water: Cf. the nymph's retreat from the youthful protagonist of "Nympholepsy": "...feeling his wet hair plastered upon his face, he saw her swing herself, dripping, up the bank" (*US* 335). The Ike episode of *Ham* shares with the early "Nympholepsy" the transcendence of ordinary reality and of the physical through a visionary erotic experience (Hönnighausen 183).

166.36 **the shape of love:** recalls "Endymion": "...yes in spite of all,/ Some shape of beauty moves away the pall/ From our dark spirits" (I.11-13).

167.16-17 **since he knew most of the adjacent countryside and was never disoriented:** Faulkner juxtaposes the instinctive orientation of the idiot with the disorientation of Mink Snopes in the next episode. Hardy, similarly, contrasts the responses to their environments of Thomasina Wildeve and Eustacia Vye in *Return of the Native*. Eustacia, confronted by the wildness of the landscape on a rainy night, finds "the wings of her soul...broken by the cruel obstructiveness of all about her" (322). Thomasina, on the same night, does not see nature as an enemy: "To her there were not, as to Eustacia, demons in the air, and malice in every bush and bough. The drops which lashed her face were not scorpions, but prosy rain; Egdon in the mass was no monster, but impersonal open ground" (331).

168.3-4 **he tried again to speak to the man with his eyes:** another of the many images of frustrated communication. See note 47.14-23.

168.17-23 **Then he would turn and mount the hill...his shadow shortening on the dust ahead...damp overalls:** The conjunction of hill and shadow suggests the early Faulkner prose poem, "The Hill." See Gresset's treatment of the hill vantage point as the "locus solus, the central dramatic location in Faulkner's work" (*Fascination* 46) and his discussion of the symbolic implications of ascent and descent in Faulkner's work. The ascent of a hill, he suggests, signals both a character's receptivity to enlightenment and his assertion of virility, given the associations of masculine and feminine with hill and valley (46-53).

168.28-32 **Because even while sweeping he could see her...integer of spring's concentrated climax, by it crowned, garlanded:** reminiscent of Eula's entry into the schoolroom, bringing with her "a moist blast of spring's liquorish corruption, a pagan triumphal prostration before the supreme primal uterus" (113.39-114.2).

168.34-174.2 He was upstairs sweeping when he saw the smoke...pale smoke on the sunny sky: Faulkner's "Afternoon of a Cow" treats parodically the rescue of the cow Beulah from a similar fire. Interestingly enough, in that story, Faulkner himself plays the part that Ike Snopes assumes in the novel. In 1937, while in Hollywood working for Twentieth Century Fox, Faulkner read aloud to some dinner guests the story, which, he reported, had been written by one Ernest V. Trueblood. His French translator, Maurice Coindreau, appreciated the joke and was given a carbon copy of the typescript. Faulkner almost certainly had in mind a send-up of some of his early poetic efforts that had been published in the University of Mississippi student newspaper seventeen years before. His first published poem, "L'Après-Midi d'un Faune," appearing in the August 16, 1919 issue of the *New Republic*, was also published later that year in the student newspaper at Old Miss, *The Mississippian*. The next year, the student newspaper published "Une Ballade des Femmes Perdues." On May 12, 1920, "Une Ballade d'une Vache Perdue," published under the name Lordgreyson, parodied the lovesick speakers of the early Faulkner poems. In the parody, a cow named Betsy strays from her home and wanders lost and alone (Blotner, *US* 702).

Adams notes that, in Faulkner's work, the purpose of disaster in the natural world is to dramatize the power of the life force as it subsumes anything less animate that gets in its way. He mentions the predominance of scenes, like this one, involving "flood, fire, wind, stampeding animals, moving crowds of people, burgeoning vegetation, hot sunshine, odors of growth and decay, flocks of birds, and swarms of buzzing insects" (*Myth and Motion* 5). Among the stories and novels in which fire plays a prominent part are "Barn," *AILD*, and *AbAb!*. In the barn fire near the end of *AILD*, there is also a cow who needs to be rescued (210-11). Gresset comments on the "inevitable presence of smoke in Faulkner's valley" and cites *LA*, where it prefigures death, and "The Hill," where it is innocuous (*Fascination* 49).

170.23-26 Because he stands in sun, visible...no darkness to flee to and from, and this is wrong: Ike, like Benjy Compson, adheres to rigid patterns of behavior and is disturbed when the pattern is varied. See the closing scene of *S&F*, when Luster drives Benjy around the square to the left, rather than to the right as is customary (399-401).

171.9 thick female thighs: While Ike is a sympathetic character and his love for the cow is genuine, his androgyny may indicate that something is not quite right with him. Faulkner's early examinations of hermaphroditism, inspired, as Hönnighausen notes, by Swinburne's "Hermaphroditis" cycle, focus on sterile and unattainable love (101). Bleikasten, too, comments on the late Romantic concern for the blurring of traditional sex role definition in such texts as Gautier's *Madamoiselle de Maupin* and Pater's "Diaphaneity," as well as in the nineteenth-century realistic French novel (8). See 86.15-17.

171.17 rimpled: wrinkled (AHD).

171.32-172.9 A mile back he had left the rich, broad, flat river-bottom...red and white with alternate sand and clay: Faulkner here compresses the already tightly compressed history of the region in the opening pages of his essay, "Mississippi" (*ESPL* 11-21).

172.24 the horse appeared, materialised furiously out of the smoke, monstrous and distorted, wild-eyed and with tossing mane, bearing down upon him: Cf. "Afternoon of a Cow": "Again a wild and monstrous shape materialised in violent motion before us, again apparently with the avowed and frantic aim of running us down" (*US* 428). Cf. also the mule that materializes out of the fog to trouble Mrs. Hait's cow in "Mule in the Yard": "...there appeared at the corner of the house and apparently having been born before their eyes of the fog itself, a mule. It looked taller than a giraffe. Longheaded, with a flying halter about its scissorlike ears, it rushed down upon them with violent apparitionlike suddenness" (*CS* 250).

172.30 fierce dragon-reek of its passage: Faulkner underscores the mock-chivalric nature of Ike's rescue of the cow through analogies like this one equating his confrontation with a horse to the knight's battle with a dragon. In medieval romance, captive ladies were often guarded by dragons. In Christian iconography of the medieval period, the dragon is presented interchangeably with the serpent as a symbol of sin. The image derives from several biblical references to dragons, among them Revelations 12.9, which refers to Satan as "the great dragon," and Psalms 91.13, which promises that "the dragon shalt thou trample under feet" (Evans, *Brewer*'s 341).

173.24-25 framed out of a swirled rigidity of forelock and mane:

Faulkner contrasts the rigid, aggressive equine and male world with the fluid bovine and female world.

173.25-26 the entire animal floating overhead in monstrous deliberation: Faulkner repeats the surreal detail of the floating animal in other episodes. The horse that invades Mrs. Littlejohn's establishment leaves solid ground: "...the horse soared above the unwinking eyes...took the railing and soared outward, hobgoblin and floating, in the moon" (303.20-26). The hound that torments Mink also seems "to float toward him interminably" (253.1) and is said to soar "like a tremendous wingless bird" (254.31). Airborne horses are twice connected with fire. Cf. *Flags*: "...the animal's whole body soared like a bronze explosion....The beast burst like unfolding bronze wings" (118-19). Cf. also "Carcasonne": "Still galloping, the horse soars outward; still galloping, it thunders up the long blue hill of heaven, its tossing mane in golden swirls like fire" (*CS* 899, noted McDaniel, *Annotations* 119.1-12).

173.28-30 the horse vanished beyond the ravine's lip, sucking first the cow and then himself after it...vacuum of its passing: Cf. "Mule in the Yard": "It [the cow] vanished, sucked into invisibility like a match flame..." (*CS* 251).

173.32-37 He made no sound as the three of them plunged down the crumbling sheer...received the violent relaxing of her fear-constricted bowels: Cf. "Afternoon of a Cow": "Mr. Faulkner and the cow were hurled violently to the foot of the precipice with Mr. Faulkner underneath....In a word, Mr. Faulkner received the full discharge of the poor creature's afternoon of anguish and despair" (*US* 430). Gresset notes other scenes in which defecation and sexuality are linked: Fairchild's memory of boyhood voyeurism in an outhouse (*Mosq* 231-34, noted *Fascination* 96) and Elmer's conflicting desires to meet Myrtle in his room and to relieve his bowels ("Portrait of Elmer" *US* 640, noted *Fascination* 97). When the young protagonist of "Moonlight" hears the "sweet high whinnying reasonless giggling" of Susan, the sound "turn[s] his bowels to water" (*US* 500).

174.7 blind paroxysm of shame: Cf. "Afternoon of a Cow": "the poor cow who now stood with her head lowered and not even trembling in utter and now hopeless female shame" (*US* 431-2).

174.14 such is the very iron imperishable warp of the fabric of love: Cf. Gavin Stevens's thoughts from the top of Seminary Hill, in which he imagines the world to be "bound, precarious and ramshackle, held together by the web, the iron-thin warp and woof of his rapacity but withal yet dedicated to his dreams" (*Twn* 316).

174.20-22 locked together and motionless, they descended once more to the floor of the ditch, planted and fixed ankle-deep in a moving block of sand like two effigies on a float: When the forces of convention sacrifice Ike's cow, he is seen by Ratliff clutching a "battered wooden effigy of a cow" (266.16-17). After her husband has bought one of the spotted horses, Mrs. Armstid is described as "mov[ing] without inference of locomotion, like something on a moving platform, a float" (294.33-34). See also the image of Flem's sisters at the well "postulat[ing] that immobile dreamy solidarity of statuary...like a figure in a charade, a carved piece symbolising some terrific effort which had died in its inception" (*Ham* 19.24-32).

175.11 maiden meditant: Cf. "Afternoon of a Cow": "freed now of anguish and shame she ruminated, maiden meditant" (*US* 433).

175.30 "Get on home, you damn whore!": continues the linkage of love and commerce that is critical in the sacrifice of Eula Varner.

176.37-39 Then Houston took a handful of coins from his pocket and chose a fifty-cent piece and came and put it into his shirt pocket and buttoned the flap: Houston's insistence on paying Ike for the loss of his love reveals his flawed understanding of the nature of love, while Ike's instinctive rejection of the payoff marks him as one of the novel's true lovers.

177.29-178.3 presently he had the coin in his hand...the coin rang dully once on the dusty planks...opening the other hand to look into it: Cf. the scene in *Crime and Punishment* in which Raskolnikov, who, like Ike, has been given money in recompense for his sufferings, throws the twenty copecks into the Neva: "He felt as though he were flying upwards and everything were vanishing from his sight. Making an unconscious movement with his hand, he suddenly became aware of the piece of money in his fist. He opened his hand, stared at the coin, and with a sweep of his arm flung it into the water; then he turned and went home. It seemed to him, he had cut himself off from everyone and from everything at that moment" (102). Ike, in rejecting payment for his beloved, continues to act out the part of the courtly lover. De Rougement points out that the cult of courtly love arose in the twelfth century in reaction to the feudal and commercial orientation of the marriage contract (33). See Mink's rejection of his wife's illicitly earned ten dollars at 240.26-29 and his disinterest in the fifty dollars that Lump says Houston carried at 241.6. Grimwood points out that many of Faulkner's books of the thirties and forties repeat a situation in which a character rejects money (*Heart in Conflict* 327). Cf. *Unv*: When Colonel Sartoris sends money to the wife of the man he killed, she "walked into the house two days later while we were sitting at the dinner table and flung the money at Father's face" (155, noted Grimwood 327). Cf. *WP* for Harry's reaction to Charlotte's offer of ten dollars, earned from the little figures she makes: "He refused. It's yours. You earned it" (87). Cf. *GDM* for Roth Edmonds's mistress's disinterest in the money he sends her through Ike McCaslin: "She went and got it, thrust the money into the pocket of the slicker's side pocket as if it were a rag, a soiled handkerchief" (362, noted Grimwood 327). Cf. "Tomorrow" for Jackson Fentry's reaction to a money purse given him by the Thorpes: "Then he raised the hand that had the money purse in it and started to mop his face with the money purse, like it was a handkerchief; I don't believe he even knowed there was anything in his hand until then, because he taken his hand down and looked at the money purse for maybe five seconds, and then he tossed it" (*KG* 103).

178.14 **an effort almost physical, like childbirth:** See note 165.3-5.

179.13 **At six oclock that afternoon, they were five miles away:** Ike elopes with his beloved.

179.18-19 **pinnacle-keep:** Cf. *WP*: "what Helen, what living Garbo, he had not dreamed of rescuing from what craggy pinnacle or dragoned keep when he and his companion embarked in the skiff" (149). McHaney sees the story of the tall convict and his pregnant consort to be another enactment of the springtime fertility ritual that Ike and the cow play out (*William Faulkner's The Wild Palms: A Study* 112).

179.35-36 **the azure bowl of evening, the windless well of night:** Cf. *GB* XVI for a similar conflation of space and time in the image of evening as a bowl: "Yes, it is I who, in the world's clear evening/ with a silver star like a rose in a bowl full of lacquer" (21-22). The ultimate source of this metaphor is certainly the opening lines of the first quatrain of Fitzgerald's first edition of "The Rubaiyat of Omar Khayyam": "Awake! for Morning in the Bowl of Night/ Has flung the Stone that puts the Stars to Flight" (1.1-2).

179.36 the portcullis of sunset: A portcullis is "a grating of iron or wooden bars or slats, suspended in the gateway of a fortified place and lowered to block passage" (*AHD*).

179.39 Then the milk came down: another instance of release, like the cow's loosened bowels and the rain.

180.4-5 each dawn the morning star burned in fierce white period to the night: Poem X of *GB*, which is closely related to "The Hill" and to Ike's episode of *Ham*, features a mythic scene punctuated by a star:
 Nymph and faun in the dusk might riot
 Beyond all oceaned Time's cold greenish bar
 To shrilling pipes, to cymbals' hissing
 Beneath a single icy star

 Where he, to his own compulsion
 -A terrific figure on an urn-
 Is caught between his two horizons,
 Forgetting that he can't return (13-20).

180.5-8 he would smell the waking's instant as he would rise, hindquarters first, backing upward out of invisibility, attenuating then disseminating out of the nest-form of sleep, the smell of milk: Onoe traces Faulkner's fondness for the verb attenuate to Eliot's "Portrait of a Lady" and lists passages in which the verb carries, as here, the sense of time passing. Cf. "Portrait of a Lady": "--And so the conversation slips/Among velleities and carefully caught regrets/Through attenuated tones of violins/Mingled with remote cornets/And begins" (*The Complete Poems and Plays: 1909-1950* 8). Cf. *Flags*: "Freed as he was of time, he was a far more definite presence in the room than the two of them cemented by deafness to a dead time and drawn thin by the slow attenuation of days" (5, noted Onoe 54). Cf. "The Big Shot": "The actual passing of time, the attenuation, had condensed into a forgotten instant" (*US* 514, noted Onoe 54). Another source for "attenuate" may be Cabell's

121

Jurgen (1919), which Faulkner knew well. While Jurgen is in the garden between dawn and sunrise, he sees approaching two giants: "Then, as the giants turned dull and harsh faces toward the garden, the sun came above the circle of blue hills, so that the mingled shadows of these two giants fell across the garden. For an instant, Jurgen saw the place oppressed by that attenuated mile-long shadow..." (32). Cf. also *The Return of the Native*: "If she had had a little more self control she would have attenuated the emotion to nothing by sheer reasoning, and so have killed it off" (106). Cf. *Tess of the D'Urbervilles*: "She knew how to hit to a hair's-breadth that moment to evening when the light and the darkness are so evenly balanced that the constraint of day and the suspense of night neutralize each other, leaving absolute mental liberty. It is then that the plight of being alive becomes attenuated to its least possible dimensions" (69).

180.15-16 **fluid and abstract earth:** Faulkner again aligns fluidity with the feminine. The earth itself is "female" (181.11).

181.7-10 **breathing in the reek...as the successful lover does that of a roomful of women:** perhaps an ironic allusion to Eliot's Prufrock, the quintessential unsuccessful lover, who finds himself in a room full of women "talking of Michelangelo" (13-14, 35-36). Faulkner associates a barn with sex in "Portrait of Elmer," when Elmer, seeing a "flash of skirt," chases Velma into the "high odorous cavern of the barn" (*US* 619) and, unpleasantly, in the rape scene of *Sanc*. Joe Christmas, on the other hand, sleeps in the barn because horses "are not women. Even a mare horse is a kind of man" (*LA* 101).

181.9 **victor's drowsing rapport:** The narrator of "Afternoon of a Cow" notes Faulkner's "curious rapport with horned and hooved beasts" (*US* 427).

181.9-11 **the victor's drowsing rapport with all anonymous faceless female flesh capable of walking the female earth:** See note 118.31-119.6.

181.16 **leaving in the wet grass a dark fixed wake:** This section of the novel retains traces of the water imagery of Poem X of *GB*. In that poem, the laborer is "lapped in azure seas" (2), "the phantoms of breath round man swim fast" (10), and the nymphs and fauns "might riot/ Beyond all oceaned Time's cold greenish bar" (13-14).

181.20-182.11 Roofed by the woven canopy of blind annealing grass roots...Troy's Helen and the nymphs and the snoring mitred bishops, the saviors and the victims and the kings...before he runs into it and through it: Faulkner's celebration of the dawn borrows from J. M. Synge's *The Playboy of the Western World*: "If the mitred bishops seen you that time, they'd be the like of the holy prophets, I'm thinking, do be straining the bars of Paradise to lay eyes on the Lady Helen of Troy, and she abroad pacing back and forward with a nosegay in her golden shawl" (p. 149). He alludes to the same passage in *GB* III.20-23:

> About him snored
> Kings and mitred bishops tired of sin
> Who dreamed themselves of heaven wearied,
> And now may sleep, hear rain, and snore again."

Finally, Mink Snopes, in the concluding lines of *Mans*, feels his life seep out of him and into the ground, "itself among the shining phantoms and dreams which are the milestones of the long human recording--Helen and the bishops, the kings and unhomed angels, the scornful and graceless seraphim" (436). The image of the luminous earth suspiring light at dawn is reversed at sunset on Seminary Hill in *Twn*: "Yet it is as though light were not being subtracted from earth, drained from earth backward and upward into that cooling green, but rather had gathered, pooling for an unmoving moment yet, among the low places of the ground so that ground, earth itself, is luminous and only the dense clumps of trees are dark, standing darkly and immobile out of it" (315, noted Pruvot, "Le Sacre de la Vache" 116).

181.33 jonquil thunder: Yonce cites Kipling's "Mandalay" as a possible source: "An' the dawn comes up like thunder outer China 'crost the Bay!" (noted 123). Cf. *LA*: "jonquilcolored sun" (314). Cf. *Unv*: "pale jonquil-colored light" (69). Cf. *WP*: "the jonquil sky at dawn" (277).

181.35 byre: In keeping with the elevated language style of this chapter, Faulkner uses a British word meaning "a barn for cows" (*AHD*).

181.36-37 fields for plowing, since sunset married to the bedded and unhorsed plow: This image picks up the receptive and feminine properties of the earth that are accentuated in the rainstorm. See note 184.27-38.

123

181.39-182.1 Then the sun itself: the silent copper roar fires the drenched grass: Cf. "Nympholepsy": "The sun was a red descending furnace mouth" (*US* 332).

182.1-11 flings long before him his shadow...the earth mirrors his antic and constant frustration...runs into it and through it: Cf. *Macbeth*'s response to the news that Lady Macbeth is dead: "Out, out, brief candle!/ Life's but a walking shadow, a poor player/ That struts and frets his hour upon the stage/ And then is heard no more. It is a tale/ Told by an idiot, full of sound and fury,/ Signifying nothing" (V.v.23-28). The protagonist of *GB* X anticipates at twilight the nightly release from time and the daily re-entry into it: "Behind him day lay stark with labor/ Of him who strives with earth for bread;/ Before him sleep, tomorrow his circling/ Sinister shadow about his head" (5-8). Cf. the shadow double that precedes the unnamed narrator of "The Hill": "His long shadow legs rose perpendicularly and fell, ludicrously, as though without power of progression, as though his body had been mesmerized by a whimsical God to a futile puppet-like activity upon one spot, while time and life terrifically passed him and left him behind. At last his shadow reached the crest and fell headlong over it" (*EPP* 90). "Nympholepsy" begins with the scene at the crest of a hill: "Soon the sharp line of the hill-crest had cut off his shadow's head; and pushing it like a snake before him, he saw it gradually become nothing. And at last he had no shadow at all" (*US* 331). Cf. *Mosq*: "life is a kind of antic shadow" (231). Cf. also Quentin's obsession with his shadow in the section of *S&F* that he narrates, culminating in a vision of absurdity and futility: "I seemed to be lying neither asleep nor awake looking down a long corridor of gray halflight where all stable things had become shadowy paradoxical all I had done shadows all I had felt suffered taking visible form antic and perverse mocking without relevance inherent themselves with the denial of the significance they should have affirmed thinking I was not who was not was not who" (211). See also 303.2.

182.10 whimple: variation of wimple: a ripple as on the surface of water; a fold or bend (*AHD*).

182.12-14 Within the mild enormous moist and pupilless globes he sees himself in twin miniature mirrored by the inscrutable abstraction: The mirroring motif is important to Symbolist and fin-de-siècle art, both influential in Faulkner's development. Cf. *Sanc*: "thinking of the expression he had once seen in the eyes of a dead child, of the other dead: the cooling indignation, the shocked despair fading, leaving two empty globes in which the motionless world lurked profoundly in miniature" (266). Cf. Charles looking into Emma's eyes in *Madame Bovary*: "As his own eyes plunged into those depths, he saw himself reflected there in miniature down to his shoulders" (37).

182.15 **Juno:** Wife of Jupiter, Juno was the Roman queen of the heavens. She protected women in childbirth and was also a goddess of war (Evans, *Brewer's* 598). Her epithet translates as "cow-eyed" (Graves 192).

182.21-23 **a hand's breadth shapes her solid and whole out of the infinity of hope:** The touch of love, so rare in Frenchman's Bend, is enough to make the cow whole, while its lack stunts her human counterparts.

182.25 **They eat from the same basket:** Weston argues that the link between pagan mystery cults and Christianity is in the central rite of a "Eucharistic feast in which worshippers part[ake] of the food of life from sacred vessels" (5).

182.26 **silage:** fodder prepared by storing and fermenting green forage plants in a silo (*AHD*).

182.27 **pig swill:** a mixture of liquid and solid foods, such as table scraps, fed to animals; slop (*AHD*).

183.3-7 **who is learning fast now, who has learned success and then precaution and secrecy...yet to acquire:** Hönnighausen includes this passage among the "ironic references to higher evolutionary stages" that imply a criticism of the civilized world (182).

183.9 **a clump of alder and beech:** An alder (*Alnus glutinosa*) is a tree of the birch family that is related to "the willows, poplars, oaks, and other plants whose flowers occur in catkins. Catkins are usually dangling strands of small flowers" (Petrides 227). A beech (*Fagus grandifolia*) is "a tall tree with distinctive smooth grey bark, slender many-scaled buds, and elliptic or egg-shaped, coarse-toothed leaves" (Petrides 263). Diana's sacred grove at Nemi was composed of beech trees (Frazer 8).

183.14 **green reflections:** Playing on the alternative meaning of reflection, Faulkner alludes to Marvell's "The Garden": "Annihilating all that's made/ To a green thought in a green shade" (47-48).

183.14-16 **with their own drinking faces break each's mirroring each face to its own shattered image wedded and annealed:** Images of narcissism, common among Symbolist poets and dramatists, often convey a character trapped within the bounds of his own psyche, unable to escape sterile self-reflexivity. Hönnighausen offers an alternative reading of reflection as conveying an image of "art's self-sufficiency" (141). Cf. *The Marble Faun*: "Pan sighs and broods upon the scene/ Beside this hushed pool where lean/ His own face and the bending sky" (*MF* 17, noted Brooks *Toward* 23, Hönnighausen 141). Cf. also *The Marionettes*:
>Marietta--How this garden has changed!
>Why has it changed so? Ah, I know, it
>is autumn that has changed the garden,
>But I am not changed. Am I changed
>very much, I wonder?
>
> She goes to the pool and
>stares in it, turning her head this way
>and that (42-3).

183.30-32 **but the cries are no longer the mystery's choral strophe and antistrophe rising vertical among the leafed altars:** Faulkner keeps the religious references that were so prominent in "Nympholepsy": "Before this green cathedral of trees he stood for a while, empty as a sheep...and he could hear the day repeating slow orisons in a green nave. Then he moved forward again, slowly, as though he expected a priest to step forth, halting him and reading his soul" (332-33). See Hönnighausen for a discussion of Faulkner's integration of religious and erotic imagery in his early work (178-79). The "leafed altars" allude to the alternative scene on Keats's Grecian urn: "Who are those coming to the sacrifice?/ To what green altar, O mysterious priest,/ Lead'st thou that heifer lowing at the skies,/ And all her silken flanks with garlands drest?" ("Ode on a Grecian Urn" 31-34).

183.28-29 **They have the same destination: sunset:** Ike exists not in space, but in time; thus his destination is not a place but an hour. His movements over the course of the day follow the pattern of the sun.

183.33-34 trunks which are the sun-geared ratchet-spokes which wheel the axled earth: The image of the wheeling world recurs often in Faulkner's work. Cf. *SP*: "the wheel of the world, the terrible calm, the inevitability of life, turning through hours of darkness, passing its dead center point and turning faster" (244). Cf. the final scene in "Barn": "The slow constellations wheeled on" (*CS* 25). Faulkner may have borrowed the image from Keats's "Endymion": "How beautiful thou art! The world how deep!/ How tremulous-dazzlingly the wheels sweep/ Around their axle!" (II.188-90).

184.11 he lays the plucked grass before her, then out of the clumsy fumbling of the hands there emerges, already in dissolution, the abortive diadem: Ike's chivalric crowning of his lady-love recalls the knight-at-arms's garlanding of the lady in the meads in Keats's "La Belle Dame Sans Merci": "I made a garland for her head,/ And bracelets too, and fragrant zone;/ She look'd at me as she did love,/ And made sweet moan" (17-20). The heifer being led to the sacrifice in "Ode on a Grecian Urn" is also garlanded. Pitavy relates the crowned cow to Botticelli's Primavera who, he says, also has a bovine look ("Idiocy and Idealism" 109).

184.17 That afternoon it rained: One of two incidents of rain in the novel. The second rainstorm immediately precedes Eula Varner Snopes's return to the hamlet from her Texas honeymoon. See note 263.35-264.3. In the Perceval and Galahad versions of the Grail legend, the task of the hero is not only to restore the ailing Fisher King to health but also to free the waters in the wasteland (Weston *passim*). Weston links the motif of freeing the waters to the *Rig Veda*, in which seven rivers are imprisoned by the evil giant Vritra, or Ahi (26).

184.22 like gauzy umbilical loops from the bellied cumulae: See note 165.3-5.

184.23-24 the sun-belled ewes of summer grazing up the wind from the southwest: Cf. *GB* III: "Where aimless clouds/ Go up the sky-hill, cropping it like sheep" (69-70). Cf. "The Cobbler": "the great stars were loud as bells in the black sky, loud as great golden-belled sheep cropping the hill of heaven" (*NOS* 134). Cf. Keats's "I Stood Tip-Toe...": "I stood tip-toe upon a little hill/...The clouds were pure and white as flocks new-shorn" (1-8).

184.27-38 The pine-snoring wind dropped, then gathered...windy uproar which had begotten and foaled them: For this vignette of the stallion wind fertilizing the mare earth, Faulkner drew on an early poem, *GB* XXXVI:
> Gusty trees windily lean on green
> eviscerated skies, the stallion, Wind,
> against the sun's gold collar stamps, to lean
> his weight. And once the furrowed day behind,
> the golden steed browses the field he breaks
> and full of flashing teeth where he has been
> trees, the waiting mare his neighing shakes,
> hold his heaving shape a moment seen.
>
> Upon the hills, clashing the stars together,
> stripping the tree of heaven of its blaze,
> stabled, richly grained with golden weather-
>
> within the trees that he has reft and raped
> his fierce embrace by riven boughs in [sic] shaped,
> while on the shaggy hills he stamps and neighs.

Cf. *MF*: "The far world's shaggy flanks and breast..." (p.33).
Cf. *WP*: "enclosed and lost within the furious embrace of flowing mare earth and stallion sun" (155-156).
Cf. *GDM*: "the last of open country, the last trace of man's puny gnawing at the immemorial flank" (195).

185.1 each brief lance: In *SP*, rain is described as running across the lawn like a "cavalry with silver lances" (119). Yonce points out that the lance, obviously a phallic symbol, is central to the ritual which restores the wounded Fisher King (*Annotations* 62). See Weston's discussion of the sexual implications of the lance, or male principle, and the cup, or female principle (75).

185.8-10 releasing in mirrored repetition the sky...falling drops had prisoned: See note 165.30-31.

185.16-17 illogical and harmless sound and fury: Faulkner again appropriates the phrase from Macbeth's great speech, which he used to title his third novel: "Life's but a walking shadow, a poor player/ That struts and frets his hour upon the stage/ And then is heard no more. It is a tale/ Told by an idiot, full of sound and fury,/ Signifying nothing" (*Macbeth* V.v.24-28).

185.26-27 the leaves and branches which globe in countless minute repetition the intact and iridescent cosmos: See note 165.30-31.

185.27-28 They walk in splendor: perhaps a variation of Byron's "She walks in beauty like the night" ("She Walks in Beauty," *Lord Byron: The Complete Poetical Works* 3:288-89).

185.32-33 the bowl of evening: See note 179.35-6.

185.35 in the womb-dimension: Cf. "Endymion": "The old womb of night" (IV.372).

185.35-36 the unavoidable first and the inescapable last: Cf. Dilsey's comment in *S&F*: "I've seed de first en de last" (371).

185.36 they descend the hill: See note 168.17-23.

186.3 ichor: Ichor is "the blood of the gods," according to Pitavy ("Idiocy and Idealism" 107).

186.12 the fierce white dying rose: Cf. Fitzgerald's annotations to the 4th edition of "The Rubaiyat of Omar Khayyam": "I think that Southey, in his Common-Place Book, quotes from some Spanish author about the rose being White till 10 o'clock; 'Rosa Perfecta' at 2; and 'perfecta incarnada' at 5" (169).

186.19-20 tender mouth: Cf. Swinburne's "In the Orchard": "Nay, take it then, my flower, my first in June,/ My rose, so like a tender mouth it is" (18-19, noted Adams, "The European Roots" 35).

186.21-22 the one fierce evening star: Venus.

186.22-23 the marching constellations mesh and gear and wheel strongly on: See note 183.33-34.

186.28-29 **Helen and the bishops, the kings and the graceless seraphim:** See note 181.20-182.11.

186.29-30 **When he reaches her, she has already begun to lie down-first the forequarters, then the hinder ones:** Hönnighausen notes the juxtaposition of highly lyrical and ornate prose with this realistic detailing of the cow's anatomy. The balance of these two elements--the stylizing and the realistic--presents, he maintains, the "great challenge" in Faulkner's writing (183).

186.33 **They lie down together:** represents a climax in the animal world equivalent to the climactic rain in the vegetable world and the culmination of the fertilizing, regenerative energies of the Ike/cow episode. The ultimate union of man and cow conveys, Hönnighausen argues, "the overcoming of the gap between man and animal and a new, vitalistic vision of innocence" as well as a contrast to the unsuccessful human sexual relations that dominate the novel (183).

187.15-25 **in conjunction with the savage fixation about females...place:** Houston joins the married and unmarried bachelors of *Ham*, including Flem, Jody, Ratliff, and Labove, who isolate themselves from love and involvement in the female world. See note 6.31. Houston's desire to escape the feminine recalls the tall convict's analogous desire to "turn his back on female life and return to the world of shotguns and shackles" (*WP* 152).

188.27-31 **it seemed to him that once more he had been victim of a useless and elaborate practical joke...prime maniacal Risibility...mile's walk in darkness:** Houston's natural antagonist, Mink Snopes, in a later volume of the Snopes trilogy, expresses contrasting views on the forces that control the universe. Houston's vision of an absurd world governed by a cosmic practical joker directly opposes Mink's sense of "fundamental justice" (*Mans* 6). If there is an "Old Moster," he "jest punishes; He dont play jokes" (*Mans* 398). Gresset lists some of the names assigned god in Faulkner's fiction as: the Supreme Player (*Sart*); the Judge or Umpire (*AbAb!*); the cosmic joker, the supreme Manipulator (*WP*); the maniacal Laugher (*Ham*); the immortal Arbiter (*GDM*)--in short, the Stage Manager (*AbAb!*) (*Fascination* 256).

190.8 **monklike iron cot:** See note 6.31.

190.9-12 the moony square of the window falling across him as it had used to fall...in place of the cot: See note 215.11-13.

190.25 crib: "a rack or trough for fodder; a manger" (*AHD*).

190.32-33 first burst of impotent wrath at the moral outrage, the crass violation of private property: The unnamed barn owner is not, it develops, interested in morality at all but, rather, in commerce. He will embark on a quest for the cow that is a minor and inferior variation of the mythic quest of Ike Snopes, the one for love and the other simply for money.

191.3-5 the ancient biblical edict... that man must sweat or have not: Cf. Genesis 3:19: "In the sweat of thy face shalt thou eat bread, till thou return unto the ground...."

191.17 ward heeler: "Informal. A worker for the ward organization of a political machine" (*AHD*).

192.1-3 the constant and unflagging round... labor by which alone that piece of earth which was his mortal enemy would fight him with: Cf. Mink's musings on the relationship of a tenant farmer to the land he works in *Mans*: "the ground, the dirt which any and every tenant farmer and sharecropper knew to be his sworn foe and mortal enemy--the hard implacable land which wore out his youth and his tools and then his body itself" (90). Nicholaisen sees this as evidence of Faulkner's ambivalent attitude toward the land: it is at once the locus of peace and fertility and, as experienced by those in close contact with it, a threatening and hostile combatant (259). It is perhaps more to the point that Faulkner realistically depicts a range of attitudes to the land as experienced by a variety of characters.

192.5 tomorrow and tomorrow: Faulkner again echoes Macbeth's speech: "Tomorrow, and tomorrow, and tomorrow/ Creeps in this petty pace from day to day/ To the last syllable of recorded time;/ And all our yesterdays have lighted fools the way to dusty death..." (5.5.19-23).

192.7-12 this until the day came when... he would stumble and plunge, his eyes still open...still clutching the brush-hook or the axe: The bitter end imagined by the anonymous farmer supports Flem's early observation that there "Aint no benefit in farming." See note 23.4.

192.12-13 marked by a cenotaph of coiling buzzards on the sky: A cenotaph is a monument to the memory of a person whose remains lie elsewhere (*AHD*). See note 4.2.

193.10 the thick, bearlike figure: Cf. Benjy's "shambling gait like a trained bear" in *S&F* (342).

195.15 Houston's dollar: the dollar pound fee.

195.26-28 They just looked at one another, not man and woman but two integers which had both reached the same ungendered peace even if by different roads: This truce in the ongoing war between the sexes is significantly occasioned by Ike's love, which, though admittedly unconventional, is still one of the purest expressions of sexual emotion by a male in the novel. Mink Snopes is the novel's other authentic male lover in that he overcomes the pull of respectability to marry and have children with the woman he loves.

195.29-30 "I dont want money," he said roughly: Again, when acting on behalf of Ike's passion, Houston forgoes the profit motive that drives the men of the novel, and, like Ike and Mink, refuses money, if only temporarily.

195.31-33 "It's his...V.K. Ratliff gave it to me. It's his": Mrs Littlejohn buys the cow with the proceeds of Ratliff's goat deal. See 87.20-27.

196.6-7 this September forenoon: The time shifts back to the present moment, when Ratliff is participating in Lump's peep show.

196.14-16 He knew not only what he was going to see but that, like Bookwright, he did not want to see it, yet, unlike Bookwright, he was going to look: Voyeurism is a basic perversion for Faulkner throughout his career. Cf. Miss Reba's description in *Sanc* of the impotent Popeye's watching Temple and Red: "the two of them would be nekkid as two snakes, and Popeye hanging over the foot of the bed without even his hat took off, making a kind of whinnying sound" (311-12). Earlier in *Sanc*, Popeye catches Clarence Snopes in the act of spying on Temple through a keyhole, and he runs him off by touching a lit match to his neck (251-52). Cf. Otis's peephole activities when he and Everbe Corinthia are still in Arkansas: "That's where I had the peephole--a knothole in the back wall with a tin slide over it that never nobody but me knowed how to work, while Aunt Fittie was out in front collecting the money and watching out. Folks your size would have to stand on a box and I would charge a nickel until Aunt Fittie found out I was letting grown men watch for a dime that otherwise might have went inside for fifty cents" (*Reiv* 156-57). Will Varner also draws a young voyeur, the fourteen-year-old boy who reports on Varner's afternoon liaison with the wife of a tenant farmer. See 140.35-36. Faulkner has been building up to this comparison between Bookwright and Ratliff. Both are decent men who have great respect for a shrewd trader, and both will succumb to the lure of buried treasure at the old Frenchman's Place; but Bookwright neither desires nor needs to look through I.O.'s peephole. Ratliff's compulsion to look through the peephole, when he admits he does not want to look, may be related to his defensiveness on the subject of sex. See note 157.34-158.2.

196.16-21 **He did look, leaning his face between two other heads; and it was as though it were himself inside the stall with the cow...words:** Ratliff's ability to identify with Ike sets him apart from the other onlookers at the barn wall but also makes more horrible his decision to deprive Ike of the only thing he has ever loved or wanted.

196.32-37 **With it he drove the nails back...This here engagement is completed:** See note 198.12-25.

197.5 **Only all you done was think:** There is a certain ambiguity in Ratliff's statement. He is either complimenting her because she, unlike him, did not need to see the Ike show for herself, or he is chiding her because she too disapproved of the peep show but did not act on her disapproval.

197.6 **Launcelot," he said. "Lump":** In the manuscript, Lump is Mordred, nicknamed Maud.

197.16 **the State Teacher's College:** This could be Mississippi State College for Women in Columbus, which, when it opened in 1885 as Mississippi Industrial Institute and College, was the first state-supported institution for women in the country. It offered programs in industrial and secretarial arts as well as in teacher training. Mississippi State Teacher's College in Hattiesburg was incorporated as Mississippi Normal College by legislative act in 1910 and opened two years later, so it would not conform with the original time frame of the novel. However, Faulkner may well have not known the date of its founding (*Mississippi: A Guide to the Magnolia State* 122).

197.24-27 and a belief that there was honor and pride and salvation and hope too to be found for man's example between the pages of books...named it Launcelot: Lump's mother finds in books two of the "eternal verities" that Faulkner catalogues in his Nobel Prize acceptance speech (*ESPL* 120). Faulkner may have had in mind, as literary predecessors to this kind of romantic retreat into books, Don Quixote or Emma Bovary. In *WP*, the tall convict relies on books, in his case copies of the *Detective Gazette*, as how-to crime manuals and considers their authors directly responsible for his predicament when he is arrested for attempted robbery (23).

198.5 man-tall, man-grim woman: Cf. Mrs. Gant, who "for twelve years had been growing into the outward semblance of a man" ("Miss Zilphia Gant" 373).

198.10-11 It's all right for it to be, but folks mustn't know it, see it: Mrs. Littlejohn proposes that Ratliff has pandered to the forces of convention in interfering with Ike's love affair. The accusation is especially biting because it follows on the heels of Ratliff's own bitter reaction to the sacrifice of Eula to respectability in the previous book.

198.12-25 I aint never disputed I'm a pharisee...at least I can go to sleep tonight: The Pharisees, who figure prominently in the Gospels and the Acts as opponents of Jesus and his disciples, were a powerful sect within Judaism about whom little is known historically. Ratliff's identification of himself as a Pharisee is germane on two grounds. First, the Pharisees were known for their strict adherence to the law and especially for their defense of purity regulations. Secondly, they were challenged as hypocrites who "say and do not" (Matthew 23:3). Cf. Christ's long diatribe against "scribes and Pharisees, hypocrites":

> But woe unto you, scribes and Pharisees, hypocrites! for ye devour widows' houses, and for a pretense make long prayer: and therefore ye shall receive the greater damnation.

> Woe unto you, scribes and Pharisees, hypocrites! for ye compass sea and land to make one proselyte, and when he is made, ye make him twofold more the child of hell than yourselves.
>
> Woe unto you, ye blind guides, which say, Whosoever shall swear by the temple, it is nothing; but whosoever shall swear by the gold of the temple, he is a debtor! (Matthew 23:13-16)... .
>
> Woe unto you, scribes and Pharisees, hypocrites! for ye pay tithe of mint and anise and cummin, and have omitted the weightier matters of the law, judgment, mercy, and faith: these ought ye to have done, and not to leave the other undone.
>
> Ye blind guides, which strain at a gnat, and swallow a camel (Matthew 23:23-24)...
>
> Even so ye also outwardly appear righteous unto men, but within ye are full of hypocrisy and iniquity (Matthew 23:28).

Christ condemns the Pharisees for vices that prevail in Frenchman's Bend, especially the inability to make distinctions between true and false visions and values.

Ratliff's decision to intervene in this incident puzzles some critics, particularly in light of his later refusal to intercede on behalf of Mrs. Armstid (See *Ham* 321.3-15). Greet, who identifies the prime conflict of the novel as that between reason and emotion, sees Ratliff's closing of the peep show as a triumph of the rational faculties over the emotional faculties, especially love. He believes that Ratliff admits the injustice of what he feels compelled to do (312). Gold agrees with Greet that Ratliff denies his own best impulses when he rescinds the gift of the cow and suggests that Ratliff at this point is motivated not by love but by power (322-23). Brooks, on the other hand, argues that Ratliff's words need not be taken at face value. He considers Ratliff to be aware of the fact that, in a world of moral relativism, rightness and wrongness are hard to prove or disprove. On a purely practical plane, he seems to say, a moral man could not let the show continue (*Yoknapatawpha Country* 407-410). Millgate praises Ratliff's complexity and intellectuality, in that he can acknowledge his own shortcomings and act on his self-knowledge (*Achievement* 197). The crucial question for Ratliff, he says, is in how far he will go to combat the spread of Snopesism, given his own adherence to the code of the trade. Millgate defines the three tenets of that code as: 1. respect for the skill of a winner, 2. lack of concern for the losses of a loser, and 3. non-interference in other men's trades (*Achievement* 198-99). Williamson records an incident of "stock diddling" in Ripley. A Jeffrey

Long was indicted secretly by a grand jury that found him guilty on January 13, 1906 of committing "that detestable and abominable crime against nature by then and there having sexual intercourse with a certain beast, to wit, a cow" (99).

198.27-38 but he was only canvassing the possibilities--or rather, discarding the faces as he called them up...Mink, Eck, I.O.: Faulkner parodies the epic catalogue in his recital of the Snopes faces. This scene also recalls Hightower at what may be his death calling up the images of faces he has encountered throughout life (*LA* 462-466).

198.35-36 painted balloon face: Brown finds the source for this image to be *The Katzenjammer Kids*, a comic strip drawn by Rudolph Dirks, "in which two brats of German extraction...performed various sorts of trickery...against the other characters. The balloon with a face and hat was one of their favorite ruses; they would paint balloons with their own features and then tie them up as if peering over a fence or hedge in order to avert suspicion while they themselves were off performing some sort of devilment" (113). Cf. *AbAb!*: "You knew that you could hit them and that they would not hit back or even resist. But you did not want to because they (the niggers) were not it, not what you wanted to hit; that you knew that when you hit them you would just be hitting a child's toy balloon with a face painted on it..." (230). Perhaps Faulkner is suggesting that each of the recollected faces is just a sham of the ur-Snopes, Flem.

199.14-18 Flem, thinking how this was probably the first time anywhere...that anyone had ever wished Flem Snopes were here instead of anywhere else: This passage looks ahead to Book Four, when both Mink and Mrs. Armstid will wait, desperately pinning their hopes on Flem Snopes.

199.26 cannas: "any of the various perennial tropical herbs of the genus *Canna*, having clusters of large showy flowers and including an edible variety" (*AHD*).

199.26 geraniums: any of various plants of the genus *Pelargonium*, widely cultivated for their rounded, often variegated leaves and showy clusters of pink, white, and red flowers (*AHD*).

200.7 paper dickey: "a man's detachable shirt front" (*AHD*).

200.11-12 Ratliff noticed that the frames had no lenses in them: Cf. Fonsiba's husband in *GDM*: "he entered the next room, the only other room the cabin owned, and found, sitting in a rocking chair before the hearth, the man himself reading...in the same ministerial clothing in which he had entered the commissary five months ago and a pair of gold-framed spectacles which, when he looked up and then rose to his feet, the boy saw did not even contain lenses..." (278).

200.17-18 like the light down which children blow from the burrs of dandelion blooms: It is a folk belief that good luck comes from being able to blow all the spores off the dandelion (*Taraxacum officinale*).

200.30-31 Bread and circuses, as the fellow says, makes hay at the poll-box: The fellow is Juvenal, who proposes in his *Satires* that *panem et circenses*, or food and entertainment, are the two things that the Roman population most desires (Evans, *Brewer's* 149).

201.5-8 "When Caesar's wife goes up to Will Varner next month to get that ere school job again, and he aint pure as a marble monument...happen?": "The name of Pompeia having become involved with an accusation against P. Clodius, Caesar divorced her, not because he believed her guilty, but because the wife of Caesar must not be even suspected of crime" (Evans, *Brewer's* 173).

201.25-28 A man cant have his good name drug in the alleys. The Snopes name has done held its head up too long...stock diddling: Faulkner parodies the concern for respectability as a means to an end that drives Flem Snopes to attend church services and wear a tie, Will Varner to marry Eula off to Flem, and V.K. Ratliff to sacrifice Ike's love and end the peep show. See notes 4.2 and 57.32-34. The concern for good name accelerates in *Twn*. Cf. Gavin Stevens's and Ratliff's exchange on Wallstreet Panic Snopes's wife's determination to clean up the Snopes name:

> "Yes," I said. "I've heard of that. I wonder why she never changed their name."
> "No no," he said. "You dont understand. She dont want to change it. She jest wants to live it down. She aint trying to drag him by the hair out of Snopes, to escape from Snopes. She's got to purify Snopes itself. She's got to beat Snopes from the inside" (149-50).

Cf. Gavin's deliberations as he waits for Linda Snopes in the drug store to tell her that they will have to stop seeing one another to preserve Linda's good name: "You see? That was it: the very words *reputation* and *good name*. Merely to say them, speak them aloud, give their existence vocal recognition, would irrevocably soil and besmirch them" (*Twn* 202). When Miss Corrie of *Reiv* decides to give up prostitution, she signals the change in behavior with a change in name: she announces that she will go by her full name, Everbe Corinthia (218).

201.34 **the minister of the village church:** This is probably not the same Reverend Whitfield as the philandering minister of *AILD* who fathered Jewel Bundren and struggled with his conscience over whether to confess his lapse to Anse Bundren while Addie is on her deathbed (169). That Reverend Whitfield was a fundamentalist Protestant circuit rider, while this one is a farmer who was made the Baptist preacher by Will Varner. The Whitfield of "Shingles for the Lord," first published in *Saturday Evening Post* CCXV (Feb. 13, 1943) is also not the Baptist preacher of *Ham*. That story takes place in the 1930's, during the WPA. In naming Whitfield, Faulkner must have had in mind the eighteenth-century English evangelist George Whitefield (1714-1770), who drew large crowds during his revivalist tours of America (*The Encyclopedia of Religion* 15:379-80).

202.7-13 **You take and beef the critter... wont want to chase nothing but human women:** Adams identifies a Provençal story appended to the biography of the twelfth-century troubadour, Guilhem de Cabestanh, as a possible source for this remedy. In the story, a knight loves the young wife of a proud and irascible aristocrat, and his admiration is returned by the beloved. The husband, who was a jealous man, learned of the attraction and killed the knight, ripping the heart out of his body. He had the heart roasted and seasoned and fed it to his wife. Only after she had eaten it did he tell her what it was. She lost her sight and hearing temporarily, but when she had recovered it, she told her husband that she would never again eat anything else. He, hearing that, lunged at her with his sword. She, however, threw herself off the balcony before he could reach her. The story turns up in a slightly altered form in the ninth tale of the fourth day of Boccaccio's *Decameron*. Stendhal translated a version of the story for his *De l'amour*. More recently, Pound used the story in his fourth canto (noted "The European Roots" 36-37). For a comic variation on Ike's eating his beloved cow, see the episode in *Twn* in which Byron

Snopes's four half-Indian children cook and eat a $500 pet Pekingese (361-63).

202.32-33 It will cost you sixteen dollars and eighty cents: See note 87.9-17.

203.12-13 And Mink aint, not to mention after that law verdict Will Varner put on him this morning: Mink is required to pay Houston three dollars in pasturage before he can recover his bull. See note 161.20-21.

204.3-12 "I'm a single man, unfortunately," I.O. said. "But you got three children"...rest of the beef: I.O. is not only not single, he is a bigamist. A wife and three children materialize (199), and later another wife and child appear, causing him to retire as schoolmaster. See 264.15-29. Faulkner undercuts the tragedy and pathos of Ike's separation from his beloved with the hilarity of I.O.'s dickering with Eck over the cow. Later, he makes no similar attempt to mitigate the tragedy of the spotted horse episode.

204.16-17 It aint the beef and the hide. That's just a circumstance. It's the moral value we are going to get out of it: Morality now joins the other abstractions, most notably love and respectability, that are up for sale in the male world of the deal.

Chapter Two: Faulkner composed the story of Jack Houston's retreat from and eventual submission to Lucy Pate in late 1938 or early 1939 when he was retyping and rearranging the Snopes material to form *Ham* (Kibler 25-27). He also at this time expanded the material from "The Hound" to include the parallel love story of Mink Snopes and his wife. The two stories examine the mystery of love as well as the ramifications of pursuit, devotion, loss, and desolation. Coming, as they do, after the best hopes for love in the hamlet have been wasted, the stories of Mink and Houston and their wives resonate with analogies within the work and also look ahead to the related love stories of *GDM*, parts of which Faulkner was also composing at this time. As bachelors who succumb to marriage, Houston and Mink provide counterpoints to Flem. Houston's reversion to monastic bachelorhood recalls Labove's self-imposed austerity in the face of his obsession. Mink's virility sets off the sterility of most sexual encounters in *Ham*. Dunn sees in Labove, Mink Snopes, and Jack

Houston three examples of enslavement: Labove to his obsession with Eula, Mink to physical passion for his wife, and Houston to marriage (419). She also cites correspondences among the passions of Buck McCaslin, Ike McCaslin, and Rider and those of Mink, Houston, and Labove (420). Blotner notes correspondences between Houston's life and Joe Christmas's. Both were thirty-three years old; both had stern fathers and understanding mothers; both were initiated into sex by Negro girls; and both fled their fates for over ten years before returning to face them (*Faulkner*, One Vol. ed. 409).

205.22 **immemorial trap:** Houston perceives marriage to be a form of bondage.

205.28 **unbitted yet:** Faulkner makes a connection between Houston in his free state and the aggressively masculine stallion that eventually kills his wife. See note 214.28-32.

206.10-11 **was the possessor of a mistress--a Negro girl two or three years his senior:** Joe Christmas at fourteen is, with his friends, slated to be initiated into sex with a "womanshenegro," but he beats her instead (*LA* 146-47).

206.14 **bulging in Lilliput:** an allusion to Part One, Chapter 1 of *Gulliver's Travels*, in which the shipwrecked hero awakes to find himself in a land that is one-twelfth the scale of his native England.

206.19-21 **Afterward, it seemed that the first thing he saw when he entered the room was that...head:** Like Labove, Houston encounters his fate in a schoolroom.

206.22-27 **it seemed to him that it had been in his life always...the two of them chained irrevocably from that hour and onward forever:** Houston's fate, which he senses as a form of bondage, is not only to marry Lucy Pate but also to encounter Mink Snopes, who is also described as being linked to him eternally. See note 217.25-28.

206.37-207.3 **What he did not comprehend was that until now he had not known what true slavery was...victimization:** Faulkner here sees slavery as a collusion between the slaver and the enslaved. Dunn examines the theme of bondage that links *Ham* to the novel that succeeds it, *GDM*, and concludes that in each novel the possibilities of freedom are illusory. Men who are shackled to women or their responsibilities to the land try to escape into a man's world, of games or horses or hunting, but they find that there is ultimately no escape from their fetters (422-23).

207.5-9 It was as though she had merely elected him out of all the teeming earth...to establish the structure of her life: Cf. "Portrait of Elmer": "At one time he believed that you can seduce them; now he is not so sure. He believes now that they just elect you when they happen to be in the right mood and you happen to be handy" (*US* 612).

207.25-28 It was a feud, a gage, wordless, uncapitulating, between that unflagging will...for the married state, and that furious...one for solitariness and freedom: another variation on the conflict between the sexes. Men and women are tragically at odds too often, and even happy unions are doomed. Faulkner's focus on the restricting and uncompromising wills of Lucy Pate and Jack Houston looks back to a major thematic emphasis of *WP*. In that novel, he adapts Schopenhauer's thesis that the life of the will is a prisonhouse to his treatment of captivity and the illusory nature of love (McHaney, *William Faulkner's The Wild Palms: A Study passim*). Houston, like Harry Wilbourne in the previous novel, becomes eventually a prisoner of love, most completely after the possibilities for love are cancelled by the death of his wife.

207.25 gage: "something, such as a glove, that is offered or thrown down as a pledge or challenge to fight; a challenge" (*AHD*).

208.12-13 she was beside him, flailing at his enemies with her book satchel: recalls Eula's defense of Hoake McCarron. See 137.36-138.3.

208.38-209.1 It was as if...they had looked upon the olden Snake, had eaten of the tree: Faulkner of course alludes to the story of Eve's temptation by the serpent in Genesis 3.

211.3-4 It took him twelve years to learn you cannot escape either of them: Joe Christmas wanders on "the street" for a comparable period of time, fifteen years (*LA* 211).

211.19-24 (Geography: that paucity of invention, that fatuous faith in distance of man...required to breathe in.): Many of the male characters of *Ham* follow the pattern of escape, or exile, and return: Labove, Mink, Houston, and Flem. Joe Christmas, like Houston, flees from possession by a woman, only to accept it as his doom finally. Faulkner thought of himself as a tramp at heart as late as 1954, when he wrote in "Mississippi": "the middleaging (now a professional fiction writer: who had wanted to remain the tramp and possessionless vagabond of his young manhood but time and success and the hardening of his arteries had beaten him)" (*ESPL* 35).

211.30 curl papered: hair rolled in pieces of soft paper for curling (*AHD*).

211.37-38 her who in her turn was loyal, discreet, undemanding, and thrifty with his money: Weisgerber sees in the story of Houston's concubine a vestige of Dostoyevsky's theme of the good prostitute. Houston's associate, however, does not have Sonya Marmeladov's power to redeem (269). Among the examples of loyal prostitutes in Faulkner's work are Ruby Lamar in *Sanc* and Everbe Corinthia in *Reiv*.

212.5-7: abolished his inherited southern-provincial-Protestant fanaticism regarding marriage and female purity: Mink, who does not give up the woman that he loves, is still convinced "that to every man...there was reserved one virgin, at least for him to marry; one maidenhead, if only for him to deflower and destroy" (237.26-29).

212.7 the biblical Magdalen: Mary Magdalene was one of the most prominent of the Galilean women who followed Jesus. While the Bible does not say where or how they met, she figures in all four gospel accounts, most importantly as a witness to the crucifixion, burial, and resurrection of Jesus. Only Luke mentions a shady past or an exorcism. In his account, she is one "out of whom went seven devils" (Luke 8:2). After the sixth century in the western church, a tradition grew up which associated Mary Magdalene with the sinful woman of Luke 7:36-50 who washed Jesus's feet with her tears and dried them with her hair (*Anchor Bible Dictionary* IV.579-581). It is to this tradition that Faulkner is alluding.

212.18-19 What do I want with money? Look at me? Do you think I will lack money?: Faulkner identifies the quality and intensity of Houston's common-law wife's love by her refusal to put a monetary value on it. When she rejects money for love, Houston's Galveston prostitute joins the other true lovers of *Ham*: Ike Snopes (see note 177.32-178.3) and Mink Snopes (241.6).

212.22-24 If she would just touch me, hit me, make me mad enough to hit her, he thought: See Labove's speech at 121.20-23.

212.33-34 the Babylonian interdict by heaven forever against reproduction: In 597 B.C., the Babylonians, in what is known as the Babylonian Captivity, captured Jerusalem, exiling thousands of Israelites, including the prophet Ezekiel (2 Kings 24; 2 Chronicles 26). When Jerusalem was destroyed in 586 B.C., most of the population was deported to Babylon (*Anchor Bible Dictionary* I:563). During their time in the Babylonian wilderness, according to the prophets, the Israelites were enjoined from reproductive activities. Cf. Isaiah's prophesy at 2 Kings 20:18 and Isaiah 39:7: "And of thy sons that shall issue from thee, which thou shalt beget, shall they take away; and they shall be eunuchs in the palace of the king of Babylon." Cf. also Jeremiah 25:10-11:

> Moreover I will take from them the voice of mirth, and the voice of gladness, the voice of the bridegroom, and the voice of the bride, the sound of the millstones, and the light of the candle.
>
> And this whole land shall be a desolation, and an astonishment; and these nations shall serve the king of Babylon seventy years.

The allusion to Babylon and to the theme of captivity draws attention to connections with *WP*, whose original title, *If I Forget Thee, Jerusalem*, comes from Psalm 137:4-6:

> How shall we sing the Lord's song in a strange land?
>
> If I forget thee, O Jerusalem, let my right hand forget her cunning.
>
> If I do not remember thee, let my tongue cleave to the roof of my mouth; if I prefer not Jerusalem above my chief joy.

212.36-39 some instant, mystical still, when the blight of those nameless and faceless men...which she had prostituted: Houston can only imagine marriage and full acceptance of his prostitute as a conditional circumstance, if she were mystically purged of her sins. Mink, with similar cultural expectations of chastity in a bride, is willing to sleep with the "ghostly embraces of thirty or forty men" (237.33-34).

214.11-12 **He was bitted now:** See note 205.28.

214.15-18 **the beast, prime solitary and sufficient out of the wild fields, drawn to the trap and knowing it to be a trap...wild:** Dunn compares this description of Houston walking into the trap to Hubert's comment in *GDM* that Buck has walked into bear country and lain down with the bear (22, noted 420).

214.28-32 **He bought the stallion too then, as if for a wedding present to her...polygamous and bitless masculinity...said that:** By establishing the horse as a symbolic replacement for what Houston has lost in marrying Lucy Pate, Faulkner prepares the way for the symbolic transference that takes place in the spotted horse episode of Book Four. In *GDM*, Rider acquires a large hound one month after marriage and tells Mannie: "Ah needs a big dog. You's de onliest least thing whut ever kep up wid me one day, leff alone fo weeks" (*GDM* 139).

214.38-215.1 **with a Negro woman to cook...was Varner's:** See note 10.15-16.

215.11-13 **they would remark how the house had been completed just in time to catch the moon's full of April...bed was placed:** See 190.9-12, 216.26-32, 307.13-26. Opie cites a consistent folk belief that the fortunes of human beings are affected by the waxing and waning of the moon. Children conceived or born during the full moon were believed to be larger, stronger, and healthier (*Dictionary of Superstitions* 260-64). Symbolically, the moon is traditionally associated with the feminine, with the mutable, with the world of imagination and dreams rather than with the manifest world and the realms of activity and reality (Cirlot 215-17).

215.14 **Then the stallion killed her:** This is the first of three incidents in which a horse initiates action that has unfortunate consequences. The second occurs when Mink shoots Houston off his horse, because Mink's feelings of anger and injustice are aggravated by the fact that Houston is on horseback. The third is the spotted horse auction and its aftermath.

215.18 **transubstantiation:** In "The Hound," it is the dog that shares Houston's identity, having "something of the master's certitude and overbearance" (*US* 153).

216.12-13 the son which perhaps next year they would have had: Ike McCaslin, too, sacrifices love, young marriage, and a future heir for the sake of a principle. Cf. *GDM* for his wife's announcement that she will leave him if he gives up his inheritance: "That's all from me. If this dont get you that son you talk about, it wont be mine" (315).

216.26-32 But sooner or later the moon would wax again...full moon of April guaranteed the fertilizing act: See note 215.11-13.

216.38-39 and he would lie rigid, indomitable, and panting: Broughton relates this passage to Labove's lying "prone and sweating" (118.10) on his monklike iron cot (noted 186).

216.38-217.2 "I dont understand it...You cant beat me": Dunn relates Houston's despair and confusion at the death of his wife to Rider's grief: "Hit look lack Ah just cant quit thinking. Look lack Ah just cant quit" (*GDM* 159, noted Dunn 420).

217.5-6 Then the orderly sequence of time as he had known it for thirty-three years became inverted: Cf. Joe Christmas's similar experience with time after he has murdered Joanna Burden: "for thirty years he has lived inside an orderly parade of named and numbered days like fence pickets" (*LA* 314). Houston, like Christmas, and also like Benjy Compson, is thirty-three years old, the age of Christ at his crucifixion. When asked about the Christian significance of Benjy's age, Faulkner acknowledged it as "a ready-made axe to use" but insisted that it was "just one of several tools" (*FU* 17).

217.15-16 he lay on his back watching the ravelled ends of sentience and will projecting into the gap: Cf. Jason after he has been robbed in *S&F*: "the man sitting quietly behind the wheel of a small car, with his invisible life ravelled out about him like a wornout sock" (291). Cf. Darl's questions in *AILD*: "How do our lives ravel out into the no-wind, no sound, the weary gestures heavily recapitulant: echoes of old compulsions with no hand on no strings: in sunset we fall into furious attitudes, dead gestures of dolls" (207).

217.19-21 But it came from the other direction: not from himself outward but, but inward toward himself out of the identifiable lost earth: When Mink Snopes dies at the end of *Mans*, Faulkner reverses the direction of the pain. Whereas, in Houston's case, the pain seems to flow inward from the earth he will lose, at Mink's death, all the pain finally flows out of his body into the earth: "...he could feel the Mink Snopes that had had to spend so much of his life having unnecessary bother and trouble, beginning to creep, seep, flow easy as sleeping; he could almost watch it, following all the little grass blades and tiny roots, the little holes the worms made, down and down into the ground already full of the folks that had all the trouble but were free now..." (435).

217.25-28 **looking...into the face which with his own was wedded and twinned forever...ten-gauge shell:** As Hightower is reflecting on his life, he sees his own face and antic gestures mirrored back at him by other watching faces: "the faces seem to be mirrors in which he watches himself" (*LA* 462), and he also sees the faces of Christmas and his murderer, Percy Grimm, merge into a single face (465-66). Cf. *Gobseck* for the lawyer Derville's comments on the doubling of antagonists: "Now, I have often noticed, and always with new wonder, that two antagonists almost always divine each other's inmost thoughts and ideas. Two enemies sometimes possess a power of clear insight into mental processes, and read each other's minds as two lovers read in either soul (297). See note 100.8-17.

217.28 **ten-gauge shell:** "the interior diameter of a shotgun barrel as determined by the number of lead balls of a size exactly fitting the barrel that are required to make one pound," in this case ten (*AHD*). See note 232.21.

217.28-30 **the dead who would carry the living into the ground with him; the living who must bear...the deathless slain:** McHaney relates this to Harry and Charlotte's experience with the cold in *WP*: "a cold which left an ineffaceable and unforgettable mark somewhere on the spirit and memory like first sex or the experience of taking human life" (183, noted *The Wild Palms* 128). Cf. *Unv*: Colonel Sartoris's "intolerant eyes which in the last two years had acquired that transparent film which the eyes of carnivorous animals have and from behind which they look at a world which no ruminant ever sees, perhaps dares to see, which I have seen before in the eyes of men who have killed so much that never again as long as they live will they ever be alone" (266). Not only is this statement metaphorically true, but it will become literally true when Mink becomes involved in hiding and recovering the corpse.

218.1-11 **The shot was too loud...empty saddle:** "The Hound" begins at this point: "To Cotton the shot was the loudest thing he had ever heard in his life" (*US* 152).

"The Hound" was the first of the stories that would be incorporated into *Ham* to be published, in *Harper's Magazine* CLXIII (August 1931), p. 266-274. The short story sending schedule that Faulkner kept during these years indicates that it was completed at least by November 17, 1930. When Faulkner turned to the material again, for inclusion in *Ham*, he converted Ernest Cotton to Mink Snopes and gave him a wife, a family, and a sex life. Houston, who had also been a bachelor in the short story, is a widower in the novel.

Cullen cites as the model for Mink's murder of Houston a crime committed in Lafayette County in 1910. Pete Callicote, Cullen's neighbor, had borrowed a ten-gauge shotgun from Cullen's father because he suspected that the Taylors, other neighbors, were planning to kill him. These same Taylors had killed an old horse in a corn field and accused Callicote of doing the killing, swearing out a warrant against him. Taylor waited in a ditch, according to court records, "by the side of a small open thicket, in a corn field and while in some thirty or forty feet of the road" [sic]. When Callicote came by on his horse, he was shot in the back of the head (104-107). Another incident of murder from ambush occurs in the version of John Sartoris's murder that is recounted in *Req*: "Sartoris and Redmond bought--probably with Redmond's money--Compson's interest in the railroad, and the next year Sartoris and Redmond had quarreled and the year after that, because of simple physical fear, Redmond killed Sartoris from ambush on the Jefferson square and fled" (205). Cf. "Mississippi" for another account of the same incident, in which Redmond is described as one "who, after the inevitable quarrel, finally shot Colonel Sartoris dead on a Jefferson street, driven, everyone believed, to the desperate act by the same arrogance and intolerance which had driven Colonel Sartoris's regiment to demote him from its colonelcy in the fall elections after Second Manassas and Sharpsburg" (*ESPL* 20). The murder of Sartoris was supposedly modeled on the murder of Colonel Falkner on the square in Ripley by Thurmond, a former business partner. Duclos notes an important difference: Thurmond approached Falkner on the square and shot him in the face (12). Balzac's peasants shoot the proud forrester Michaud in the back after first killing his pet greyhound (*Les Paysans* 342, noted Cohen, "French Peasants" 384). Michaud's horse is described in terms similar to Houston's:."in the frantic gallop of the horse and the clank of the empty stirrups, there had been a mysterious sound which told of something wrong" (*Les Paysans* 341).

218.5 the vindication of his rights and the liquidation of his injuries: Mink sees in the act of murder a redress of wrongs he has suffered from Houston and an expression of his outraged pride. In this act of revenge, he is animated by many of the same factors that cause Ab Snopes to exact revenge by burning the barns of landowners who don't give him his due. Mink's demand for revenge finally plays itself out in *Mans* when he murders Flem for failing to save him from conviction for Houston's murder (415). The question of whether or not justice is possible is one that comes up often in *Ham*, especially in the three trials of Book Four: Tull v. Snopes, Armstid v. Snopes, and The People v. Mink Snopes. In the short story version, Cotton does not experience the satisfaction of revenge. Lying on his pallet after the ambush, he feels "no triumph, no vindication, nothing" (*US*, "The Hound" 153).

218.6-7 the thicket where he crouched and the dim faint road that ran beside it: The setting of Mink's ambush shares many of the characteristics of the image cluster that Faulkner employed often in his novels involving one or more characters surprised by others who come upon them in a thicket by a stream, usually on a spring evening (*Fascination* 183-198). The scene in "The Hound" includes a stream: "a fading grass-grown trace along the edge of the river bottom" (*US* 153).

218.24-25 It was no blind, instinctive, and furious desire for flight which he had to combat and curb: In the story, Ernest Cotton has to coach himself to resist his instinctive desire for flight: "Right after it you'll want to run," he told himself. "But you can't run. You got to finish it. You got to clean it up. It will be hard, but you got to do it..." (*US* 152).

218. 26-29 What he would have liked to do was leave a printed placard on the breast itself: *This is what happens to the men who impound Mink Snopes's cattle*, **with his name signed to it:** In *Mans*, Mink is illiterate: "Now he held the letter himself, the page of foolscap out of school writing pad, pencilled over, spidery and hieroglyph, not one jot less forever beyond him than Arabic or Sanskrit" (50). Cf. *Mans* for an alternative reason for killing Houston: "I aint shooting you because of them thirty-seven and a half four-bit days. That's all right; I done long ago forgot and forgive that. Likely Will Varner couldn't do nothing else, being a rich man too and all you rich folks has got to stick together or else someday the ones that aint rich might take a notion to raise up and take hit away from you. That aint why I shot you. I killed you because of that-ere extry one-dollar pound fee" (39).

218.32-219.1 He must rise and quit the thicket...not to finish it but merely to complete the first step of what he had started...slain a corpse to be hidden: Kartiganer believes that Mink is shown to grow into tragic wisdom because he acts in the face of fatality, knowing that he is responsible for setting in motion a train of events that will never be completed (123). Cf. to "The Hound": "You got to set there in the bushes and shut your eyes and count slow until you can make to finish it" (*US* 152).

219.19 his meager and sorry corn: The corn motif, so expressive of the impoverishment of Mink's life, is new to the novel version of his story.

219.10-27 the paintless two-room cabin with an open hallway...roof over his head: See Ratliff's approach to the same cabin 72.27-73.8. Cf. Ab Snopes and family's arrival at the De Spain tenant shack: "In the early afternoon the wagon stopped before a paintless two room house identical almost with the dozen others it had stopped before even in the boy's ten years" (*CS*, "Barn" 8). The outrage that both Ab Snopes and Mink Snopes feel has its origin in a class and economic system that relegates them to an endless cycle of poverty and brutality. In "The Hound," Cotton seems to own the shack he lives in, or he has, at least, built it. He leans against "the wall which he had built log by log" (*US* 155).

219.23 since his marriage: Cf. "The Hound": "Cotton was a bachelor" (*US* 153).

219.38-220.4 once more framed by an opening...nine years ago: a flashback to Mink's first encounter with the woman who would become his wife. See 236.7-12.

220.11-12 the incredible spring of which the dry summer was the monstrous abortion: This image of aridity, sterility, and stunted promise follows on the episode of Ike and the cow, with its strong associations of fertility and birth, in which the entire natural world seems to celebrate their union.

220.14 as if the zodiac too had stacked cards against him: Mink's doom is signaled by the opposition of the stars just as Ike's triumph is signaled by his identification with the forces of cosmological order.

221.10-18 He struck her across the mouth..."Go. Go": The impoverishment of these bleak lives often vents itself in violence toward women. Henry Armstid also strikes his wife twice. See 295.14-15.

221.25-26 surrounded by the loud soundless invisible shades of the nameless and numberless men: Cf. Horace's observation on Belle in *Flags*: "She had ghosts in her bed" (347). Cf. the shades that haunt Hightower in *LA*: "The son grew to manhood among phantoms and side by side with a ghost" (449). Cf. Quentin in *AbAb*: "He was a barracks full of stubborn, back-looking ghosts still recovering, even forty-three years afterward, from the fever which had cured the disease" (12).

222.6-7 the immitigable discrepancy between will and capability: See note 235.14-17.

223.24-25 Then he heard the hound: Cf. "The Hound": "He had heard...how negroes claimed that a dog would howl at the recent grave of its master" (*US* 154). Rider's hound begins to howl after Mannie's death (*GDM* 139). The hound, while realistic enough at this point, begins to take on supernatural characteristics. The increasingly surreal atmosphere of the episode links it to the stories in the Beyond section of *Collected Stories*, particularly "The Leg."

224.12-17 So he followed it, slipping and plunging in the mud...midhowl: After an analogous description of the treacherous footing, "The Hound" version continues with this line suggesting that the material world opposes Cotton's progress: "They possessed the perversity of inanimate things, seeming to spring out of the darkness and clutch him with spiky tentacles" (*US* 154).

225.7-9 He followed it for better than a mile, dragging the body which outweighed him by fifty pounds: In the novel, the Herculean nature of Mink's effort to transport Houston's body is conveyed by the emphasis on distance and weight, both absent from the short story version.

225.18 pin oak: a medium-sized tree (*Quercus palustris*) that attains a height of 60-80 feet and a diameter of 1-3 feet. It displays pyramidal growth with drooping lower branches that do not prune neatly (Preston 199). In the short story, Cotton stores the body in a hollow cypress (155).

226.4 snuff: "a preparation of finely pulverized tobacco that can be drawn up into the nostrils by inhaling" (*AHD*).

226.25 His days and nights were now reversed: Kidd points out that from the moment he fires the shot that kills Jack Houston, Mink is "out of synch with time." He is driven by the conviction that time, moving at an accelerating pace, is running out. Kidd argues that his failed suicide attempt is one final effort to control time by escaping from it forever (316).

226.26 morning star: "a planet, especially Venus, visible in the east just before or at sunrise" (*AHD*).

226.29-30 would eat standing from the pot of cold peas on the stove: Rider eats "cold and glutinous peas" after the death of Mannie (*GDM* 141).

226.37-38 by then he realized it could have but one ending and so it would last forever, and he stopped being hungry: See note 87.6-7.

226.38-39 He would merely rouse, wake, to tell himself, You got to eat: Rider, who is also intent, finally, on killing himself, also forces himself to eat: "But Ah needs to eat," he said" (*GDM* 139).

227.22-23 the round-headed periwinkle-eyed son of his kinsman who operated Varner's blacksmith shop: Wallstreet Panic Snopes.

228.9-13 He knew, even in the midst of the unreality which was not dream but a barren place where his mind, his will, stood like an unresting invincible ungrazing horse while the puny body which rode it renewed its strength: This complex image pulls together several patterns of theme and imagery that have been developing in the novel. First, the dissociation of the will from the body marks Mink as a double character, like Eula. See note 100.10-17. Joe Christmas, likewise, at a critical moment in his life, experiences a separation from his body. Cf. *LA*: "He stood over the bed. He held the razor in his hand. But it was not open yet. But she did not speak again and then his body seemed to walk away from him" (266). By dividing into a mind and a body, Mink allows himself to accept the dictates of his will while ignoring the demands of the body. He subsists on meal and then seemingly on almost nothing; he reverses his sleep pattern; and he will try to commit suicide. Significantly, the will is a horse, equated with the active male principle, which in this novel is often a destructive one. Also significantly, it is only in the abstract sense that Mink is ever construed to be on horseback. He is one of life's pedestrians as opposed to Jack Houston, who is the archetypal man on a horse. Cf. *Crime and Punishment* for the obverse of this image. Raskolnikov, who experiences what he considers to be a failure of will after he commits murder, quivers "like an overdriven horse" (102).

228.29 the sheriff's: In *Ham*, the sheriff is Hope Hampton, who also holds that office in *Intruder*. Hubert (Hub) Hampton, Sr. is the sheriff in *Twn* and is succeeded by his son, Hubert (Hub) Hampton, Jr., in *Mans* and *Reiv*. The sheriff is unnamed in "The Hound" (156).

228.32-34 the metal shield smaller than a playing card, on which he had gambled not only his freedom but perhaps his obliteration too: Even the minor male characters are portrayed as carrying on the game tradition. Matters of life and death, as here, are undertaken in the context of the contest for dominion.

229.19-23 and again he watched the night emerge...two up-opening palms releasing the westward-flying ultimate bird of evening: Kartiganer contrasts Mink's observance of night forming with Ike's witnessing the splendor of sunrise. See 181.17-33. Cf. "The Priest" for similar avian imagery representing nightfall: "How like birds with golden wings the measured bell notes fly, passing with clear and faint regret the ultimate slender rush of cross and spire; and how like the plummet lark the echo, singing, falls. Ave Maria...Ah God, ah god, that night should come so soon" (*NOS* 39).

229.25-26 the steady booming of the frogs was the steady pulse and beat of the dark heart of night: Cf. Conrad's description of the river in *Heart of Darkness*: "the river...seemed to beckon with a dishonouring flourish before the sunlit face of the land a treacherous appeal to the lurking death, to the hidden evil, to the profound darkness of its heart" (105).

229.31-32 He reached his hand backward and took up the gun: Mink at this point in the action is both hunter and quarry. He commences his hunt for the grief-stricken hound at the same time that he is also being hunted by the law. The double hunts of this episode follow the double hunts of the previous episode, in which Ike Snopes is, on the one hand, a quester and courtly lover, and, on the other hand, the human prey of both Jack Houston and the unnamed farmer whose feed basket he raids. *GDM*, Faulkner's next novel, is built on a series of hunts: the mythic hunt for the bear, the ritual hunt of "Was," Lucas Beauchamp's hunt for gold, the hunt for the still, Gavin Stevens's hunt for Samuel Beauchamp in "Go Down Moses," and the black woman's hunt for Roth Edmonds in "Delta Autumn."

231.3-5 Then it splashed, not sinking but disintegrating among that shattered scurrying of broken stars: Cf. "Nympholepsy": "He saw the broken water of his endeavor crested with stars" (*US* 335).

231.8-9 and lay down on the pallet: In the short story version, Cotton "[takes] to spending the nights sitting up in a chair in the door, watching the fireflies and listening to the frogs and the owls" (*US* 159).

231.17 roaring silence: Faulkner inverts Mallarmé's image of silent thunder. Cf. Mallarmé's quote, noted in Symons, that he condemns inclusion of anything in literature but "for example, the horror of the forest, or the silent thunder afloat in the leaves" (71). Cf. "Carcasonne": "...the galloping horse filled his mind again with silent thunder" (*CS* 898).

231.18-19 the random and velvet-shod fireflies drifted and winked: Cf. *Twn* for the fireflies on Seminary Hill: "Then as though at signal, the fireflies--lightning bugs of the Mississippi child's vernacular--myriad and frenetic, random and frantic, pulsing; not quiring, but choiring as if they were tiny, incessant appeaseless voices, cries, words. And you stand suzerain and solitary above the whole sum of your life beneath that incessant ephemeral spangling" (315).

231.39 the buzzards: "any of various North American vultures, such as the turkey vulture" (*AHD*).

232.10 he mounted to the empty gallery: In "The Hound," Ernest Cotton goes to town, makes the sixth in a group on the veranda of Varner's store, and finds himself compelled to join in a choral discussion of Houston: "'He warn't no smarter than nobody else,' he said. Then he wished he had not spoken...'Swelling around like he was the biggest man in the county. Setting that ere dog on folks' stock'....'Maybe I'll have to kill them all,' he said to himself....'Not them; just the words, the talk.' But the talk was familiar, the intonation, the gestures; but so was Houston. He had known Houston all his life; that prosperous and overbearing man. 'With a dog,' Cotton said...'A dog that et better than me. I work, and eat worse than his dog. If I had been his dog, I would not have....We're better off without him,' he said, blurted" (*US* 157). At this point in the story, the reader also learns that Cotton in the past won a lawsuit against Houston over the quartering of a hog. Houston's hog wandered into Cotton's lot one October; when Cotton could not find the hog's owner, he wintered the animal on his own corn. In the spring, Houston claimed the hog, but a court assessed him for the wintering and fined him one dollar pound fee (*US* 157-58).

232.16 **pussel-gutted:** When asked about the meaning of pussel-gutted at the University of Virginia in 1957, Faulkner replied: "I've heard it all my life. It means someone that is bloated, that has a tremendous belly that he shouldn't have" (*FU* 126). Cf. Jewel's address to his horse in *AILD*: "Get the goddamn stuff out of sight while you got a chance, you pussel-gutted bastard" (13). Luce cites a variant spelling of the word in Zora Neale Hurston's *Seraph on the Suwanee* (1948): "Raine and her mother were up to baiting a hook for the puzzle-gutted slob" (9, noted 11).

232.17 **grabbling:** feeling around with the hands, groping (*AHD*). Brown says that in Mississippi, "grabbling is a standard method of fishing in which a person wades along the edge of a creek or river, groping in holes, under logs, and overhanging banks, etc., and seizing any fish they can" (94).

232.21 **hammer-lock ten-gauge Hadleys:** a Hadley is a make of shotgun (Brown 97). According to Brown, the gauge of a shotgun measures the size of the bore. The smaller the number, the larger the bore, since the gauge is actually the number of lead balls of that size that it takes to weigh a pound. The common shotgun gauges at the time of *Ham* were twelve and sixteen" (197-98). See note 217.28.

232.28 **squirl:** squirrel.

233.1 trace chains: chains used as traces, which are the straps that connect a horse or mule to the vehicle he is pulling. They are attached to the hames, or breast strap, at the front and run along the animal's sides (Brown 201-2).

233.38-39 "Do you mean to tell me that you never even looked? never even looked?: Mink Snopes and his cousin Ike Snopes are the only males in *Ham* who are, if not disdainful, at least unconcerned with money. Kartiganer, while noting this link between the two, argues that Mink's section of the novel achieves its effects through contrasts with the chapter that precedes it. While Ike and the cow carry on their love affair in harmony with the natural world, Mink is physically at odds with a world that seems to block him at every step. The course of Ike's journey follows naturally the course of the moving sun, while Mink struggles to outrun the night. Ike woos a cow; Mink battles a hound (122).

234.38-39 it was as if he were standing outside of himself: See note 228.9-13.

235.1-4 All them days and nights that looked like they wasn't going to have no end, come down to the space...door: Faulkner repeats the essential elements of this scene again twice in Mink's narrative. See Mink's first glimpse of his future wife at 236.7-12 and his approach to Mrs. Littlejohn's house at 242.35-243.1.

235.14-17 He merely wished he did not have to remember the fiasco which had followed the act...failed the will to do: Cf. *Crime and Punishment* for Raskolnikov's speculations on why so many criminals leave obvious traces: "Almost every criminal is subject to a failure of will...at the very instant when prudence and caution are most essential. It was his conviction that this eclipse of reason and failure of will-power attacked a man like a disease developed gradually..." (63). In Mink's case, it is the aftermath of his crime that is unsettling, not the recollection of the murder itself.

235.29-30 He was seeking the sea....He had never seen it: Cf. *LA*: "Calvin Burden...ran away from home at the age of twelve, before he could write his name (or would write it, his father believed) on a ship" (228). Cf. Sutpen's flight to sea in *AbAb!*: "a boy of fourteen or fifteen who had never

155

seen the ocean before, going to sea in 1823" (239).

235.33-37 what of repudiation of the land, the earth...availing himself: See note 306.15-18.

236.1-7 Perhaps he was seeking only the proffer of this illimitable space...dreamed intact golden galleons and the unattainable deathless seamaids: Nicholaisen relates this passage to Conrad's Lord Jim, who also escapes the limitations of the earth by setting out for the sea (noted 268). The image of the mermaids perhaps alludes to Prufrock's ecstatic vision at the end of "The Love Song of J. Alfred Prufrock": "We have lingered in the chambers of the sea/ By sea-girls wreathed with seaweed red and brown/ Till human voices wake us, and we drown"(130-32).

236.12 He went no further: Nicholaisen argues that Mink's decision to forsake his plans to reach the sea and to remain on solid ground is a surrender to the power of the feminine force, which is associated with the earth (269).

236.27 quadroon: a woman whose ancestry is one-fourth Negro.

237.5-9 That is what he saw: the habit of success--that perfect marriage of will and ability...not a nympholept but the confident lord of a harem: Mink identifies his own problem after the murder as a rupture between will and ability. See 235.14-17.

237.25-29 He had been bred by the generations to believe invincibly that to every man...there was reserved one virgin, at least, for him to marry...deflower and destroy: Cf. Anderson's "The Man Who Became a Woman": "I had been dreaming and thinking about women, and I suppose I'd always been dreaming about a pure innocent one, for myself, made for me by God, maybe" (391). Faulkner's accentuation of Mink's culturally bred expectation that his bride will be a virgin highlights an essential difference between Mink and Jack Houston. Each of them believes he deserves to marry a virgin; each of them condemns female promiscuity; each of them nevertheless becomes involved with a woman who does not conform to society's sexual standards for women. In love with a socially stigmatized woman, Mink marries her anyway and has a family. Houston does the opposite. There is no question that the Galveston prostitute, with whom he lived for seven years, loves him, but Houston discards her and does the respectable thing: he returns home to marry Lucy Pate, whom he has known all his life. See note 212.36-39.

237.35-38 no room, no darkness, no desert even...stallion ramp of those inexpugnable shades: See note 221.25-26.

238.18-25 Afterward it seemed to him that that afternoon's bedding...ravished acres...the lopped dead limbs and tree butts and all the grief of wood: Dimino notes that Mink voices the same connection made in the Eula section between exploitation of a woman and exploitation of the land (166). See note 118.31-119.6.

238.32 shuck mattress: a mattress stuffed with corn shucks.

238.34-37 She said: "I've had a hundred men, but I never had a wasp before. That stuff comes out of you is rank poison. It's too hot. It burns itself and my seed both up. It'll never make a kid": Cf. the connection Rosa Coldfield makes between wasps and the male principle in *AbAb!*: "the male predacious wasps and bees of later lusts" (144). Cf. *WP*: Charlotte has heard "that when people loved, hard, really loved each other, they didn't have children, the seed burned up in the love, the passion" (205). Eula is like a peach around which wasps swarm. See note 127.4-5.

239.3 threadless and headless plow bolts: "nuts and bolts used for fastening the various parts of the plow together...These bolts are countersunk so that the head of the bolt is flush with the surface of the plowshare" (Brown 150).

239.11-14 They served to shackle her too...letting her hair grow out again and dyeing it: See note 206.37-207.3.

239.37-38 "I know you didn't have any money, just like I know you haven't had anything to eat except the dust in that barrel: In "The Hound," Cotton goes to the store "to purchase food. He bought it: crackers, cheese, and a tin of sardines" (*US* 160).

240.21-22 Did you sell Will something for it, or did you just take

it out of his pants while he was asleep? Or was it Jody?: In *Sanc*, Horace Benbow refuses the kind of payment that Mink believes Will Varner to have accepted: "You said tonight was the time to start paying you."

For a while longer, he looked at her. "Ah," he said. "O tempora! O mores! O hell! Can you stupid mammals never believe that any man, every man--You thought that was what I was coming for? You thought that if I had intended to, I'd have waited this long?" (330).

240.26-29 she saw only the slight jerk of his hand and wrist--no coin to wring against his thumbnail...where dusty cotton clung: See note 177.29-178.3.

241.28-29 puke-stomached: nauseated, squeamish.

242.25-31 suddenly, now that it was too late, now that he had lost all hope of alternative between planned and intelligent escape...would be given him: See note 229.31-32. Mink's reduction to a beast challenges the animal/human hierarchy, as does Ike's love affair with the cow. Men are susceptible to backsliding along the animal/human continuum, while animals, like Houston's hound and Ike's cow, are depicted as behaving with more grace and delicacy than their human counterparts. The pattern of shifting hierarchies, whether involving animals and humans, men and women, or insiders and outsiders, carries through the novel at all levels.

242.35-243.1 It began to seem to him now that that puny and lonely beacon ... period to hope...advancing foot: See note 235.1-4.

243.1-2 I thought that when you killed a man, that finished it, he told himself. But it dont. It just starts then: Mink discovers what Dostoyevsky's Raskolnikov also learns, that murder is merely the prelude to suffering, not the antidote to it. Weisgerber compares this passage to Raskolnikov's thoughts shortly after the murder: "Surely it isn't beginning already! Surely it isn't my punishment coming upon me? It is!" (81, noted 268-69).

243.32-33 feed corn: "mature, hard corn kept for stock feed--not normally edible for people unless ground into meal and made into bread, but can be parched and eaten" (Brown 80).

245.12 **fob pocket:** "a small pocket at the front waistline of a man's trousers or in the front of a vest, used especially to hold a watch" (*AHD*).

245.20 **checkers:** This image of contained, ritualized competition points up the pathos and irony of Mink's situation. In his ploy to stall Lump, he resorts to a mode of behavior that comes easily to the other men of the hamlet but that is out of line with his own character.

248.8 **tit for tat:** "a variation of tip for tap, one stroke in return for another; retaliation" (*Oxford Dictionary of English Proverbs*).

248.20 **white oak:** *Quercus alba*, "a tall tree with rather evenly lobed hairless leaves that may be somewhat whitened beneath. Twigs hairless; end buds red-brown, small, blunt, and hairless" (Petrides 216).

248.21 **a twister which Houston had used with his stallion:** Brown identifies the twister as "a device used to control a dangerous or unruly horse, much as a nose ring is used to control a bull. The loop of rope is slipped over the horse's nostrils, and the stick is twisted to tighten it and cut off its breath" (204).

248.24 **cudgel:** "a short heavy stick; a club" (*AHD*).

248.28 **hame-string:** According to Brown, "strictly speaking, the hames may be fastened together above and below a horse's collar either by hame strings (leather thongs, which are tied) or by hame straps (leather straps, which are buckled). In practice, the distinction is often ignored, and Faulkner uses hame string for either system" (98).

248.28 **check rein:** "a short strap used to hold a horse's head up or back" (Brown 50).

248.28 **plow gear:** "a general term for anything needed in connection with plowing: plowlines, harness, plowshares, nuts and bolts, etc. More specifically, the complete harness put on a mule for plowing: bridle, collar, hames, trace chains, and plowlines" (Brown 150).

249.6 **roar not of silence but of time's friction:** Cf. *Sanc*: "The voice of the night--insects, whatever it was--had followed him into the house; he knew suddenly that it was the friction of the earth on its axis, approaching

the moment when it must decide to turn on or be forever still..."
(Corrected Text 233).

249.27-28 Now he was in corn again, better than his: The ultimate blow to Mink's pride is that a Negro should succeed where he has failed. See his reaction to being fed after the "nigger" convicts at 258.30-32.

250.5-6 admitted at last that he was lost: In "The Hound," Ernest Cotton is not lost; he goes straight to the hollow cypress tree (*US* 160).

250.16.17 avalanche of accumulating seconds which was now his enemy: Quentin Compson, another time-obsessed character, is given a watch by his father and counseled to give up his war with time: "I give it to you not that you might remember time but that you might forget it now and then for a moment and not spend all your breath trying to conquer it" (93).

250.34-36 until suddenly there was no earth under his feet; he made another stride, running upon nothing, then he was falling: Nicholaisen cites this literal loss of footing as symbolic evidence that Mink is not in control of his environment and is, literally, not on solid ground (255).

251.10-12 the bizarre erst-fluid earth became fixed and stable in the old solid dimensions and juxtapositions: Nicholaisen links Mink's return home from the bottom land to Vernon Tull's accession to dry land after crossing the river in *AILD*. Each is experienced as a "return from the abyss," he suggests (255). Cf. Tull's surprise to find himself on "something tame like the hard earth again" (*AILD* 131).

252.1-2 keep telling lies just to save your neck: The irony is that Mink does not want to save his own neck and that it is his strong neck muscles that botch his suicide attempt after he is captured and is being transported to Jefferson. See note 256.22-257.10.

252.22-23 It's like just about everything is in cahoots against one man killing another: Cf. *Oliver Twist*: "Let no man talk of murderers escaping justice, and hint that Providence must sleep. There were twenty score of violent deaths in one long minute of that agony of fear" (368). Murder violates the natural order, thus the entire physical universe seems to rebel against it.

252.39-253.1 He could see its eyes now as it leaped the second time. They seemed to float toward him interminably: After Sikes kills Nancy in Dickens's *Oliver Twist*, he embarks on a three-day flight from the authorities that shares many characteristics with Mink's. Cf. his vision of Nancy's haunting eyes: "For now a vision came before him, as constant and more terrible than that from which he had escaped. Those widely staring eyes, so lustreless and so glassy, that he had better borne to see them than to think upon them, appeared in the midst of the darkness; light in themselves, but giving light to nothing. There were but two, but they were everywhere" (368). Sikes's efforts to shake off the phantom Nancy look ahead both to Mink's efforts to rid himself of the hound and to his struggle to evade Lump Snopes. Both Sikes and Mink are affiliated with women who were at one time promiscuous, if not prostitutes. Both are hunted down, and both are likened to beasts; the chapter heading above Sikes's capture is entitled "The Wild Beast Laid Low." Although there is no one-to-one correspondence between the dogs in each narrative, a loyal dog does figure in each. Sikes's dog, like Houston's, seems invincible and resists Sikes's own plot to kill him. Once Sikes is dead, however, the animal, like Houston's, begins to howl. Finally, each attempts to escape capture. Sikes, attempting to get away, commits suicide. Mink attempts to escape through suicide but is unsuccessful.

252.31-32 the darkness itself merely sighed and flowed behind him: Cf. "The Hound": "something flowed silent and savage out of the darkness behind him and struck him a slashing blow" (*US* 160). In Faulkner's revision, the darkness itself is a palpable medium.

253.1 They seemed to float toward him interminably: See note 173.25-26.

253.13 felt the axe strike and leap spinning from his hands: Faulkner's revisions reinforce the eery sense that the earth and all of the things, animate and inanimate, on it dynamically resist Mink's will. Cf. "The Hound": "felt the axe strike and whirl from his hands" (*US* 161).

253.14-19 where the animal thrashed and groaned in the underbrush, leaping toward the sound...hunting the axe: Cf. "The Hound" where neither the hound nor Mink is particularly agitated: "He heard the dog whimper, he could hear it crawling away. On his hands and knees he hunted for the axe until he found it" (161).

254.10-12 he was actually seeing the animal and that dawn had come, the animal visible now, gaunt, thin, with a fresh bloody gash across its face, howling: Contrast this with the emergence into visibility at dawn of Ike's beloved cow. See 165.36-39.

254.31-33 he saw it in midair like a tremendous wingless bird soar out and vanish into the mist: See note 173.25-26.

255.6 the surrey: "a four-wheeled horse-drawn pleasure carriage having two or four seats" (*AHD*). In the short story, Ernest Cotton is taken to the county seat in a "battered Ford" (162). In December of 1956, Saxe Commins gave the proofs of *Twn* to James B. Meriwether and told him that Faulkner wanted to eliminate all discrepancies between *Twn* and *Ham*. In the typescript of *Twn*, and therefore in the galleys that Meriwether read, Faulkner reverts to the Ford. When Commins, alerted by Meriwether, called Faulkner's attention to the inconsistency, Faulkner instructed him to make the vehicle a surrey. Commins later wrote on the galleys, after the fact, "Ask Jim Meriwether" (Meriwether, Interview 6/2/94).

255.33 gunny sacks: a bag made of a coarse, loosely woven fabric such as jute or hemp (*AHD*).

255.34-38 Then the road came down out of the hills...cotton pickers still moving through the spilling rows: Gavin Stevens, returning to Jefferson from a meeting with the governor over the pardoning of prisoners, has a similar vision of the land that glosses Mink's: "but he started back to Jefferson at once, riding across the broad, heat-miraged land, between the cotton and the corn of God's long-fecund, remorseless acres, which would outlast any corruption and injustice" (59-60).

255.37 the fired and heavy corn: According to Brown, corn is fired when the ears turn yellowish as they mature (87).

256.5-8 They went on, pacing in the thick, soft dust the long, parched summer afternoon, though actually they could not keep pace with it...surrey where he sat: See 183.31: "They pace the ardent and unheeding sun..."

256.15-16 the long shadows of the pines wheeled slowly over the slow surrey in the now setting sun: See a similar image at 183.33-34.

256.18 the poised fierce ball of the sun dropping down beyond it: Cf. *Heart of Darkness*: "blazing little ball of sun hanging" over the jungle (114).

256.22-257.10 gathered and hurled himself feet foremost out of the moving surrey...and the three faces: Only Mink's strong neck muscles prevent him from committing suicide by breaking his neck. In *GDM*, another strong man, Rider, declaring twice that he is "snakebit and bound to die" (152), accomplishes his own suicide in a less direct fashion. Ab Snopes also seems to be on a suicide path, as does young Bayard Sartoris in *Flags*. Characters who successfully commit suicide in Faulkner's work include Sir Galwyn of *Mayday*, Quentin Compson of *S&F*, and Mr. Coldfield of *AbAb!*.

257.15-21 the surrey moving now beneath an ordered overarch of sunshot trees, beneath the clipped and tended lawns...twilight: Millgate comments on the richly evocative nature of this passage. First, the vision of order and prosperity points up the economic deprivation of Mink's life and of the lives of all Frenchman's Bend's inhabitants. Instead of a neatly clipped lawn, Mink's house sits in a "muck-trodden lot" (73.2). His gate is not only paintless but broken (222.30). His wife's garments are grey and nondescript, and his children are never heard to speak. Secondly, the glimpse of Jefferson creates a context for Flem's rise (*Achievement* 193).

258.30-32 Are they going to feed them niggers before they do a white man? he thought, smelling the coffee and ham: See note 249.27-28. Cf. "The Hound": "(he had never known a negro himself because of the antipathy, the economic jealousy, between his kind and negroes)" (*US* 154).

258.35-36 The summer's heat--the blazing days beneath which even the oak leaves turned brown and died: Cf. "Dry September": "the bloody September twilight, aftermath of sixty-two rainless days" (*CS* 169).

258.36-259.1 the nights during which the ordered stars seemed to glare down in cold and lidless amazement: Cf. the final sentence of

"Dry September": "The dark world seemed to lie stricken beneath the cold moon and the lidless stars" (*CS* 183).

259.3-5 ardor-wearied earth, ancient Lilith, reigned, throned and crowned amid the old invincible courtesan's formal defunction: According to Jewish legend, Lilith was Adam's first wife. She refused subordinate sexual positions because she believed herself to be Adam's equal. She has come down in Hebrew teachings as one of the two harlots of Jerusalem who presented themselves to Solomon and asked him to arbitrate the custody of the son that each of them claimed for her own. The woman who favored that the child be slain and divided is said to have been Lilith (1 Kings 3: 16-28, noted McHaney 93). Lilith's daughters, the Empusae, could change themselves into beautiful maidens or cows, because Lilith was identified with Aphrodite, or cow-eyed Hera (Graves 190). Blotner notes that in the 1925 sketch, "New Orleans," Faulkner used similar imagery to depict the city: "New Orleans...a courtesan whose hold is strong on the mature, to whose charm the young must respond" (49, noted 1 Vol. 409). Cf. *WP*: "*It was the Indian summer that did it. I have been seduced to an imbecile's paradise by an old whore; I have been throttled and sapped of strength and volition by the old weary Lilith of the year*" (114-15).

259.8-9 the two small grimed hands, immobile and clasping loosely the bars of the jail window: Cf. Darl's hands in *AILD*: "Our brother Darl in a cage in Jackson where, his grimed hands lying light in the quiet interstices, looking out he foams" (254). Cf. the Negro murderer in *Sanc* who occupies a barred window in the Jefferson jail in the days remaining before his execution: "The jail faced west; a last, faint copper-colored light lay upon the dingy grating and upon the small, pale blob of a hand..." (159).

259.9 the jail: Faulkner recounts the history of the Jefferson jail in *Req*, where it is founded almost simultaneously with the town. Not fully aware of the potential for evil in the new world, the town's founders erect a ramshackle structure that proves too flimsy for the Natchez Trace bandits who are its first inhabitants. The jail is rebuilt when the bandits steal not only Alex Holsten's lock but a wall of the jail itself. The jail figures prominently in: *Sanc*, where it houses a Negro wife-murderer who sings spirituals to mark the time until his execution, Lee Goodwin, who will be lynched, and for a time Goodwin's wife and their child; the "Pantaloon in

Black" chapter of *GDM*, where Rider spends a few hours in jail before he is lynched by the Birdsongs; and *Req*, where Nancy Manigoe does time for murdering Temple Drake's baby, and Gavin Stevens sings spirituals with her in her cell.

259.15 **his sister:** In *Mans*, Ratliff is "a damned good cook, living alone in the cleanest little house you ever saw, doing his own housework" (206).

259.35 **suttee:** the practice in India of a Hindu widow's throwing herself on her husband's funeral pyre to be cremated in order to prove fulfillment of her wifely obligation *(AHD)*.

260.1-4 **the four of them sitting in the close cell rank with creosote and old wraiths of human excreta--the sweat, the urine, the vomit discharged of all the old agonies: terror, impotence, hope:** Cf. *Intruder*: "jails were the true records of a county's, a community's history, since not only the cryptic forgotten words and even phrases cries of defiance and indictment scratched into the very walls but the very bricks and stones themselves held...intact and biding and potent and indestructible, the agonies and shames and griefs with which hearts long since unmarked and unremembered dust had strained and perhaps burst" (49-50). Cf. *Req* for a similar association of the jail with the history of human travail: "...if you would peruse in unbroken...continuity the history of a community, look not in the church records and the courthouse records, but beneath the successive layers of calcimine and creosote and whitewash on the walls of the jail, since only in that forcible carceration does man find the idleness to compose in the gross and simple terms of his gross and simple lusts and yearnings, the gross and simple recapitulations of his gross and simple heart" (214).

261.13-14 **an iron cold which locked the earth in a frozen rigidity:** The bitter winter of Book Three relates to Flem's removal of Eula, a Persephone figure, to Texas. See note 118.31-119.6.

261.39 **axle-grease:** "thick black grease used where wheels of wagons turn on their axles" (Brown 23).

262.15 **wafer of sun:** Cf. *The Red Badge of Courage*: After Henry witnesses the death of his friend, the tall soldier, he shakes his fist at the battlefield and notices the sun: "The red sun was pasted in the sky like a fierce wafer" (58).

263.4 After all, blood is blood: Mink's wife expresses the conviction first voiced by Ab Snopes in the excised first chapter of the novel: "You got to stick to your own blood or you ain't going to have any blood to stick to you" (*CS*, "Barn" 8). Mink is certain that he will not be abandoned by his kin until the point that he is convicted of Houston's murder without Flem's intercession.

263.18 Mottstown: Because Brown assumes that Oxford is Jefferson, he associates Mottstown with Water Valley, a town "some 20 m. SSW of Oxford by highway Miss. 7" (133). If Jefferson is Ripley, and this is more likely, Mottstown would be New Albany.

263.25-26 It aint hardly big enough to be chewing tobacco yet I reckon: There is a standing joke in the earliest versions of the spotted horses story about the size and accomplishments of Eula's baby. Cf. *FA*: "It was a fine child, remarkably wellgrown..." (21). Cf. "Spotted Horses": "Then one day last month, Eula come back, with a baby. We figgered up, and we decided that it was as well-growed a three-months-old baby as we ever see. It can already pull up a chair. I reckon Texas makes big men quick, being a big place. Anyway, if it keeps on like it started, it'll be chewing tobacco and voting time it's eight years old" (*US* 167). Cf. "Spotted Horses": "...he had went on to see his wife I reckon, and to see if that ere baby had done gone on to the field to help Uncle Billy plow maybe" (*US* 167). In *Twn*, Gavin recalls Ratliff's having told him that the baby was walking when Eula and the baby returned from Texas: "Ratliff would have invented the walking, being Ratliff. In fact, if there had been no child at all yet, Ratliff would have invented one, invented one already walking for the simple sake of his own paradox and humor, secured as he was from uncheckable fact" (134).

263.35-264.3 Then even that winter was over at last. It ended as it had begun, in rain...warm water washing out the earth...plow: The arrival of the belated spring, with its warm, lush rainfall coincides with Eula's Persephone-like return to the hamlet. See note 118.31-119.6 and note 184.17.

264.4 school was already closed for the planting year:
In rural school districts, the necessity that every member of the family

help out with the planting and harvesting took precedence over education. School terms did not begin until the fall harvest, and they ended in spring before planting.

264.15-29 "His wife come in one day...done that: See note 204.3-12.

264.30 Wallstreet: oldest son of Eck Snopes. Wallstreet, because of his innocence, is immune to the dangers of the spotted horse auction. See 283.18-20 and 303.18-22. See 266.30-38 for a description of how Wallstreet got his name. In *Twn*, Wallstreet is industrious and honest. He takes the thousand dollars his mother gets for Eck's death and buys half-interest in a grocery store (128), which he refuses to allow Flem to invest in or to loan him money for (146). Eventually, he becomes sole owner of the first self-service grocery in Jefferson. In *Mans*, Wall comes to Flem's funeral, and his life is summarized thus: "...and yes, Wallstreet Snopes, Wallstreet Panic Snopes, who not only had never acted like a Snopes, he had never even looked like one: a tall dark man except for the eyes of an incredible tender youthful periwinkle blue, who had begun as the delivery boy in a side-street grocery to carry himself and his younger brother, Admiral Dewey, through school, and went from there to create a wholesale grocery supply house in Jefferson serving all the county; and now, removed with his family to Memphis, owned a chain of wholesale grocery establishments blanketing half of Mississippi and Tennessee and Arkansas too" (420).

265.15 Mrs. Flem Snopes sat...not a tragic face: it was just damned: recalls the photographed face of Caddy Compson in "Appendix: Compson": "the woman's face hatless between a rich scarf and a seal coat, ageless and beautiful, cold serene and damned" (746).

266.16-18 Upon the overalled knees Ratliff saw the battered wooden effigy of a cow such as children receive on Christmas: The tragic diminishment of things is epitomized in the toy wooden cow that replaces Ike's bovine love. It, along with the damned face of Mrs. Flem Snopes, stands in for all the lost possibilities for love in the Frenchman's Bend world.

266.30-38 "Oh," the other said. "No sir, it wasn't changed....He figured if we named him Wallstreet Panic it might make him get rich like the folks that run that Wallstreet Panic: John D. Brown notes that the "last great mercantile and credit crisis of the nineteenth century smashed the market in 1893" (*101 Years on Wall Street: An Investor's Almanac* 20), due mainly to the collapse of the railroads, which fell one after another into receivership. The market at the close of the year was down 39% from the January high. This is undoubtedly the panic that Faulkner had in mind when writing *Ham*, as it is consistent with the original timetable of the novel. With the movement of the action of the novel up to the early twentieth century for the 1964 edition, the 1893 panic becomes problematical. Dimino notes that there were also Wall Street panics in the years 1903 and 1907 (156). The decade in which Faulkner revised and pulled together his Snopes material was not a good one for the market either. In 1930, after the preceding year's great crash, the market was down 33.8%; in 1931, it was down 52.7%; and in 1937, it lost 32.8% (John D. Brown 58-65). No year since has exceeded the losses of 1937, only the third worst year of the decade (John D. Brown 65).

267.5 Three more besides Wall: In *Twn* only Wallstreet Panic and Admiral Dewey are mentioned as children of Eck.

Book Four: The Peasants: Faulkner appropriates as the title of Book Four the working title of the entire novel, almost certainly derived from Balzac's *Les Paysans*. After the emphasis on love and loss in Book Three, Faulkner reasserts the economic theme in Book Four. In Chapter One, the men of Frenchman's Bend respond to the pony auction because the animals represent something that is missing from their lives, some quality of freedom or imagination or sexual energy or masculinity. In Chapter Two, Ratliff, the only formidable opponent to Flem's machinations, responds to the salted mine trick because he is attracted to the dream of the old Frenchman's Place and to the vision of humankind in harmony with natural order as was Sarty Snopes in "Barn." What distinguishes the commercial episodes of Book Four from earlier treatments of the economic theme, especially the fool about a horse episode and the goat trade of Book One, is the reader's increasing awareness that these surrogate experiences mask a profound emptiness in the lives of *Ham*'s men.
Chapter One: There is no doubt that the seed of *Ham* was the spotted horse episode. Faulkner told the story first in *FA*, an unfinished and only posthumously published manuscript written in 1926. The essential elements of the story, while expanded on and invigorated with sharper detail, remained consistent through multiple retellings. Faulkner

experimented with point of view in later versions, but his basic vision remained the same. His second attempt at the story, *Abraham's Children*, an unfinished typescript, retains the third person narration of *FA*. He next wrote two versions under the title "As I Lay Dying." The first of these was a daring experiment in the possibilities of the country vernacular, narrated by V.K. Suratt. It was rejected by Scribner's in November 1928. The second cannot be precisely dated but probably originated around the same time. It is narrated by the young nephew of a judge in Jefferson who is campaigning for re-election. The boy is reminiscent of Quentin Compson, but Meriwether notes that a probable model for the uncle/judge pairing was the Uncle Abner series of detective stories by Melville Davisson Post, about the escapades of a judge detective and his nephew, who narrates the series ("As I Lay Dying" 370). This rejected title, later taken up as the title of the novel begun in October 1929, may indicate the intended metaphorical locus of the story. Its source is Agamemnon's ghost's speech to Odysseus in Book IX of *The Odyssey*: "As I lay dying the woman with the dog's eyes would not close my eyelids for me as I descended into Hades" (noted Collins, "The Pairing of *The Sound and the Fury* and *As I Lay Dying*" 123, Howell 217). Faulkner next submitted to Scribner's, in August 1930, a longer version, entitled "The Peasants." The final version, then entitled "Aria Con Amore," to be retitled "Spotted Horses," was submitted February 13, 1931 and published in the June 1931 number of Scribner's. It is also told in the vernacular by an unnamed narrator, whom Faulkner identified as Surratt, the prototype of Ratliff (noted Meriwether, *Literary* 41). When he began to write the first volume of the Snopes trilogy in 1939, Faulkner recognized the primacy of the spotted horses material, as he recalled in a 1945 letter to Malcolm Cowley: "...one day I decided that I had better get started on the first volume or I'd never get any of it down. So I wrote an induction *toward* [emphasis mine] the spotted horse story, which included BARN BURNING and WASH, which I discovered had no place in that book at all. Spotted Horses became a longer story, picked up THE HOUND (rewritten and much longer and with the character's name changed from Cotton to Snopes), and went on with JAMSHYD'S COURTYARD" (*SL* 197).

Several commentators establish a factual basis for the incident of the pony auction. Cullen remembers that when they were young, a man from Texas brought in some mustangs and sold them in a lot next to the old Jeff Cook boardinghouse (63). John Faulkner not only remembers auctioneers with ponies, but he also locates Faulkner as a witness watching the whole thing from a boardinghouse porch:

One day Uncle John was scheduled in Pittsboro so they decided to spend the night there. There was no hotel, so they got rooms in a boardinghouse late that evening when some men brought in a string of calico ponies wired together with barbed wire. They put them in a lot just across the road from the boardinghouse and the next morning auctioned them off, at prices ranging from about five dollars apiece on up.

Just like in Bill's story, the men sold all the horses, put the money in their pockets and left. When the buyers went in to get their purchases, someone left the gate open and those ponies spread like colored confetti over the countryside.

Bill sat there on the porch of the boardinghouse and saw it all. One of them ran the length of the porch and he had to dive back into the hallway to get out of its path. He and Uncle John told us about it the next day, when they got home (158-59).

Stark Young also mentioned calico ponies being exported to the area every year from Texas (*The Pavilion* 55-56), as did Faulkner in his interviews at UVa. When asked if he had ever seen an auction like the one in the novel, Faulkner responded:

"Yes'm. I bought one of these horses once. They appeared in our country, every summer somebody would come in with another batch of them. They were Western range-bred ponies, pintos--they never had a bridle on them, they had never seen shelled corn before, and they'd be brought into our town and auctioned off for prices from three or four dollars up to six or seven. And I bought this one for $4.75. I was, oh I reckon, ten years old. My father at the time ran a livery stable, and there was a big man, he was six feet and a half tall, he weighed two hundred pounds, but mentally he was about ten years old, too. And I wanted one of those horses, and my father said, Well if you and Buster can buy one for what money you've saved, you can have it. And so we went to the auction and we bought one for $4.75. We got it home, we were going to gentle it, we had a two-wheeled cart made out of the front axle of a buggy, with shafts on it, and we fooled with that critter--it was a wild animal, it was a wild beast, it wasn't a domestic animal at all. And finally Buster said that it was about ready, so we had the cart in a shed--Estelle probably remembers this--we put a croker sack over the horse's head and backed it into the cart with two Negroes to fasten it in, to buckle traces and toggles and things, and me and Buster got in the seat and Buster said, All right boys, let him go, and they snatched the sack off the horse's head. He went across the lot--there was a big gate, the lane, it turned it at a sharp angle--it hung the inside wheel on the gatepost as it turned, we were down on one hub then, and about that time Buster caught me by the back of the neck and threw me just like that and then he jumped out. And the cart was scattered up that lane, and we found the horse a mile away, run into a dead-end street. All he had left on him was just the hames--the harness gone. But that was a pleasant experience. But we kept that horse and gentled him to where I finally rode him. But I loved that horse because that was my own horse. I bought that with my own money (*FU* 29-30).

The pony auction recurs in other novels, sometimes obliquely and sometimes in direct re-telling. In Chapter One of *Twn*, Chick Mallison admits that Flem was not the first person to bring in wild ponies: "Every year or so someone brought into the county a string of wild unbroken plains ponies from somewhere in the west and auctioned them off" (6-7). Ratliff alludes to "them wild Texas ponies" in *Mans* (123). Jewel buys "a descendent of those Texas ponies Flem brought here twenty-five years ago and auctioned off for two dollars a head and nobody but old Lon Quick ever caught his and still owned some of the blood because he could never give it away" (*AILD* 134). In *GDM*, Ike McCaslin remembers " the wild, never-bridled Texas paint pony which he had persuaded McCaslin to let him buy and which he and Boon had bought at auction for four dollars and seventy-five cents and fetched home wired between two gentle mares and pieces of barbed wire and which had never even seen shelled corn before and didn't know what it was" (232).

Many critics note Faulkner's debt to the southwestern humor tradition (Bungert, passim; Adams, "Apprenticeship" 38; McHaney, "What Faulkner Learned" 124; Hoffman, passim; Jehlen 144).

271.10 **It's a circus:** Cf. *AILD*, where Jewel Bundren's horse, a descendent of the Texas ponies is referred to as "a durn circus animal" (105).

271.24-30 **the horses stood in a restive clump, larger than rabbits and gaudy as parrots...quiet as doves:** Eddins relates this episode to the metamorphosis of the dogs in the Proteus chapter of Joyce's *Ulysses*. The humor, he points out, arises from the ridiculous prospect of transforming these insubstantial, exotic creatures into farm animals. The men of Frenchman's Bend are mistaken in believing that the stuff of illusion can be subsumed for the purposes of reality (24).

272.4 you broom-tailed, hay-burning sidewinders: A sidewinder is "a rattlesnake of the...deserts of the southwest (*Crotales cerastes*), named for its way of progressing over loose sand. The Texan would know about sidewinders...but the word would not be in the vocabulary of Frenchman's Bend" (Brown 178).

272.20 "Hipps," the other said. "Call me Buck": See Richard Parker for an examination of the implications of Buck Hipps's name. He is associated primarily with sexual potency: the buck is a male animal, the hips are located in the region of sexual activity, and the pearl-handled pistol is symbolically suggestive. Parker argues that Flem, who is sexually impotent, must contract surrogates to carry out his aggressive programs (11-12). Meriwether remembers an English bawdy song, common among soldiers, with the refrain: "No balls at all,/No balls at all,/She had married a man who had no balls at all." The euphemized version of the song substitutes "hips" for "balls" (Meriwether, Interview 6/2/94).

273.10 the yellow teeth cropped: Onoe examines Faulkner's recurrent use of this image, borrowed from Eliot's "Sweeney Erect," in an essay on the Eliotic influence on Faulkner (51-52). Cf. "Sweeney Erect":
>This withered root of knots of hair
>Slitted below and gashed with eyes
>This oval O cropped out with teeth...(13-15, noted Onoe 51).

The image in the Eliot poem is associated with illicit, diminished sexuality. While Sweeney lathers his face, the prostitute on the bed has an epileptic seizure. Cf. *AILD*: "Jewel kicks him in the stomach; the horse arches his neck back, crop-toothed; Jewel strikes him across the face with his fist and slides onto the trough and mounts upon it" (13, noted Onoe 51). Cf. *AILD*: "*Its head flashes back, tooth-cropped; its eyes roll in the dusk like marbles on a gaudy velvet cloth as he strikes it upon the face with the back of the curry comb*" (183, noted Onoe 51). In both of the *AILD* allusions to Eliot's poem, Faulkner carries over the connotation of sexuality in relation to Jewel's relationship with his horse. Cf. the description of one of Popeye's cohorts in *Sanc*: "...the whole lower part of his face seemed to be cropped with teeth of an unbelievable whiteness and size" (282, noted Onoe 51). Cf. Elmer's visit to the schoolteacher in "A

Portrait of Elmer": "She was grinning now as if her thick face had been wrung and fixed in that tragic image, and Elmer, unable to move, seemed to drag his eyes heavily up the black, shapeless skirt, up the white shirtwaist pinned at the throat with a barpin of imitation lapis lazuli, meeting her eyes at last. He grinned too and they stood facing one another, cropping the room with teeth" (618, noted Onoe 52). Cf. the glances of two Paris streetwalkers in "A Portrait of Elmer": "...the grave one stares at Elmer in stoic invitation, the other one crops her goldtrimmed teeth at him before he looks quickly away" (631, noted Onoe 52). Onoe finds that the *Ham* appropriation of the image is not sexually allusive (52). I find its use at this point in the *Ham* narrative to be highly suggestive. The men are attracted to the horses as surrogates for their diminished virility, and the use of this image, with its connotations of raw attraction, points up the debasement of love in their world.

273.22-24 a second horse slashed at his back, severing his vest from collar to hem...severs a floating veil with one stroke: Cf. Sir Walter Scott's *The Talisman*: "...he undid the veil he had hitherto worn, laid it double along the edge of the sabre, extended the weapon edgeways in the air, and drawing it suddenly through the veil...severed that also into two parts, which floated to two different sides of the tent" (329, noted Harkness 164). Showett suggests an alternative source for the quote from Scott, Edward Mayes's *Lucius Q. C. Lamar: His Life, Times, and Speeches*. In 1875, Lamar, who was a Congressman, addressed a crowd in Tippah County at Falkner's Station. Faulkner's great-grandfather then made a speech after Lamar's. Mayes's biography records a speech made during the same campaign to the state legislature in which Lamar, in defending the color line in southern life, compared it to the battle between King Richard and Saladin: "When Richard reared his battle-ax on high and made the fearful blow, Saladin drew his scimitar, snatched a gauzy silken veil, threw it in the air, and with one stroke of his keen and trenchant blade cut its fold asunder as it descended" (noted 153). *FA* points toward another source for the image: "...as he sprang free, a second horse slashed his vest down the back from neck to hem as neatly as ever D'Artagnan could have done it with his rapier..." (25). One of Dumas père's three musketeers is called D'Artagnan.

273.33-34 you transmogrified hallucinations of Job and Jezebel: Job, the eponymous protagonist of the Book of Job, in the third division of the Hebrew Bible, is a righteous man whose faith is tested by his creator. God

173

visits on Job and his family a series of calamities that shake the foundations of his belief. After he has suffered inordinately, Job bemoans his plight to three friends who come to console him. Their discussion takes up the problem of continuing evil in the world and the possibilities for justice, both pertinent to the concerns of *Ham*. Next, the young Elihu offers advice, and finally God himself arrives to chastise Job for his shaky faith and to restore him and his family to their former prosperity (*Anchor Bible Dictionary* 3:858-67). Jezebel is the foreign wife of Ahab, herself a powerful queen who is presented negatively in biblical narrative. Upon hearing that her entire family has been annihilated, she is said to have "painted her eyes and adorned her hair" (2 Kings 9:30-37) and ridiculed her enemy from an upstairs window. Traitorous harem eunuchs pitched her to her death from the window. Although Jehu ordered a burial for her, the dogs had already eaten everything but her feet, skull, and hands (*Anchor Bible Dictionary* 3:848). Hipps's humorous comparison of the ponies to metamorphosed biblical figures associated with anguish, defilement, and betrayal implicitly acknowledges their dangerous potential.

274.4-5 managed to saw the mules about and so lock the wheels: According to Walton, "a mule-drawn wagon is built so that the wheels on the front of the wagon will not go under the bed of the wagon without rubbing on the bottom of the wagon bed. By pulling the wagon lines strongly and forcing the animals to turn more sharply than they should, one can cause one of the wagon wheels to lock itself because of its rubbing the underside of the bed of the wagon" (66).

274.9 blacksnake whip: "a long whip made of braided leather" (Brown 32).

274.22-23 as though trying to hang itself: See 39.21-23 for similar association of horses and the male desire to own them as antithetical to life.

274.32 tail-gate: "the removable plank forming the back of a wagon box" (Brown 196).

275.8-9 They whipped and whirled about like dizzy fish in a bowl: The association of horses and fish was part of the spotted horses material from its inception in *FA*: "The ponies yet streaked like wild fish back and forth through the growing dusk..." (28). The *Scribner's* version of the story

eliminates the image. Howell traces the complex literary pedigree of this metaphor to the mermaids envisioned by Prufrock in the final lines of Eliot's poem:
> I have seen them riding seaward on the waves
> Combing the white hair of the waves blown back
> When the wind blows the water white and black.
>
> I have lingered in the chambers of the sea
> By sea-girls wreathed with seaweed red and brown
> Till human voices wake us and we drown (p.7, noted Howell 214).

When Faulkner appropriated the sea-girl image as a figure for the fantastical, which can be life-denying, he converted the mermaids to ponies:
> Soft the breeze, a steady flame...
> ...comb[s] the wave-ponies' manes back
> Where the water shivers black... (*MF* p. 37, noted Howell 215).

The aspiring poet of "Carcassonne" again links horses and the sea: "Bones might lie under seas, in the caverns of the sea, knocked together by the dying echoes of the waves. Like bones of horses cursing the inferior riders who bestrode them....But somebody always crucified the first-rate riders. And then it's better to be bones knocking together to the spent motion of falling tides in the caverns and the grottoes of the sea" (897, noted Howell 217). Cf. *AILD*: Vardaman's repeated assertion that *"Jewel's mother is a horse. My mother is a fish"* (196, noted Howell 222).

276.6-14 The moon was almost full then...treacherous and silvery receptivity...mirage-like clumps...hooves: Eddins identifies two modes of experience and image in the "Spotted Horses" episode. The first is associated with utility, reality, and pragmatism and is best exemplified by Mrs Littlejohn, with her wash pot and dinner bell. The second mode is represented by most of the males of Frenchman's Bend and is tied to images and objects suggesting illusion, frivolity, and ephemera: moonlight, mirage, camouflage, phantoms, pinwheels, kaleidoscopes, etc. (passim). The men are emotionally and physically endangered when they mistake one form of experience for another.

The mule that invades Mannie Hait's yard in the 1934 short story, later incorporated into *Twn*, shares characteristics with the spotted horses. It appears with "apparition-like suddenness" (*CS* "Mule in the Yard" 250) and it is "wraithlike" (251).

277.6-11 The pear tree across the road opposite was now in full and frosty bloom...like the separate upstreaming hair of a drowned woman...windless and tideless sea: Faulkner regularly associates trees and women. Cf. *Marionettes*: "She is like a slender birch tree stripped by a storm, she is a birch tree shivering at dawn upon a dim wood; no, she is like a young poplar between a white river and a road" (43-44). Cf. Margaret's connection of Cecily with a pear tree in *SP*: "Across the garden, beyond a street and another wall, you could see the top of a pear tree like a branching candelabra, closely bloomed, white, white...She stirred, crossing her knees. 'That girl fainting though'..." (107). Elmer's sister Jo stands watching their rented house burn, "starkly poised as a young ugly tree" (*Elmer* 6). In *Mosq*, Mr. Talliaferro is "conscious of the clean young odor of [Patricia Robyn], like that of young trees" (22). Caddy Compson also "smell[s] like trees" (*S&F* 7), according to Benjy, and she climbs a blooming pear tree in her muddy drawers. Cf. Benjy's image of her in the tree: "*Then I saw Caddy, with flowers in her hair, and a long veil like shining wind*" (47). Cf. *SP* for an early linkage of trees and the sea: "...trees were rigid as coral in a mellow tideless sea" (290).

277.37 a mockingbird: The state bird of Mississippi, the mockingbird (*Mimus polyglottos*) is a medium-sized, gray and white thrush that is famous for its vigorous and versatile song. It sings continuously, with night singing especially prominent during the breeding season. It is a skilled mimic, and typically incorporates mocked sounds into its own species-specific song pattern (Brown 131, Campbell and Lack 357-58). The irony of the mockingbird's singing its mating song while the men of Frenchman's Bend fall prey to the treacherous allure of the ponies is apparent. In *FA*, a mockingbird sings "like a resurgent phantom of old forgotten springs" in an apple tree (29).

278.3 gum: "a large tree (*Liquidambar styraciflua*) which exudes from wounds or cuts, a viscous, highly aromatic gum that is chewed like chewing gum by children and country people" (Brown 195).

278.4 Gum is the first tree to put out: bud: the sweet gum puts out winter buds (Preston 241).

278.7 willow: any of a number of swamp and moisture-loving trees and shrubs of the genus *Salix*. Most can be easily recognized by their long, narrow leaves. The willow also buds in winter. Although the genus comprises around 170 species, only fifteen of them could be classified as trees (Preston 130).

278.10 **grub up:** To grub up is to excavate with a grubbing hoe, or mattock, a digging tool with a strong, thin, flat blade set at right angles to a handle.

278.23 **Wallstreet:** Admiral Dewey in *FA*.

279.5-8 **I would be afraid to touch it for fear it would turn out to be a painted dog or a piece of garden hose...possession of it:** Eddins focuses on the unbridgeable gap between the items of comparison: tiger/dog and snake/garden hose (24). The difference, he argues, points up the mistake of trying to convert illusions into reality.

279.13-14 **purled:** flowed or rippled with a murmuring sound.

280.4 **trim:** swindle.

280.21 **without:** unless.

280.22 **staid:** variant spelling of stayed.

281.5 **wagon stakes:** "a stake driven vertically into a metal bow (stake iron) mounted on the side of a wagon bed or box or both" (Brown 210).

282.11 **snapping turtle:** "a savage turtle (*Chelydra serpentina*) which snaps with lightning speed and hangs on tenaciously. It weighs up to 30 lbs..." (Brown 182).

282.11 **moccasin:** a generic term for cottonmouths (water moccasins) and copperheads (highland moccasins) (Conant and Collins 226). Here, it is a water moccasin.

282.24 **shelled corn:** grains removed from the cob (Brown 174).

283.6 **downrush of flames:** Howell connects flames to the image complex that Faulkner early in his career came to associate with horses and ponies (216). See note Book Four, Chapter One for "As I Lay Dying" source material.

283.18-20 revealing at last the gaping orifice and the little boy still standing in it, unscathed, his eye still leaned to the vanished knothole: In *FA*, the wave of ponies rushes over Admiral Dewey, leaving him "untouched in the center of the doorway" (36). Cf. Ratliff's retrospective narration of this incident in "Spotted Horses": "It ain't no need to worry about that boy," I says. "He's charmed." He was right behind Eck last night when Eck went to help feed them. The whole drove of them jumped clean over that boy's head and never touched him. Eck snatched him into the wagon and taken a rope and frailed the tar outen him" (*US* 174).

283.34-35 If you're going to whip him, you better whip the rest of us too and then one of us can frail hell out of you: In *FA*, Admiral Dewey gets a spanking: "'Aint I told you?' Eck repeated whitely, laying on Admiral Dewey with the doubled rope, 'Aint I told you?' Admiral Dewey lifted his voice and wept, and his father presently exhausted his justified paternal relief and the boy wriggled free and tenderly caressed his diminutive overalls with two dirty hands, and presently his tribulation had passed away and beneath his pale golden thatch his periwinkle eyes were like two patches of spring after rain" (36).

283.35 frail: chiefly southern: to thresh, as grain (*DARE*); to whip, flail.

285.17-19 with an impenetrable surface quality like flint, as though the surface were impervious or perhaps there was nothing behind it: See note 22.4.

285.17 flint: "a very hard, fine-grained quartz that sparks when struck with steel" (*AHD*). Flint is also used colloquially to refer to the hard grains of early corn that will not dent (*DARE*).

285.21 forked: bestrode (Brown 85).

285.23 crowbait: "horses good only for carrion to attract crows into range for shooting" (Brown 64).

287.1 four bits: fifty cents.

287.3 **fiddle-head horse:** "having a head shaped like a violin" (*DARE*).

287.14 **cockle-burrs:** "the spring seeds of either one of two species of *Xanthium*. They are distributed (and make nuisances of themselves) by sticking to clothing and to the hair of dogs, the manes and tails of horses, etc." (Brown 55).

287.15 **the sawn half of a wooden hogshead:** A hogshead is a large wooden container for vinegar or cider, a barrel, a cask (*DARE*).

287.21 **wall-eyed:** "having eyes showing an abnormal amount of white" (Brown 211); "a form of strabismus in which the visual axis of one eye deviates from that of the other" (*AHD*).

288.13 **metal-ridged washboard:** "a board with a ridged metal surface on which clothes are rubbed when being washed" (Brown 211).

288.26 **a kaleidoscope:** "a tube-shaped optical instrument that is rotated to produce a succession of symmetrical designs by means of mirrors reflecting the constantly changing patterns made of bits of colored glass at one end of the tube" (*AHD*). Eddins connects the fluctuant reality of the toy to the theme of metamorphosis that he foregrounds (25).

289.2-3 **You couldn't buy that much dynamite for just fifteen dollars:** Buck's advertisement supports the view that this sort of dreaming is dangerous.

289.32 **over-topped:** outbid (Brown 143).

289.34 **baling wire:** "the thin, flexible wire with which bales of hay are fastened. It is the general-purpose light wire for temporary or clumsy repairs about a farm" (Brown 24).

289.37-39 **It contained a woman in a shapeless gray garment and a faded sunbonnet, and a man in faded and patched though clean overalls:** Mr. and Mrs. Henry Armstid make their first appearance. The roles they play in the novel do not differ in any substantial way from their function in *FA* (40-68), "As I Lay Dying" (372-79), "Spotted" (168-82), "Lizards" (136-151), *Twn* (7-8, 34, 271, 292), or *Mans* (138). However, in other works they are not the downtrodden and crazed characters that they remain in the Snopes material. In *AILD*, Armstid puts the Bundrens up after they have crossed the river; his hospitality includes offers of whiskey and of his team (173-175). In *LA*, Lena Grove is picked up by the Armstids and taken home with them for the night. Although Mrs. Armstid does not approve of her condition, she nevertheless breaks into the money she earns selling eggs and gives the savings to Lena (6-21). The current dates of *AILD* and *LA* are the years in which they were published: 1930 and 1932. Because *Ham* was originally set in the 1890's, the Armstid family of *AILD* and *LA* is probably not the same one. Will Varner also appears in *AILD*, so it is also possible, in that novel, that Faulkner transferred characters without considering the time differential between the novels. It is the heightened role of the Armstids in *Ham* that allows the spotted horse story the dualistic effect that some critics have noted (Jehlen 144, Wheeler 80). Alongside the hilarity and mayhem caused by the escaped ponies, Faulkner sets the serious and painful consequences suffered by the Armstid family.

290.14-15 **One dollar? Did I actually hear that?**: In *FA*, Buck Hipps adds: "Why a dollar wont pay fer the vest that hoss cut offen me yistiddy" (43).

291.1 **he aint no more despair**: *DARE* cites Brown (70): "...my colleague, Mrs. Tyus Butler, tells me that about 1920 she had an old Negro nurse who had been brought up near Griffin, Ga....who frequently said of someone: 'He ain't no more to spare than to' do something foolish. The word to be understood after more was something like sense, gumption, or brains. I feel certain that this is the expression intended here and that to spare was mistaken for despair somewhere along the line of transmission."

291.23-24 **"Then if you were just starting the auction off by giving away a horse, why didn't you wait till we were all here?"**: The dramatic effect of the Armstids' arrival is heightened in *Ham* by their delayed entrance. In *FA* and "Spotted Horses," they are already present among the onlookers when the Texan gives Eck a horse.

291.25-27 **He raised the empty carton...or perhaps a deadly insect**: Cf. "Spotted Horses": "He taken out that gingersnap box and held it up and looked into it, careful, like it might have been a diamond ring in it, or a spider" (*US* 170).

291.33-34 **"So Eck's going to get two horses at a dollar a head,"** the newcomer said: Buck Hipps makes this comment in both *FA* and "Spotted Horses." Cf. *FA*: "Y'all are foolin', boys. I ask you, now: Is that any way fer a man to act at a arction sale of livestock guaranteed sound and hearty and willin'? Two dollars is bid: I got to except it, but are you boys goin' to stand thar and see Eck git two hosses fer a dollar a head? Air you?" (43). Cf. "Spotted Horses": "'Well. Two dollars. Two dollars. Is your pulse all right, Eck?' he says. 'Do you have ager-sweats [chills and fever; ague] at night, maybe?' he says. 'Well,' he says, 'I got to take it. But are you boys going to stand there and see Eck get two horses at a dollar a head?'" (*US* 170).

291.37 **not looking at anything:** *FA* continues: "a quiet tragic figure with eyes that saw nothing and held nothing but the dead ashes of an instinct become habitual and compulsory" (43).

291.38 **chaps:** babies or children (Wentworth, *American Dialect Dictionary*).

292.7 **the woman said:** *FA* adds: "with her dull and infinite patience" (43).

292.17 **"Mister," she said:** *FA* follows with: "without passion, and she raised her gaunt face and looked at Buck soberly with her faded and empty eyes" (43).

292.24 **hisn:** colloquial: his.

292.36-37 **get me a box of gingersnaps:** In *FA*, the Texan's request is followed with a lyrical passage: "Again the sun came level across the earth and into the apple tree among the blooms and bees and upon the wagons lined along the road, and the horses and mules tethered among them and among the locust trees. Buck yet on his gate post, the loungers in faded negligent blue in easy inert attitudes beyond the spaces between whose heads, ceaseless fluid gleams like gaudy and patched calico" (44).

292.38-293.4: **Flem Snopes was there now...standing there in his small but definite isolation:** Flem Snopes is absent from the auction in *FA*. See also note 71.8-13.

293.9 **three dollars and a half to eleven and twelve dollars:** "a dollar and seventy-five cents to eight dollars" in *FA* (45). Faulkner follows this in *FA* with another lyrical passage: "The beasts were weary too, after the long foodless day of sunlight and voices in monotonous rise and fall and quiet constant human faces watching them always. Above, the bowl of the sky hushed itself into mysterious ineffable azures and the apple tree where tethered horses stamped and gnawed was like a candelabra tinged faintly with pink and gold. No mockingbird, though. The bystanders stood and lounged timelessly and patiently one with the grave rhythm of the earth, talking among themselves in sparse monosyllables" (45).

293.17-18 **she sat grey in the grey garment:** Millgate contrasts the shapeless, colorless dresses of Mrs. Armstid and her ilk with the "fresh dresses of afternoon" (257.18-19) that the Jefferson ladies wear as they rock on their porches (193).

293.24 **the mad look in his eyes:** In "Spotted Horses," Armstid looks "more like a mad dog than ever" after the auction (*US* 171).

293.31 **"Take your horse then":** *FA* continues with an emphasis on the contest of wills between Buck and Henry: "Buck answered coldly, and their glances clashed, and it was Henry who looked away. He stood with his head slightly bowed, tasting despair and rage, swallowing it like a delicate warm salt, brooding his baffled eyes upon the drooping gaudy huddle of the beasts without seeing them" (46).

294.6 **chinaberry tree:** "an oriental tree (*Melia azedarach*) often planted in dooryards in the South and often escaped into the wild." It produces purple flowers that have an unpleasant odor and that cluster in May and June (Petrides 147).

294.7 **swallows:** "1. any of various small, graceful swift-flying passerine birds of the family Hirundinidae, having long, pointed wings, a usually notched or forked tail, and a large mouth for catching flying insects and noted for their regular migrations in large numbers, often over long distances 2. Any of various similar birds, such as a swift" (*AHD*).

294.24-25 **The wife stood motionless between them:** *FA* follows with: "It was as though she had left her body for the time" (47).

294.27-28 The other men did not look at her at all, at her or Henry either: Gold cites this passage as evidence that Snopesism is not an alien force in Frenchman's Bend. The inhabitants are, like Flem, self-interested and unwilling to involve themselves in the lives of others (318). See note 71.8-13.

294.32-34 the wife followed... she moved without inference of locomotion, like something on a moving platform, a float: See 174.20-22.

295.14-15 the husband turned and struck her with the coiled rope: Mink also strikes his wife twice. See 221.10-18.

295.20-22 Only Flem Snopes was still watching...standing in his little island of isolation: At this point in the action of *FA*, Flem appears among the bystanders (48). See note 292.38-293.4.

295.22 it soared past her: See note 173.25-26.

296.39 snuff-colored dust: Snuff is a warm reddish-brown, the color of tobacco.

297.11-12 That leaned along the fence...as though the fence were in another land, another time: Faulkner continues to stress the dreamy insubstantiality of the action. This metaphor paraphrases Marlowe's *Jew of Malta*:
>Thou hast committed-
>Fornication: but that was in another
>>country,
>
>And besides, the wench is dead.

Faulkner would have been familiar with the phrase in the original, but he would also have seen it as the epigraph to Eliot's "Portrait of a Lady" and as the title to a Hemingway short story, "In Another Country" (Adams, *Myth and Motion* 11). Faulkner appropriated the entire Marlowe quote in *A Fable* (70). See Bartlett, "Other Countries, Other Wenches" for a discussion of twentieth century borrowings of the quote.

298.8-9 "If it dont suit you, you can ride one of the mules back to Texas": Parker comments on the aptness of Buck Hipps's being provided with a vehicle that no one would want, since he has just done the same thing to the men of Frenchman's Bend (12). In *FA*, the Texan swaps his remaining two mules for a buckboard, satisfied to trade for anything with four wheels (50). The sense in that story is that he has determined that it is time to move on, while in *Ham*, Flem is obviously clearing him out. In "Spotted Horses," he also swaps for a buckboard.

298.17 **vigilance committee:** "a voluntary association of men professing to supplement the efforts of the police and the courts in maintaining order, punishing crime, etc." (Matthews, *A Dictionary of Americanisms*).

298.20 **look-see:** "a look around, an inspection" (Partridge).

299.5-7 **"He'll be lighter when he gets there...His pockets wont rattle:** The men of Frenchman's Bend know that Buck Hipps is Flem Snopes's proxy, and they assume that Flem will have collected the profits of the horse transactions from the Texan.

300.2-3 **The pear tree before Mrs. Littlejohn's was like drowned silver now in the moon:** See 277.6-11. Cirlot notes that silver is the metal that is symbolically associated with moonlight (217).

300.10-11 **the ponies, huddled again, were like phantom fish:** See note 275.8-9.

300.30 **Them things will kill you:** Eck is the only man who consistently voices the danger inherent in the ponies. That, of course, does not stop him from spending the night trying to catch his own. The other voice of caution belongs to Mrs. Littlejohn.

302.7-8 **the gate which the last man through it had neglected to close:** In *Twn*, Ratliff identifies the man who left the gate open as Henry Armstid (34).

302.11 **hitch-reins:** "hitching strap, a strap that was used for hitching a horse to a post, tree, etc. but was not a part of the regular harness" (Brown 103).

302.30-33 **They saw the horse the Texan had given them whirl and dash back and rush through the gate into Mrs Littlejohn's yard and run up the front steps...vanish through the front door:** The violation of order suggested by the intrusion of an animal into the house recalls George Washington Harris's "Sicily Burns's Wedding." The bull Sock, provoked to hysteria by Sut Lovingood, bursts through a wall of the Burns house during Sicily's wedding banquet and wreaks havoc (90-97). Cf. also Harris's "Mrs. Yardley's Quilting," in which a wall-eyed horse escapes confinement, heads for the house, and leaves behind a path of destruction (134-148). The narrator of "The Liar," known for his "fabling" (*NOS* 173), recounts the story of a hill family that runs over Old Man Mitchell's buggy, tears it apart, and scares his horse off. All night long, according to the liar, they can be heard "whooping and hollering" as they try to "head that hoss into something with a fence around it. They say he run right through old Mis' Harmon's house" (173). Cf. a 1943 story outline that Faulkner completed for Warner Brothers in which a pet pig invades the local church: "One Sunday the pig gets out, follows the family to church, enters the church. A scene follows, in which the congregation and the two boys try to catch the pig, which darts among the pews, until the whole church is in an uproar. At last the pig is captured" (*Country Lawyer* 33).

302.38 **melodeon**: a small reed organ (*AHD*).

302.38-303.1 **it produced a single note, almost a chord, in bass, resonant and grave, of deep and sober astonishment**: Cf. the sound engendered when Mrs. Hait's cow is chased into the cellar by I. O. Snopes's mule in "Mule in the Yard": "there came an indescribable sound of shock and alarm by shed and beast engendered, analogous to a single note from a profoundly struck lyre or harp" (*CS* 251).

303.2 **antic shadow**: See note 182.1-11.

303.3-8 **It was a bedroom; Ratliff in his underclothes and one sock and with the other sock in his hand....Then he sprang through the window as the horse backed out of the room and into the hall again**: Ratliff's encounter with the horse figures more prominently in "Spotted Horses":

Anyway, I was in my room, in my underclothes, with one sock on and one sock in my hand, leaning out the window when the commotion busted out, when I heard something run into the melodeon in the hall; it sounded like a railroad engine. Then the door to my room come sailing in like when you throw a tin bucket top into the wind and I looked over my shoulder and see something that looked like a fourteen-

foot pinwheel a-blaring its eyes at me. It had to blare them fast, because I was already done jumped out the window (*US* 174-75).
Ratliff repeats the story of his escape from the runaway horse in *Twn* 34.

303.14.17 "**Get out of here, you son of a bitch," she said. She struck it with the washboard....Eck and the boy now stood**: The two worlds of *Ham*, masculine and feminine, come together dramatically when Mrs. Littlejohn crowns the spotted horse, emblem of frivolity and dream, with her washboard, emblem of utility and reality.

304.11 **slewed:** "to swing around" (Partridge).

305.11-13 "**I'll declare," she said. "You men**": Mrs. Littlejohn, with her steady, purposeful activity, is opposed throughout the spotted horse episode to the kaleidoscopic motion of the men. She maintains a detached and contemptuous attitude toward the prevailing masculine folly. Hoffman compares Mrs. Littlejohn's domestic business to Andromache and her women washing clothes in the stream as Hector and the Trojan warriors prepare to go to war in *The Iliad* (noted 102-3).

305.23-25 "**Go get Will Varner," Mrs. Littlejohn said. "I reckon you can tell them it's still a mule**": Following this comment in "Spotted Horses," Mrs. Littlejohn adds: "Except maybe a mule's got more sense" (177). Faulkner often joins mules and men in opposition to the female. Cf. "Mule in the Yard": "Toward this sound Mrs. Hait sprang, immediately, as if by pure reflex, as though in invulnerable compact of female with female against a world of mule and man" (*CS* 251).

305.25 **crossed the veranda:** *FA* continues: "into the pallid refulgence of the moon. The apple tree raised its virginal transience, haunting as a forgotten strain of music frozen into fragile and fleeting permanence, still as a dream, as austere and passionate and fine" (60).

305.32-33 "**He went through that house quick," Ratliff said. "He must have found another woman at home**": Ratliff suggests that even the horse instinctively recognizes the feminine world as the antithesis of the masculine and as a curb on freedom.

306.8-18 **suddenly someone was standing in one of them. It was Flem Snopes's wife...waiting for no one**: The whole tragedy of the spotted horse episode is summed up in this image. While the men of Frenchman's Bend pursue phantoms in the moonlight, Eula Varner Snopes, the sacrificed local goddess, languishes lonely, distant, and abandoned, above the fray, waiting for no one. In positioning her at the window, Faulkner not only frames her in a static attitude that contrasts with the frenetic chase of the men, but he evokes other literary heroines who also gaze down from windows. In his own work, Morell suggests, Faulkner poses trapped women at windows to distinguish the barriers that separate "the interior world of the imagination and the blunt reality of the world outside" (305). Cf. "Miss Zilphia Gant," written in 1928 but not published until 1932: "The window was barred and in it...the farmers...would see a wan small face watching them, or, holding the bars, coughing" (US 371). Cf. "A Rose for Emily": "As they recrossed the lawn, a window that had been dark was lighted and Miss Emily sat in it, the light behind her, and her upright torso motionless as that of an idol" (CS 120). Cf. the third stanza of Poe's "To Helen" :

Lo! In yon brilliant window-niche
How statue-like I see thee stand!
The agate lamp within thy hand,
Ah! Psyche, from the regions which
Are Holy Land! (l. 11-15)

The "marble-like fall" of Eula's garment suggests a favorite poem of Faulkner's, "Ode on a Grecian Urn," and the distinction the speaker finally makes between real life and the "marble men and maidens overwrought" (l.42) on the urn. The adjective implies that Eula is subsumed into the perfection and permanence of art but at the expense of her life. Her detachment and supra-terrestrial position at the window also recall Rossetti's "The Blessed Damozel," who "lean[s] out/ From the gold bar of heaven" (ll. 1-2).

Balzac's Augustine, also partner in a mismatched marriage to a shopkeeper, is watched by the adoring eyes of an admirer as she is framed at a third story window in a state of undress. She, too, is compared to a work of art: "No expression of embarrassment detracted from the candor of her face, or the calm look of eyes immortalized long since in the sublime works of Raphael; here were the same grace, the same repose as in these Virgins, and now proverbial" ("At the Sign of the Cat and Racket" 701). The appearance of a face in the window of the desolate house also recalls the opening paragraph of *Eugenie Grandet*:

In some country towns there are houses more depressing to the
sight than the dimmest cloister, the most melancholy ruins, or

the dreariest stretch of sandy waste. Perhaps such houses as these combine the characteristics of all three, and to the dumb silence of the monastery they unite the gauntness and grimness of the ruin, and the arid desolation of the waste. So little sign of life or of movement is there about them, that a stranger might take them for uninhabited dwellings; but the sound of an unfamiliar footstep brings someone to the window; a passive face suddenly appears above the sill, and the traveler receives a listless and indifferent glance--it is almost as if the monk leaned out to look for a moment on the world (1).

After her marriage to Charles Bovary, Emma Bovary also sits at the window on an April evening, as the mist rises among the poplar trees, and thinks about her past (*Madame Bovary* 124-25).

Prior links the figure of Eula at the window on this April night to the parallel figure of Mink at the window of his jail cell (259.8-10).

306.15-18 to those below what Brunhilde, what Rhinemaiden on what spurious river rock...what topless and shoddy Argos: Onoe attributes the rhythmic interrogative pattern of this passage to King Pericles' addresses to his daughter Marina at the beginning and end of Eliot's poem of that title ("Some T. S. Eliot Echoes in Faulkner" 56):

What seas what shores what grey rocks and what islands
What water lapping the bow
And scent of pine and the woodthrush singing through the fog
What images return
O my daughter (ll.1-5).

What seas what shores what granite islands towards
    my timbers
And woodthrush calling through the fog
My daughter (ll.33-35).

Onoe notes Faulkner's first use of the pattern in a speech of Mr. Compson's in *AbAb!*: "what act of fate, destiny, what irrevocable sentence of what Judge or Arbiter between them since nothing less would do, nothing halfway or reversible would seem to suffice" (124, noted 57). He again adopted the pattern in *WP*: "who to say what Helen, what living Garbo, he had not dreamed of rescuing from what craggy pinnacle or dragoned keep" (124, noted Onoe 58). Onoe also links this passage to Dr. Faustus's famous speech in Marlowe's play: "Was this the face that launched a thousand ships,/ And burnt the topless towers of Ilium?"

(*Doctor Faustus* 7.1328-30, noted 61). See also 235.33-37.

306.16 **Brunhilde:** See note 146.38-147.3. Brünhilde was one of the Norse Valkyries, arbiters of fate whose power extended only to the field of battle. The Valkyries determined the victor in a battle and chose the slain warriors who were invited to feast with Odin afterward in Valhalla. In one version of the story, when Brünhilde incurs Odin's wrath, he pricks her with a magic thorn which plunges her into the deepest sleep. He then encloses her in a dwelling place surrounded by flames from which she can never escape. From that time on, Brünhilde is exiled from Valhalla and forced to live the life of a mortal woman, rather than a divine goddess (*New Larousse Encyclopedia of Mythology* 278-79). In Wagner's tetralogy, *The Ring of the Nibelung*, Wotan takes to wandering and fathers a child by the First Mother. This daughter, Brünhilde, is conceived by Wotan to be his helpmate, his true self. She is his dearest and most capable child. When Brünhilde rebels against her father, he is forced to punish her by depriving her of her immortality. He casts her into a deep sleep, protects her with her war shield, and abandons her within a wall of fire. The fire can only be penetrated, and Brünhilde rescued, by a hero, who will recognize that the flames are only illusory (Shaw, *The Perfect Wagnerite* 33-41).

306.16-17 **Rhinemaiden on what spurious river rock:** See note 146.38-147.3. Wagner's *Das Rheingold* opens in the depths of the Rhine river, where the Rhinemaidens cavort and sing in the vicinity of a rock of Rhine gold. This treasure can only be taken from the Rhine by a man who forswears love. When the maidens repulse the dwarf Alberic, he steals the gold instead. Wotan, at the same time, has commissioned the giants to build a castle for him, with the promise that he will deliver the goddess Freya and her love apples to them when the job is done. Wotan, with the help of the trickster, Loki, acquires Alberic's gold and offers it to the giants in lieu of Freya; they accept, and, for the second time, love is forfeited for money (Shaw, *The Perfect Wagnerite* 7-24).

306.17 **Helen:** The wife of King Menelaus of Sparta, Helen, was the most beautiful woman on earth. At the marriage of Peleus and Thetis, Eris, the uninvited goddess of discord, threw out a golden apple inscribed "For the fairest." Venus, Minerva, and Juno each claimed the apple and were sent to Mount Ida, where the shepherd Paris was instructed to award the apple to the fairest. The goddesses immediately set about bribing him for the prize; Venus, with her promise that the fairest woman in the land should be his, won. Protected by Venus, Paris sailed immediately for Helen and Sparta, where he was hospitably received by Menelaus. He eventually abducted the beautiful Helen, thereby causing the Trojan War (Bullfinch 251-175).

306.18 **Argos:** According to Euripides, before Helen and Menelaus, retreating from the Trojan War, reached Sparta, they landed at Argos, on the day that Orestes had just slain Clytemnestra and Aegisthus. Orestes wanted to kill Helen as well, because he held her responsible for all the disaster that had befallen his family. Apollo dissuaded him, carried Helen off, and, in this version, made her immortal (Grimal 177).

306.27 **drenched:** made an animal swallow a medicine (Brown 74).

306.27 **wormed:** "treat[ed] for an infestation of parasitic worms" (Brown 218).

306.27 **blistered:** applied a "blistering ointment to a horse as a form of veterinary treatment" (Brown 32).

306.28 **floated:** "file[d] down the points of a horse's teeth" (Brown 83).

307.1-3 **The moon...a pearled and mazy yawn in the soft sky, the ultimate ends of which rolled onward, whorl on whorl...surrounded:** The image of the whorling night sky suggests Van Gogh's "La Nuit etoilée" to Adams (*Faulkner: Myth and Motion* 124).

307.8-11 **Then the pear tree came in sight...make this year, sho:** See note 277.6-11.

307.8 **that tree:** an apple tree in *FA* (62).

307.9 **like exploding snow:** Cf. *MF*: "slow exploding oak and beech/ Blaze up" (p.41).

307.12 **"Corn'll make this year too," one said:** Brooks suggests that Faulkner's setting this practical comment against the "dreamily erotic" landscape impresses the reader with the potential for mystery in even the most mundane lives (*The Yoknapatawpha Country* 170). Millgate also believes that, within its lyrical context, the observation about the corn indicates that the men, for all their inarticulateness, are not insensitive to beauty (190). Prior, however, links the comment to the sacrifice of love and beauty to commerce, particularly in its juxtaposition with the image of Eula at the window, waiting for no one (244).

307.13-26 **A moon like this is good for every growing thing outen earth...feeling the moon:** Jack Houston and Lucy Pate also subscribe to the fertilizing properties of the full moon of April. See note 215.11-13. In *FA*, the Varners have only two sons at the time they conceive Eula and insure her gender in the moonlight (62). Varner continues by relating the fact that he and his wife were married in April, that he built their house himself, and that "there was a apple tree jest outside the winder. We used to lay there in the dark, a-watchin' it. Smellin' it, too" (62).

307.15 **mess of:** many.

307.26 **scrouging:** pushing, crowding, pressing (Brown 170).

308.7 **"There's another one on the creek bridge," one said:** *FA* continues: "The earth dreamed on, mysterious, rapturous, like a chord hushed, like an unborn chord held in suspension: the grave and tragic rhythm of the world" (62-63).

308.9-16 **"They'll get the money back in exercise and relaxation...provided he gets back home by then:** Varner's interpretation of the spotted horse shenanigans as a surrogate experience is original to *Ham*. Kartiganer proposes an unconventional reading of the spotted horses episode on the basis of this passage. Varner's comment, he argues, acknowledges that the men's participation in the auction is a sign of the "health and vitality of the community" (127).

308.19 **field trials:** "a test for young... hunting dogs to determine their competence in pointing and retrieving" (*AHD*).

309.23 **miniature ballet skirts:** miniature doll skirts in *FA* (63).

308.27 **Dead-eye Dick:** "a dead shot, an expert marksman" (Brown 69).

308.39 **sight draft:** a draft, or check, payable on presentation (*Dictionary* *of Americanisms).*

309.33 varmint: derived from vermin, a wild, unwanted, or destructive animal (Brown 208).

309.33-34 blaring its eyes at me: "to open the eyes widely; to stare widely" *(DARE).* Cf. *AILD:* "'You wont help me,' Jewel says, them white eyes of his kind of blaring and his face shaking like he had the aguer" (179).

310.1-311.19 If Flem had known how quick you fellows was going to snap...rope and catch it: In *FA,* the corollary to this discussion focuses not only on whether the horses were Flem's but on how much money he made in profits from the horse auction:
"Flem claims he never had no interest in them hosses."
Surratt emitted a crude abrupt sound of disparagement. "Does anybody yere believe that?"
The man with the peach spray removed it and spat. "Will anybody yere ever know no better? Flem haint a-goin' to tell."
I.O. Snopes cackled again, with a kind of secretive glee. "Aint he a beatin' feller, now?" he said with frank admiration. "Yes, sir, Flem aint a-goin' to tell how much he made on them hosses."
"And you needn't to pretend like you knowed, neither," Surratt told I. O. Snopes. "Flem aint a-goin' to tell you no quicker'n anybody else." I. O. Snopes continued to shake with niggard and secret mirth, rubbing his palms on his thighs. "Yes, sir," Surratt continued fretfully, "They wont nobody ever know how much he made on them hosses, but I got my opinion of a feller that'll bring a herd of wild cattymounts into a place and sell 'em to his neighbors, and ef I was..." (64-65).

309.37 Lump Snopes: I. O. Snopes in *FA* (64).

310.38-39 We done all admitted that you are too smart for anybody to get ahead of: See note 365.29-31.

311.11 Burtsboro Old Town: According to Brown, an imaginary place with no corresponding counterpart in northern Mississippi. The appended "Old Town," he notes, is a common Mississippi indicator that the location is "the early site of a town that has been moved or abandoned" (41).

313.9-11 You ought to know. This wont be the first time I ever saw you in their field doing plowing Henry never got around to. How many days have you already given them this year?: Beck cites this passage as one of many examples in which "the unassuming virtue of simple people provides the foil to evil" (*Faulkner* 12). Faulkner's "deep pessimism," he continues, "does not proceed from a denial of values but from a melancholy recognition of the great weight of evil opposition to very real values" (13).

313.15-16 "They're unlucky," the third said. "When you are unlucky, it dont matter much what you do": Cf. Faulkner's definition of luck in the early story, "Moonlight": "luck: that instant when desire and circumstance coincide" (*US* 495).

313.19-21 "He aint lazy," the third said. "When their mule died three or four years ago, him and her broke their land working time about in the traces with the other mule. They aint lazy": Henry Armstid provides the supreme example of a man whose humanity has been warped and distorted by poverty to the point that he has metamorphosed into an animal. See note 33.17. Cf. "Sut Lovingood's Daddy Acting Horse" for a comical model of this transformation: "I'll be hoss myself and pull the plow" (Harris 22). Cf. "Sut Lovingood's Chest Story" for its metaphorical linkage of a married couple to a team in harness: "I told you, George, that Sicily and her hoss, ole Capshaw, warn't agwine ter pull well in the same yoke, as soon as I seed that orful misfortinate start they got" (Harris 98). Cf. "Mississippi": "...and Sullivan's Hollow, a long narrow glen where a few clans or families with North Ireland and Highland names feuded and slew one another in the old pre-Culloden fashion yet banding together immediately and always to resist any outsider in the pre-Culloden fashion too: vide the legend of the revenue officer hunting illicit whiskey stills, captured and held prisoner in a stable and worked in traces as the pair to a plow mule" (*ESPL* 33).

314.2-3 the biggest gal gets the bar up and gets into bed herself with the axe--: In "Spotted Horses," Ratliff reports verbatim the overheard conversation in which Mrs. Armstid conveys this information to Mrs. Littlejohn (179).

193

314.32-33 But asking him wont do no hurt: "Spotted Horses" adds: "It might shame him. I dont reckon it will, but it might" (179).

315.18-317.26 Then he stopped, and all of them watched Mrs. Armstid approach...you cant beat him: Flem's refusal to refund Mrs. Armstid's money and his compensatory offering of sweetening for the chaps did not become part of the spotted horse material until Faulkner's 1928 attempts to tell the story under the title "As I Lay Dying."

315.29-30 Motionless, the gray garment hanging in rigid, almost formal folds like drapery in bronze: Faulkner continued to use the frieze, or statuary motif, which was central to his first published book, *MF*, to suggest questions of freedom and bondage.

316.10 locust: *Gleditsia triacanthos*, an erect, thorny tree with compound leaves. It bears small, clustered greenish-white flowers May-July (Petrides 126-27).

316.17 mourning doves: A soft, sandy-colored bird with a long tail bordered in white, the mourning dove, *Zenaida macroura*, is an abundant bird that is distinguished by its low, mournful cry (Bull and Ferrand 542).

317.3-5 "Here," he said..."A little sweetening for the chaps": McDaniel notes that "candy is a special, inexpensive treat in Yoknapatawpha to sweeten bitter days or console for loss or injury" (48). Old Bayard gives Old Man Falls a present of some tobacco and "a small sack of peppermint candy, of which he was inordinately fond" (*Flags* 70) whenever he walks into town. Roth Edmonds takes "a small sack of the soft cheap candy which he knew she [Molly] loved" (*GDM* 90, noted Taylor 81) when he stops for his monthly visit with Molly. After Lucas announces to the judge that he does not, after all, want a divorce, he makes Molly a present of "a small sack--obviously candy, a nickel's worth" (*GDM* 129, noted McDaniel 48). Ike McCaslin likewise leaves a present of "a small sack of peppermint candy which Sam had used to love" (*GDM* 328, noted McDaniel 48) at the grave of Sam Fathers. In *Reiv*, a woman injured by a shot in the buttocks is compensated by a bag of candy (11). See note 57.32.

317.22-24 a grey and blasted tree trunk moving, somehow intact and upright, upon an unhurried flood: Cf. the Captain in Cather's *A*

Lost Lady: "He looked like an old tree walking" (115).

318.1 St. Elmo: The candy-stealing episode survives intact from *FA*, but the perpetrator is Clarence in the earlier version.

318.3-38 Aint I told you...the gin and the blacksmith shop: St. Elmo literally enacts the metaphorical grazing activity of the Snopes clan. See note 70.8-10.

318.17-18 the tight overalls undulant and reluctant across his flabby thighs: See note 86.15-17.

318.36-319.4 a resemblance intangible, indefinite, not in figure, speech, dress, intelligence; certainly not in morals....Ratliff never: See note 42.31-27.

319.36 helling: causing a tremendous disturbance, noise, or great trouble (Partridge).

319.37 hen-hawk: More commonly known as the cooper's hawk, *Accipiter cooperii*, the hen hawk is an uncommon woodland species, blue-grey in coloration, that is prone to attacks on farm poultry, hence the name (*Terres* 480-81).

320.14-18 He was gone all day yesterday...I dont care if his name is Snopes, going to let his own blood kin rot in jail: Flem violates the code of his class and caste: the fealty to family over all other forms of social organization. Ab Snopes's warning to his son Sarty in "Barn" holds true for Flem: "You got to learn to stick to your own blood or you ain't going to have any blood to stick to you" (*CS* 8). Grimwood points out that Faulkner was writing the stories of *KG*, which also involve the concept of justice as it applies to the rural poor, at the same time that he was pulling together *Ham*. In the story "Tomorrow," Jackson Fentry upholds the kinship bond by shielding a foster son (Grimwood 188).

320.27-321.15 "I reckon you gave Henry Armstid back his five dollars too....I could do more, but I wont. I wont, I tell you!: Ratliff's outburst is inconsistent with his criticism of the apathetic response to Flem's intrusion at 71.8-13 (see note) and with his involvement in shutting down the Ike/cow peep show. See note 198.12-25.

In *FU*, Faulkner outlines three possible responses to the discovery of evil in *A Fable*: "What I was writing about was the trilogy of man's conscience represented by the young British Pilot Officer, the Runner, and the Quartermaster General. The one that said, This is dreadful, terrible, and I won't face it even at the cost of my life--that was the British aviator. The Old General who said, This is terrible but we can bear it. The third one, the battalion Runner who said, This is dreadful, I won't stand it, I'll do something about it" (62). Ratliff, at points in the Snopes work, embodies each of the available reactions. Millgate believes that Ratliff's agonized cry at the conclusion of this speech reveals the depth of his dilemma. He knows, on the one hand, that, as Millgate recognizes, "involvement hurts," and that he can protect himself from suffering by refusing to participate in the problems of Frenchman's Bend. On the other hand, he is a morally decent person who feels called to act (*Achievement* 199). Cf. Quentin's similarly negative response when Shreve asks him why he hates the South: "*I dont. I dont! I dont hate it! I dont hate it!*" (*AbAb!* 378, noted Millgate 198). Cf. the old Justice's final words in the trial of Tull v. Snopes: "I cant stand no more!...I wont! This court's adjourned!" (*Ham* 332.9-10, noted Beck, *Faulkner* 130). Greet links Ratliff's rejection of responsibility to Ike McCaslin's rejection of his inheritance in *GDM* (315).

321.16-17 **Hook your drag up; it aint nothing but a hill:** A drag is "any device for locking a wheel of a wagon or carriage making a steep descent" (Brown 73). Bookwright, as Brown notes, uses the expression metaphorically in urging Ratliff to calm down and not to exaggerate the significance of the situation.

323.8-10 **her clasped and motionless hands on her lap resembling a gnarl of pallid and drowned roots from a drained swamp:** Cf. Molly's hand in *GDM*: "she...raised one gnarled hand, like a tiny clump of gnarled and blackened roots, before her eyes" (101, noted Taylor 83).

323.26-28 **an outrage...directed...not at any other man in particular but at all men, all males:** Cf. the doctor's realization in *WP*: "it was not at him the hatred was directed. *It's at the whole human race*, he thought. *Or no, no. Wait. Wait*--the veil about to break, the cogs of deduction about to mesh--*Not at the race of mankind but at the race of man, the masculine*" (11). See note 149.20-21.

327.33 **far piece:** great distance. Cf. *LA*: "Sitting beside the road, watching the wagon mount the hill toward her, Lena thinks, I have come from Alabama: a fur piece" (1).

329.9-12 That's the law...within the definition of the law as provided: The inadequacy of the law in establishing order over the complexity and, often, chaos of human life is a subject that interested Faulkner. He often makes a distinction between the conflicting claims of legality and justice. While the outcome in Armstid v. Snopes hinges on perjury, in the second trial, Tull v. Snopes, it is the law itself, not human interference, that stands in the way of justice. See Polk's study of the law in Faulkner's work, "I Taken an Oath of Office Too." See note 150.21.

332.9-10 "I cant stand no more!" the old Justice cried. "I wont! This court's adjourned! Adjourned!": See note 320.27-321.15.

332.11-333.39 There was another trial then....Is Flem Snopes in this room? Tell that son of a bitch---: Flem's violation of the kinship bond sets in motion the chain of events that eventually leads to his murder in *Mans*. When retelling the story through the limited third person point of view of Mink Snopes in *Mans*, Faulkner excises the hope and faith that Flem will come back from Texas in time to save Mink from a certain guilty verdict:

> So he knew that Flem would not be there when he would need him, since he knew that Flem and his new wife would have to stay away from Frenchman's Bend at least long enough for what they would bring back with them to be able to call itself only one month old without everybody that looked at it dying of laughing. Only, when the moment finally came, when the instant finally happened when he could no longer defer having to pull the gun and aim the trigger, he had forgot that...and that too was one more injury which Jack Houston in the very act of dying had done him: compelled him, Mink, to kill at a time when the only person who had the power to save him and would have had to save him whether he wanted to or not because of the ancient immutable laws of blood kinship, was a thousand miles away (4-5).

332.22-23 having exhausted all his challenges before the State had made one: When drawing a jury in a criminal case, each side is allowed a certain number of peremptory challenges, or strikes without cause. It is not unusual for the defense lawyer to use up his peremptory challenges before the prosecuting attorney needs to use his.

333.28 **murder in the second degree:** voluntary manslaughter, an intentional killing committed in the heat of passion and so not subject to the more severe penalties reserved for murder, which is an intentional killing committed with malice aforethought.

333.29-30 **State Penal Farm:** Parchman Prison.

Book Four, Chapter Two: The story of Flem's ultimate triumph in Frenchman's Bend, the gulling of Ratliff, was the third of the Snopes stories to be published, in the February 27, 1932 issue of the *Saturday Evening Post* (12-13, 52, 57, noted Meriwether, *Literary* 41). The short story version, which was revised extensively for the novel, is titled "Lizards in Jamshyd's Courtyard," after the eighteenth quatrain of Fitzgerald's *Rubaiyat of Omar Khayyam*. In manuscript, the story was titled "Omar's Eighteenth Quatrain":

They say the Lion and the Lizard keep

The courts where Jamshyd gloried and drank deep:

And Bahram, the great Hunter--the Wild Ass

Stamps o'er his Head, but cannot break his Sleep (4th ed.).

The allusions to Jamshyd, a mythical "King Splendid" of Persia, and to Bahram, a Sassanian sovereign who had seven castles, each a different color (Fitzgerald 169), enhance the sense that the once-great Frenchman's Place is now inhabited by lesser creatures unable to appreciate its glorious past. The nineteenth quatrain is also significant:

I sometimes think that never blows so red

The Rose as where some buried Caesar bled;

That every Hyacinth the Garden wears

Dropt in her Lap from some once lovely Head (4th ed.)

The ironic counterpoint of the past's buried Caesars and the present's foolhardy diggers, creating their own graves, is certainly intended. Stark Young, a fellow Mississippian, alluded to the nineteenth quatrain in the title of his novel, *So Red the Rose*, which Faulkner also knew.

This chapter exposes Ratliff's vulnerability to certain kinds of pressures, after the previous chapter's proof of his invulnerability to others. He is correct in recognizing that the Frenchman's Place conceals wealth, but he is wrong in defining it in monetary terms. He gropes for but can't quite grasp the agrarian dream of harmony and order in a pastoral setting. However, the fact that he can dream links him to the other dreamers of the novel and separates him from Flem, who prospers because his mind is never befuddled by dreams. Faulkner highlights Ratliff's affinity for the gutted mansion in an excised passage from "Lizards": "Suratt knew the place. He knew it better than anyone suspected. Perhaps once a year he drove three or four miles out of his way to pass the place, entering from the back. Why he took that precaution he could not have said; he probably would have believed it was not to be seen doing something by which he had no expectation of gaining anything. Once a year he halted his buckboard before the house and sat in the buckboard to contemplate the austere skeleton somnolent in the summer sunlight, a little sinister, thinking of the generations of men who had dug for gold there, contemplating the inscrutable desolation of cedar and brier and crapemyrtle and calycanthus gone lush and wild, sensing out of the sunny and sinister silence the ancient spent and hopeful lusts, the optimism, the effluvium of the defunct greed and despair, the spent and sweet nocturnal sweat left upon the place by men as quiet now as the man who had unwittingly left behind him a monument more enduring than any obituary either carved or cast" (140). Ratliff recounts the tale of the buried money in the first chapter of *Twn* (7-8) and again in *Mans* (127, 138).

1: "Lizards in Jamshyd's Courtyard" begins with the conclusion of the salted mine story: the wagons of onlookers who arrive to watch Henry Armstid dig. Its section two is the germ of the goat deal that became Book One, Chapter Three, section two of *Ham*. Section three treats the divining scene with Uncle Dick. Section four brings in Eustace Grimm and Ratliff's realization that he has lost in the contest with Flem.

334.1 **Ratliff:** Suratt in the short story.

334.1 **Bookwright:** Vernon Tull in the short story.

334.22 **black-and-tan hounds:** a breed of coon hound (Brown 31).

335.9 **he's plumb crazy now:** Bookwright traces the causes of Armstid's insanity not to any inherent defect but to external stimuli: the forfeited five dollars, the vanished horse, the broken limb. See last glimpse of Henry Armstid at 366.24. In *Twn*, Henry Armstid is said to be "now locked up for life in a Jackson asylum" (292).

335.12 **There's something there:** Ratliff responds to the spell cast by an age-old dream. There is great wealth in the earth, but it is not what Flem planted there or what Armstid got out of it. See note 4.9-10. Cather achieves the same effect in Book Two of *My Ántonia* by juxtaposing the failed quest of the treasure hunter Coronado with the heroic potential of the life symbolized by a magnified plough. Jim Burden and the hired girls are picnicking on a summer Sunday, when Ántonia asks him to tell the story of Coronado and the search for the Seven Golden Cities. After Jim's recounting of Coronado's unsuccessful quest, the group looks toward the setting sun and sees "a great black figure": "On some upland farm, a plough had been left standing in the field. The sun was sinking just behind it. Magnified across the distance by the horizontal light, it stood out against the sun, was exactly contained within the circle of the disk; the handles, the tongue, the share--black against the molten red. There it was, heroic in size, a picture writing on the sun" (156). Caldwell's *God's Little Acre* begins with the figure of Ty Ty Walden, knee-deep in a hole he has dug while searching for buried gold on his land. He, like Ratliff, fails to perceive the true wealth of the land, so that "year by year the area of cultivated land had diminished as the big holes in the ground increased" (14).

335.20-24 **And I knowed it for sho when Flem Snopes took it...hardly raise goats:** In "Lizards," Flem actually purchases the old Frenchman's Place from Will Varner (140), while he obtains the deed in *Ham* as part of Eula's dowry.

336.25-36 **the old scar almost healed now where nearly fifty years ago a courier...time of the battle of Jefferson:** The first edition reads "thirty" (386), thus placing the action closer in time by twenty years to the Civil War. Kibler notes that the time scheme Faulkner intended calls into question the old Frenchman's anonymity. He would presumably have been living in his mansion in 1861, when the courier arrived with the news of Sumter, and he is said to have buried the money when "Grant overran the country" (*Ham* 4.9-11), so he must have remained at least until 1863. Will Varner, whose age is given as sixty (*Ham* 3.24), would have been around thirty-five at that time and would probably have known the Frenchman. See notes 3.24 and 98.26-7. Clearly, the relatively wealthy antebellum South is meant to seem remote from the bitter poverty of these poor white tenant farmers. The two references to slavery in this short passage may also call into question idealized versions of the southern past.

336.28 **news of Sumter:** The first shots of the Civil War were fired at Fort Sumter, off the coast of Charleston, South Carolina on April 12, 1861. After a thirty-four hour siege, the undersupplied Union forces under Major Robert Anderson surrendered (Foote, *Fort Sumter to Perryville* 44-50).

336.28 **barouche:** "a four-wheeled carriage with a collapsible top, two double seats inside opposite each other, and a box seat outside in front for the driver" (*AHD*).

336.33 **portmanteau:** "a large leather suitcase that opens into two hinged compartments" (*AHD*).

336.33 **body servant:** personal servant, as opposed to house servant or field hand.

336.36 **battle of Jefferson:** As Jefferson is a fictional place, there was, of course, no Battle of Jefferson, but the Union did suffer a debilitating loss at nearby Holly Springs. On 20 December 1862, Pemberton sent a division of mounted brigades, with General Earl Van Dorn in charge, against Grant's supply depot at Holly Springs. The daybreak raid destroyed approximately 1.5 million dollars in Union supplies (Foote, *Fredericksburg to Meridian* 20). The courthouse and other public buildings in Oxford were burned by withdrawing Federal troops on 22 August 1864, but no battle took place there. Ripley, a likely model for Jefferson, was in the vicinity of action in 1864. Union troops moved through Ripley and were met and defeated by Confederate General Bedford Forrest on the Ripley-Guntown Road at the battle of Brice's Crossroads (Foote, *Red River to Appomattox* 363-74).

337.17 **the garden:** Cf. the plantation garden, symbol of order in *Unv*: "the garden where Aunt Jenny puttered beside old Joby...among the coaxed and ordered beds, the quaint and odorous old names" (251). Kibler cites Miss Jenny's successful transplantation of Cape Jessamine (gardenia) cuttings from her Carolina garden as evidence that the decent and gentle style of life associated with cultivation of a garden will continue after the war (16). The assault on the Frenchman's garden suggests perhaps that the plantation ideal is no longer viable.

338.1 **persimmon:** *Diospyros virginiana*, a small to medium tropical tree with shiny, dark green leaves and a globous orange to purple fruit that is edible after the first frost (Preston 341).

338.11-12 The slope had probably been a rosegarden: The rose figures prominently in *The Rubaiyat*, not only in quatrain nineteen's connection with the soil where buried Caesars bled but also in its traditional association with evanescence: "Each Morn a thousand Roses brings, you say;/ Yes, but where leaves the Rose of Yesterday?" (IX).

339.17-18 His arms felt no larger than sticks: See Uncle Dick Bolivar's arms at 345.9-10. Taylor notes a similarity to Molly Beauchamp's arm in *GDM*: "no larger than the reed stem of the pipe she smoked" (100).

340.29-32 What do you suppose that old Frenchman did with all the money...silver spoons and jewelry: See note 4.9-10.

340.38-39 Uncle Dick Bolivar: The old mystic is unique to "Lizards" and to *Ham*. Braswell connects Uncle Dick Bolivar to the "oold man and a povre" (l. 713) of Chaucer's "Pardoner's Tale" who directs the "riotoures three" (l. 716) to a hoard of florins under a tree in a grove when they ask him to point the way to death (Braswell 68). See note 346.2-6. When Buck, one of Ty Ty Walden's sons in *God's Little Acre*, suggests "what we need is a diviner," his father dismisses the idea as a darky superstition (5).

343.18 frock coat: "a man's dress coat or suit with knee-length skirts" (*AHD*).

343.27-29 "Wait," he said. "There air anger in the yearth. Ye must make that ere un quit a-bruising hit": Armstid abuses the relationship that should exist between a farmer and the earth he works. Faulkner's concern with despoliation of the land reaches a peak in his next published novel, *GDM*.

343.37-38 "For what's rendered to the yearth, the yearth will keep until hit's ready to reveal hit": Cf. Molly's concern about Lucas's money hunting in *GDM*: "Because God say, 'What's rendered to My earth, it belong to Me unto I resurrect it. And let him or her touch it and beware'" (102, noted Taylor 82-3).

344.6-9 a forked peach branch, from the butt-end of which

something dangled on a length of string...a gold-filled human tooth: The forked branch is, according to Brown, standard in a rod like this, but the charms are "optional and highly idiosyncratic" (85). Uncle Dick Bolivar's divining rod is a less sophisticated version of the divining machine that Lucas Beauchamp buys with Roth Edmonds's mule. Cf. the description of the St. Louis salesman's divining machine in *GDM*: "an oblong metal box with a handle for carrying at each end, compact and solid, efficient and business-like and complex with knobs and dials" (81). Taylor notes that fake metal detectors were often advertised in pamphlets and newspapers as early as 1849 (74).

344.19-22 **They moved like a procession...mounting the slope gradually in overlapping traverses:** A similar procession scans the orchard in *GDM*: "all three of them watched the small cryptic dials in the flashlight's contracted beam as they worked back and forth across the orchard in parallel traverses" (93).

344.25 **agin:** against.

344.27-28 **That black one:** In *Mosq*, the character Faulkner is described as a "little kind of black man" (45). Temple Drake also describes Popeye as a "black man" (*Sanc* 48).

345.7-14 **Tech my elbers....You that didn't believe:** Elbers are elbows. Uncle Dick parodies Christ's injunction to Thomas: "Reach hither thy finger and behold my hands; reach hither thy hand, and thrust it into my side: and be not faithless, but believing" (John 20:27).

345.9-10 **arms thin and frail and dead as rotten sticks:** See note 339.17-18.

346.2-6 **They struggled for it, jerking it back and forth among them....Stop it! Aint we all three partners alike?:** Braswell finds several points of connection between the "Pardoner's Tale" in Chaucer's *Canterbury Tales* and "Lizards in Jamshyd's Courtyard." Both stories develop the Pardoner's explicit theme: *Radix malorum est Cupiditas* (l. 426). In both stories, the discovery of treasure leads to an outcome that is the reverse of what the participants expect. In "The Pardoner's Tale," the youngest of the riotoures is knifed by the other two, who in turn die by drinking from poisoned bottles. In "Lizards," the end is not quite so violent: madness for Armstid, financial and moral embarrassment for the other partners. Both stories feature a trio of hunters who vow allegiance to one another and to share equally the coins they find. The intervention of the supernatural is important to each; in both stories, this intervention comes in the person of an old man who has no interest himself in possessing the riches the younger men find. Finally, each story is set in motion by a ruthless character: the Pardoner, whose sole purpose is "for to wynne" (l. 461), and Flem, who has similar aims (Braswell 66-69). The dialect spelling in "Lizards," "pardners," is perhaps meant to hint at the Chaucer source.

346.19-20 "I feel four bloods lust-running," the old man said. "Hit's four sets of blood here lusting for trash": The fourth is Flem. Cf. Marlowe, *Dr. Faustus*: "This study fits a mercenary drudge/ Who aims at nothing but external trash" (I.i.32-33).

346.23 **Uncle Dick dont care nothing about money**: In "Lizard," this proves to be an accurate statement, but in *Ham*, the old man also gains, if only a dollar fee. See 348.26.

348.9-11 **The old man lay under a tree beside the ditch, asleep...the increasing dawn**: "Lizards" stresses Uncle Dick's innocence: "He slept quiet as a child, not even snoring" (147).

348.26 **paid the old man his dollar**: See note 346.23.

348.36 **Eustace Grimm**: Grimm's role in *Ham* and "Lizards" is the same. In Eustace Grimm's only other appearance in Faulkner's work, he brings a span of mules from Snopes to the Bundrens (*AILD* 183).

349.21-24 **I used to think I was too smart to be caught by anybody around here. But I dont know now...as bland and quizzical and impenetrable as ever**: Ratliff repeats this comment at 353.9-10. Cf. this scene in "Lizards": "Surratt joined the laugh readily. 'I reckon not. I reckon I'm still smart enough not to be caught by nobody around here except Flem Snopes. 'Course I take a back seat for Flem'" (147).

349.29-351.22 "**Eustace**," he said. "**You're strayed**"...."**See you boys tomorrow**": This scene is compressed and much more forthright in "Lizards":

Suratt looked briefly from face to face, his gaze pausing for an instant at Eustace Grimm, then going on. "To tell the truth, I am getting pretty durn tired of traipsing all over the country to make a living. Be durn if I ain't sometimes a good mind to buy me a piece of land and settle down like folks."

"You might buy that Old What-you-call-it place from Flem," Grimm said. He was watching Suratt. Suratt looked at him. When he spoke his tone was immediate, far superior to merely casual.

"That's a fact. I might do that." He looked at Grimm. "What you doing way up here, Eustace? Ain't you strayed a right smart?" (147).

349.27 **Lump Snopes:** In "Lizards," Flem himself plays the part assumed by his proxy, Lump, in *Ham*. In *Ham*, Ratliff is told by Freeman that Flem, his father-in-law, and their womenfolks have been in Jefferson and were expected back that morning (350.28-30).

350.12 **Winterbottom's:** Mrs. Littlejohn's in "Lizards" (147).

350.15 **druv:** drove.

351.19-20 **how even a Snopes was not safe from another Snopes:** See 88.4-10.

353.9-10 **I used to think I was smart, but now I dont know:** See note 349.21-24.

353.31 **"How much are you going to ask him for?" Snopes told him:** In "Lizards," the figure is set at three thousand dollars. Suratt offers to pay instead three hundred (148).

354.13 **"To start a goat ranch," Ratliff said:** Ratliff's comment, which is original to *Ham* version of the story, is a reminder to Flem that he has not yet proved himself superior to Ratliff.

354.18-20 **"That fellow, that teacher you had three-four years ago. Labove. Did anybody ever hear what became of him?":** The reference to Labove, who never went head-to-head with Flem but who nonetheless lost to him, is a reminder of the roster of the defeated in

Frenchman's Bend: Houston, Mink, Eula, Labove, Ike, the cow, the Armstids, Tull, all the horse traders. The final glimpse of Eula, in her tailor-made suit, serves the same purpose. See 362.15-37.

354.21-27 **A little after six that evening, in the empty and locked store, Ratliff and Bookwright and Armstid bought the Old Frenchman Place from Snopes...paid his third in cash:** In the "Lizards" version, Armstid trades not only the mortgage on his farm and "a chattel mortgage on his stock and fixtures," along with the fencing wire, but also, listed among the fixtures, a "new stove which his wife had bought with her weaving money" (150). *Mans* specifies the amount of Armstid's mortgage as $200, "less them five or six dollars or whatever they was where Henry's wife tried to keep them buried from him behind the outhouse" (138). Millgate comments on the irony that Ratliff, Flem's most dedicated opponent, should facilitate his move to Jefferson (196).

354.37 **Bookwright's house (he was a bachelor):** See inconsistency at 68.33-34: "'We all missed him,' Bookwright said. 'My wife aint mentioned nobody's new sewing machine in almost a year.'"

355.15 **It was Eustace Grimm:** At this point in the short story version, Faulkner reveals the kinship between Eustace Grimm and Flem Snopes.

357.35-37 **as though, still sleeping, they fled the weightless shadow of that for which, awake, they had betrayed themselves:** See note 55.4-6.

358.13 **while the familiar stars wheeled overhead:** A recurring image in Faulkner's work of circularity and re-enactment, the wheeling stars place the actions of humans within a cosmological framework. See note 183.33-34.

358.34-359.11 **Because something had clicked in his mind again...and the room had only the glow of the dying fire:** The click in Ratliff's mind is caused by his simultaneous realization of two things. First, he remembers, and Bookwright confirms, that "Eustace's ma was Ab Snopes's youngest sister" (360). Secondly, he realizes that no cloth sack would remain intact for so many years after it was buried. His suspicions are validated when he and Bookwright examine the dates on the coins. At this point, Ratliff knows that the dream is dead, its impossibility suggested by the high ruined room, the dying sun, the dying fire, and the dying year. Shakespeare uses, successively, the metaphors of the dying year, the dying day, and the dying fire in his "Sonnet 73" to convey the brevity of life.

359.29-34 **he could now see Armstid waist-deep in the ground as if he had been cut in two at the hips, the dead torso...as Armstid dug himself back into the earth...until he died:** This brilliant image ties in with the motif of metamorphosis that runs through the novel. Instead of becoming an animal, Armstid is a half-man becoming a dead man.

359.32 **metronome:** automaton in "Lizards" (150)

360.2-23 **"Odom," Ratliff said, "who was Eustace Grimm's wife?"..."I'm finished":** This twist of the plot, explaining the mysterious and suggestive presence of Eustace Grimm in the Frenchman's Bend environs, hinges on kinship. See note [Manuscript Opening]. See also note 320.14-18.

360.30-31 **"I reckon we ought to knowed wouldn't no cloth sack...fifty years":** Ratliff and his partners have fallen for the old salted mine scam. Cf. *Twn*: "'A salted gold mine,' Uncle Gavin said. 'One of the oldest tricks in the world and you fell for it. Not Henry Armstid: you'" (8). The salted mine trick works only when the victim's greed overcomes his judgment, as it has in this case. Lucas Beauchamp pulls off a successful salted mine scheme in *GDM*. Having traded Roth Edmonds's mule for a divining machine, Lucas then withdraws fifty dollars from the bank, salts an old orchard in two separate places, and tricks the salesman into returning the mule and giving him a bill of sale for the machine along with half the money he finds in the orchard (78-96). Hoffman suggests Mark Twain's youthful adventure at the Wide West silver ledge in *Roughing It* as a literary model for the "Lizards" episode (209ff, noted 105). Grimwood interprets the salted mine as the perfect metaphor for the "metamorphosis of the land from fertility to profitability, from subsistence farming to cash farming" (167).

360.31 **fifty:** thirty in the first edition (414).

361.3 **1891:** 1871 in first edition (414). 1896 in "Lizards" (151).

361.4 **1901:** 1879 in first edition (414). 1901 in "Lizards" (151).

361.19 **Get out of my hole," he said. "Get outen it":** These are the final words of the short story (151).

362.1 **ewer:** "a pitcher, especially a decorative one with a base, an oval body, and a flaring spout" (*AHD*).

362.1 **slop jar:** "a large, bucket-shaped chamber pot, used in the absence of plumbing, both for urine and for waste water from the wash basin. Sometimes there was a separate chamber pot" (Brown 180).

362.15-37 **then Flem Snopes and then his wife came out...and that was all:** See note 354.18-20.

363.19 **Grover Cleveland Winbush:** Aaron Rideout in the first edition (417).

363.23 **Winbush:** Rideout in the first edition (417).

363.29 **fifty:** thirty in the first edition (417). See notes 3.24 and 336.25-36.

363.39-364.2 **the countless overlapping prints of rims and iron shoes were like shouts in a deserted church:** Faulkner insists that, in violating the land, the diggers and onlookers are defiling a sacred spot. See other references to violation at 336.25 and 343.27-29.

364.34-5 **dishing and ungreased wheels:** Brown explains that "when a wagon [wheel] is made, it is deliberately 'dished' i.e. made with one side concave. This is the side toward the wagon, and the structure of the wheel is such that it is straightened into one plane by the addition of weight." The wheels of these ramshackle wagons, however, are becoming concave on the outside and will soon fall apart" (71).

365.16 **snuff sticks:** "a small stick about the size of a large kitchen match, made of green wood, often of blackgum. One end of the stick is chewed until it is moist and soft; then it is dipped into a box or bottle of snuff, and the end is either chewed or rubbed about the teeth and gums. This practice is known as dipping snuff" (Brown 182).

365.29-31 "Couldn't no other man have done it. Anybody might have fooled Henry Armstid. But couldn't nobody but Flem Snopes have fooled Ratliff": Ratliff is nobody's fool, as the speaker acknowledges. He is the most level-headed of the traders in *Ham*, and the reader at this point in the novel has come to rely on his good judgment and on his capacity to resist foolish temptations. It is then a measure of Flem's superior skill that he can best Ratliff at his own game in this ultimate episode. See notes 87.33-39 and 71.8-13.

366.14-27 **Armstid continued to run until he stumbled and fell headlong..."Come up," he said:** The explicit juxtaposition of Flem Snopes, moving up and out after having conquered Frenchman's Bend, and Henry Armstid, literally falling down after having lost everything, including his sanity, concludes the novel on a somber note. Flem's final words recall Ratliff's address to his team, "Come up rabbits. Let's head for town" (50.7). Finally, Flem's advance toward Jefferson echoes Sarty Snopes's advance toward the future in "Barn": "He did not look back" (25).

Works Cited

Adams, Richard. "The Apprenticeship of William Faulkner." *Faulkner: Four Decades of Criticism.* Ed. Linda Wagner. East Lansing: Michigan State UP, 1973. 7-44.

----------. "Faulkner: The European Roots." *Faulkner: Fifty Years After the Marble Faun.* Ed. George H. Wolfe. University, Ala.: U of Alabama P, 1976.

----------. *Faulkner: Myth and Motion.* Princeton: Princeton UP, 1968.

The American Heritage Dictionary of the English Language. Third edition. Boston: Houghton Mifflin, 1992.

Anderson, Sherwood. *The Portable Sherwood Anderson.* Ed. Horace Gregory. New York: Viking, 1949.

Arnold, Edward. *Annotations to William Faulkner's* Mosquitoes. New York: Garland, 1989.

Balzac, Honore de. *At the Sign of the Cat and Racket. Balzac: Complete Novelettes.* New York: Collier, 1926. 698-735.

----------. *Eugenie Grandet.* Trans. Clara Bell. Philadelphia: Avil Publishing Co, 1901.

----------. *Gobseck. Balzac: Complete Novelettes.* New York: Collier, 1926. 265-305.

----------. *The Peasantry.* Trans. Ellen Marriage. Philadelphia: Avil Publishing Co, 1901.

Bartlett, Phyllis. "Other Countries, Other Wenches." *Modern Fiction Studies* 3 (Winter 1957-58): 345-49.

Beck, Warren. *Faulkner.* Madison: U of Wisconsin P, 1976.

----------. *Man in Motion.* Madison: U of Wisconsin P, 1963.

Benét, Stephen Vincent. "The Devil and Daniel Webster." *Twenty-Five Short Stories of Stephen Vincent Benet.* Garden City, N.J.: Sun Dial P, 1943. 162-183.

Bleikastan, Andre. *The Ink of Melancholy.* Bloomington: Indiana UP, 1990.

Blotner, Joseph. *Faulkner: A Biography.* 2 vols. New York: Random House, 1974.

----------. *Faulkner: A Biography.* 1 vol. ed. New York: Random House, 1984.

----------, ed. *The Selected Letters of William Faulkner*. New York: Random House, 1977.

----------, comp. *William Faulkner's Library: A Catalogue*. Charlottesville: UP of Virginia, 1964.

---------- and Gwynn, Frederick, eds. *Faulkner in the University: Class Conferences at the University of Virginia 1957-1958*. Charlottesville: UP of Virginia, 1959.

Boswell, George. "The Legendary Background in Faulkner's Work." *Mississippi Folklore Register* 21 (Spring/Fall 1987): 29-39.

Braswell, Mary. "'Pardners Alike': William Faulkner's Use of *The Pardoner's Tale*?" *English Language Notes* 23 (September 1985): 66-70.

Brodsky, Louis Daniel, and Robert Hamblin. *A Comprehensive Guide to the Brodsky Collection II*. Jackson: UP of Mississippi, 1984.

Brooks, Cleanth. *Toward Yoknapatawpha and Beyond*. New Haven: Yale UP, 1978.

----------. *William Faulkner: The Yoknapatawpha Country*. New Haven: Yale UP, 1963.

Broughton, Panthea Reid. "Masculinity and Menfolk in *The Hamlet*." *Mississippi Quarterly* 22 (Summer 1969): 181-89.

Brown, Calvin. *A Glossary of Faulkner's South*. New Haven: Yale UP, 1976.

Brown, John. *101 Years on Wall Street: An Investor's Almanac*. Englewood Cliffs, N.J.: Prentice Hall, 1991.

Browning, Robert. *The Poetical Works of Robert Browning*. Boston: Houghton Mifflin, 1974.

Bull, John, and John Ferrand, eds. *Audubon Society Field Guide to North American Birds*. New York: Knopf, 1977.

Bullfinch, Thomas. *The Age of Fable*. 1855. New York: New American Library, 1962.

Bungert, Hans. *William Faulkner und die humoristische Tradition des amerikanischen Suden*. Heidelberg: Carl Winter Universitatsverlag, 1971.

Butterworth, Keen. "A Census of Manuscripts of William Faulkner's Poetry." *A Faulkner Miscellany*. Ed. James B. Meriwether. Jackson: UP of Mississippi, 1974.

Butterworth, Keen and Nancy. *Annotations to William Faulkner's A Fable*. New York: Garland, 1989.

Byron, George Gordon. *Don Juan*. 1819, 1823-24. Boston: Houghton Mifflin, 1958.

----------. *Lord Byron: The Complete Poetical Works*. 3 vols. Ed. Jerome J. McGann. Oxford: Clarendon, 1981.
Cabell, James Branch. *Jurgen*. New York: Robert McBride, 1919. rpt. 1928.
Caldwell, Erskine. *God's Little Acre*. New York: Modern Library, 1933.
Campbell, Bruce and Elizabeth Lack. *A Dictionary of Birds*. Bath: Buteo Books, 1985.
Campbell, Harry Modean, and Ruel E. Foster, *William Faulkner: A Critical Appraisal*. New York: Cooper Square, 1970.
Cason, Clarence. *90° in the Shade*. Chapel Hill: U of North Carolina P, 1935.
Cassidy, Frederic, ed. *Dictionary of American Regional English*. Cambridge: Belknap P, 1991.
Cather, Willa. *A Lost Lady*. New York: Knopf, 1923.
----------. *My Ántonia*. 1918. Boston: Houghton Mifflin, 1988.
----------. *O Pioneers!* 1913. Boston: Houghton Mifflin, 1988.
----------. *One of Ours*. New York: Knopf, 1922.
Chaucer, Geoffrey. *The Canterbury Tales*. 1388-1400. *The Riverside Chaucer*. 3rd ed. Ed. Larry D. Benson. Boston: Houghton Mifflin, 1987. 3-328.
Cirlot, J. E. *A Dictionary of Symbols*. Trans. Jack Sage. London: Routledge and Kegan Paul, 1962.
Cohen, Philip. "French Peasants and Southern Snopeses: Balzac's *Les Paysans* and Faulkner's *The Hamlet*." *Mississippi Quarterly* 40 (Fall 1987): 383-92.
----------. "The Influence of *La Comedie Humaine* on *Flags in the Dust* and the Snopes Trilogy." *Mississippi Quarterly* 37 (Summer 1984): 325-51.
Collins, Carvel. "The Pairing of *The Sound and the Fury* and *As I Lay Dying*." *Princeton University Library Chronicle* 18 (Spring 1957): 114-123.
The Compact Edition of the Oxford English Dictionary. 3 vols. Ed. R. W. Burchfield. Oxford: Clarendon P, 1987.
Conant, Roger and Collins, Joseph. *Field Guide to Reptiles and Amphibians*. New York: Houghton Mifflin, 1991.
Conrad, Joseph. *Heart of Darkness*. 1902. *Youth: A Narrative and Two Other Stories*. New York: Doubleday, 1959. 67-163.
----------. "The Nigger of the 'Narcissus.'" 1897. *Typhoon and Other Stories*. New York: Signet, 1962. 17-144.
Craigie, William and James R. Hulbert, eds. *A Dictionary of American*

English on Historical Principles. 4 vols. Chicago: U of Chicago P, 1938-44.

Crane, Stephen. *The Red Badge of Courage*. Ed. Fredson Bowers. Charlottesville: U Press of Virginia, 1975.

Cullen, John B. *Old Times in the Faulkner Country*. Chapel Hill: U of NC Press, 1961.

De Rougement, Denis. *Love in the Western World*. Revised Ed. Trans. Montgomery Belgion. New York: Pantheon, 1956.

Dickens, Charles. *Oliver Twist*. Oxford: Oxford UP, 1949. rpt. 1987.

Dimino, Andrea. "Why Did the Snopes Name Their Son 'Wallstreet Panic'? Depression Humor in Faulkner's *The Hamlet*." *Studies in American Humor* 3 (1984): 155-72.

Dostoyevsky, Fyodor. *The Brothers Karamazov*. Trans. Constance Garnett. New York: Modern Library, 1950.

----------. *Crime and Punishment*. Trans. Constance Garnett. New York: Bantam, 1981.

Dunn, Margaret. "The Illusion of Freedom in *The Hamlet* and *Go Down, Moses*." *American Literature* 57 (October 1985): 407-23.

Eby, Cecil. "Ichabod Crane in Yoknapatawpha." *Georgia Review* 16 (Winter 1962): 465-69.

Eddins, Dwight. "Metahumor in Faulkner's 'Spotted Horses.'" *Ariel* 13 (January 1982): 23-31.

Eliade, Mircea, ed. *The Encyclopedia of Religion*. 16 vols. New York: Macmillan, 1987.

Eliot, T. S. *The Complete Poems and Plays 1909-1950*. New York: Harcourt Brace, 1971.

Evans, Ivor. *Brewer's Dictionary of Phrase and Fable*. Centenary Edition. New York: Harper and Row, 1970.

Faulkner, John. *My Brother Bill: An Affectionate Reminiscence*. New York: Trident P, 1963.

Faulkner, William. *Absalom, Absalom!* New York: Random House, 1936.

----------. *As I Lay Dying*. 1930. New York: Random House, 1964.

----------. "As I Lay Dying." Ed. James B. Meriwether. *Mississippi Quarterly* 39 (Summer 1986): 369-85.

----------. *Collected Stories*. New York: Random House, 1950.

----------. *Country Lawyer and Other Stories for the Screen*. Eds. Louis Daniel Brodsky and Robert W. Hamblin. Jackson: UP of Mississippi, 1987.

----------. *Early Prose and Poetry*. Ed. Carvel Collins. Boston: Little, Brown, 1962.

----------. *Elmer.* Ed. Diane L. Cox. Northport, Ala.: Seajay P, 1983.
----------. *A Fable.* New York: Random House, 1954.
----------. *Father Abraham.* Ed. James B. Meriwether. New York: Random House, 1984.
----------. *Flags in the Dust.* Ed. Douglas Day. New York: Random House, 1973.
----------. "The Flowers That Died." *Contempo* 3 (June 25, 1933): 1.
----------. *Go Down, Moses.* New York: Random House, 1942.
----------. *The Hamlet.* New York: Random House, 1940.
----------. *The Hamlet.* 3rd ed. New York: Random House, 1964.
----------. *Intruder in the Dust.* New York: Random House, 1948.
----------. *Knight's Gambit.* New York: Random House, 1949.
----------. *Light in August.* New York: Harrison Smith and Robert Haas, 1932.
----------. *The Mansion.* New York: Random House, 1959.
----------. *The Marionettes.* Intro. Noel Polk. Charlottesville: UP of Virginia, 1977.
----------. *The Marble Faun and A Green Bough.* New York: Random House, 1965.
----------. *Mayday.* Intro. Carvel Collins. Notre Dame: UP of Notre Dame, 1978.
----------. *Mosquitoes.* New York: Boni and Liveright, 1927.
----------. *The Portable Faulkner.* Ed. Malcolm Cowley. New York: Viking, 1946.
----------. *New Orleans Sketches.* Intro. Carvel Collins. London: Sidgwick and Jackson, 1959.
----------. *Pylon.* 1935. New York: Vintage, 1987.
----------. *The Reivers.* New York: Random House, 1962.
----------. *Requiem for a Nun.* New York: Random House, 1951.
----------. *Sanctuary.* New York: Modern Library, 1932.
----------. *Sanctuary: The Corrected Text.* 1985. New York: Vintage, 1987.
----------. *Sanctuary: The Original Text.* Ed. Noel Polk. New York: Random House, 1981.
----------. *Soldier's Pay.* New York: Boni and Liveright, 1926.
----------. *The Sound and the Fury.* New York: Random House, 1929. rpt. 1956.
----------. "Spring." *Contempo* 1 (February 1, 1932): 2.
----------. *The Town.* New York: Random House, 1957.
----------. *Uncollected Stories of William Faulkner.* Ed. Joseph Blotner.

New York: Random House, 1979.

----------. *The Unvanquished.* New York: Random House, 1938.

----------. *The Wild Palms.* 1939. New York: Modern Library, 1984.

Festa-McCormick, Diana. *Honoré de Balzac.* New York: G. K. Hall, 1979.

Fitzgerald, Edward. "The Rubaiyat of Omar Khayyam." 1859-1879. *The Letters and Literary Remains of Edward Fitzgerald VII.* 7 vols. New York: AMS P, 1966. 1-186.

Flaubert, Gustave. *Madame Bovary.* Trans. Francis Steegmuller. New York: Random House, 1957.

----------. *The Temptation of St. Anthony.* Trans. Lafcadio Hearn. New York: Williams Belasco, 1930.

Foote, Shelby. *Fort Sumter to Perryville.* New York: Random House, 1958. Vol. 1 of *The Civil War: A Narrative.* 3 vols. 1958-1974.

----------. *Fredericksburg to Meridian.* New York: Random House, 1963. Vol. 2 of *The Civil War: A Narrative.* 3 vols. 1958-1974.

----------. *Red River to Appomattox.* New York: Random House, 1974. Vol. 3 of *The Civil War: A Narrative.* 3 vols. 1958-1974.

Franklin, Malcolm. *Bitterweeds: Life at Rowan Oak with William Faulkner.* Irving, Tex.: Society for the Study of Traditional Culture, 1977. .

Frazer, Sir James. *The Golden Bough.* 1 vol. abridged ed. New York: Macmillan, 1922. rpt. 1941.

Freeman, David, ed. *Anchor Bible Dictionary.* 6 vols. New York: Doubleday, 1992.

Galewitz, Herb and Don Winslow, eds. *Fontaine Fox's Toonerville Trolley.* New York: Weathervane Books, 1972.

Gidley, Mark. "One Continuous Force: Notes on Faulkner's Extra-Literary Reading." *Faulkner: Four Generations of Criticism.* Ed. Linda Wagner. East Lansing, Mich: Michigan State UP, 1973. 55-67.

Goethe, Johann Wolfgang von. *Faust.* Trans. Bayard Taylor. New York: Modern Library, 1950.

Gold, Joseph. "The Normality of Snopesism." *Faulkner: Four Decades of Criticism.* Ed. Linda Wagner. East Lansing, Mich: Michigan State UP, 1973. 318-326.

Graves, Robert. *The Greek Myths.* 1 vol. ed. Mt. Kisco, New York: Moyer Bell, 1988.

Greene, Wilhelmina and Hugo Blomquist. *Flowers of the South: Native and Exotic.* Chapel Hill: U of North Carolina P, 1953.

Greet, Thomas. "The Theme and Structure of Faulkner's *The Hamlet.*"

Faulkner: Four Decades of Criticism. Ed. Linda Wagner. East Lansing, Mich: Michigan State UP, 1973. 302-317.

Gresset, Michel. *Fascination: Faulkner's Fiction, 1919-1936*. Adapted from the French by Thomas West. Durham: Duke UP, 1989.

Grimal, Pierre. *The Concise Dictionary of Classical Mythology*. Trans. A. R. Maxwell-Hyslop. New York: Basil Blackwell, 1990.

Grimwood, Michael. *Heart in Conflict: Faulkner's Struggles with Vocation*. Athens: U of Georgia P, 1987.

Guerard, Albert J. *The Triumph of the Novel*. New York: Oxford UP, 1976.

Guirand, Felix. *New Larousse Encyclopedia of Mythology*. Trans. Richard Aldington and Delano Ames. New York: Prometheus P, 1959.

Hammond, N. G. L. and H. H. Scullard. *Oxford Classical Dictionary*. Oxford: Clarendon P, 1970.

Hardy, Thomas. *Jude the Obscure*. Boston: Houghton Mifflin, 1965.

----------. *The Mayor of Casterbridge*. Boston: Houghton Mifflin, 1962.

----------. *The Return of the Native*. New York: Macmillan, 1961.

----------. *Tess of the D'Urbervilles*. London: Chatto and Windus, 1981.

Harkness, Bruce. "Faulkner and Scott." *Mississippi Quarterly* 20 (Summer 1967): 164.

Harris, George Washington. *Sut Lovingood: Yarns Spun by a Nat'ral Born Durn'd Fool*. Memphis: St. Luke's P, 1987.

Harvey, Paul and Heseltine, J. E. *Oxford Companion to French Literature*. Oxford: Clarendon P, 1959.

Heck, Francis. "Zola's Nana: A Source for Faulkner's Eula Varner." *Arizona Quarterly* 40 (Winter 1984): 293-304.

Hoffman, Daniel. *Faulkner's Country Matters*. Baton Rouge: Louisiana State UP, 1989.

Hönnighausen, Lothar. *William Faulkner: The Art of Stylization in His Early Graphic and Literary Work*. Cambridge: Cambridge UP, 1987.

Hooper, Johnson Jones. *Some Adventures of Captain Simon Suggs, Late of the Tallapoosa Volunteers, Together with "Taking the Census" and Other Alabama Sketches*. Philadelphia: Carey and Hart, 1846.

Howatson, M. C., ed. *Oxford Companion to Classical Literature*. 2nd ed. Oxford: Oxford UP, 1989.

Howell, John. "Faulkner, Prufrock, and Agamemnon: Horses, Hell, and High Water." *Faulkner: The Unappeased Imagination*. Ed. Glenn O. Carey. Troy, N.Y.: Whitson, 1980. 213-30.

Inge, M. Thomas. *Faulkner, Sut, and Other Southerners*. West Cornwall, Ct.: Locust Hill P, 1992.

Irving, Washington. "The Legend of Sleepy Hollow." *Selected Writings of Washington Irving*. Ed. Saxe Commins. New York: Modern Library, 1945. 21-50.

Irwin, John. *Doubling and Incest/ Repetition and Revenge: A Speculative Reading of William Faulkner*. Baltimore: Johns Hopkins UP, 1975.

Jarrett, David W. "Eustacia Vye and Eula, Olympians: The Worlds of William Faulkner and Thomas Hardy." *Novel* 6 (Winter 1973): 163-74.

Jehlen, Myra. *Class and Character in Faulkner's South*. New York: Columbia UP, 1976.

Johnson, Gerald. *The Wasted Land*. Chapel Hill: U of North Carolina P, 1937.

Kartiganer, Donald. *The Fragile Thread*. Amherst: U of Massachusetts P, 1979.

Keats, John. *Poetical Works*. Ed. H. W. Garrod. London: Oxford UP, 1956.

Kendrick, Benjamin Burks. *The South Looks at Its Past*. Chapel Hill: U of North Carolina P, 1935.

Kibler, James. *A Study of the Text of William Faulkner's The Hamlet*. Diss. U of South Carolina, 1970.

Kreiswirth, Martin. *William Faulkner: The Making of a Novelist*. Athens: U of Georgia P, 1983.

Leach, Maria. *Standard Dictionary of Folklore, Mythology and Legend*. 2 vols. New York: Funk and Wagnalls, 1949-50.

Lind, Ilse Dusoir. "Faulkner Studies and Women's Studies." *Faulkner and Women: Faulkner and Yoknapatawpha 1985*. Ed. Doreen Fowler and Ann Abadie. Jackson: UP of Mississippi, 1986. 21-40.

Longstreet, Augustus Baldwin. *Georgia Scenes*. 1835. Atlanta: Cherokee Publishing, 1971.

Luce, Diane. *Annotations to William Faulkner's* As I Lay Dying. New York: Garland, 1990.

Mallarmé, Stephane. *Poems*. Trans. Roger Fry. New York: New Directions, 1951.

Marlowe, Christopher. *Doctor Faustus*. *Christopher Marlowe: The Complete Works*. Ed. Fredson Bowers. 2 vols. Cambridge: Cambridge UP, 1973. II: 121-272.

----------. *Jew of Malta*. *Christopher Marlowe: The Complete Works*. Ed. Fredson Bowers. 2 vols. Cambridge: Cambridge UP, 1973. I: 253-352.

Matthews, Mitford, ed. *A Dictionary of Americanisms on Historical*

Principles. 2 vols. Chicago: U of Chicago P, 1951.

McDaniel, Linda Elkins. *Annotations to William Faulkner's* Flags in the Dust. New York: Garland, 1991.

McHaney, Thomas. "The Falkners and the Origin of Yoknapatawpha County: Some Corrections." *Mississippi Quarterly* 25 (Summer 1972): 249-264.

----------. "What Faulkner Learned from the Tall Tale." *Faulkner and Humor.* Eds. Doreen Fowler and Ann J. Abadie. Jackson: UP of Mississippi, 1986. 110-35.

----------. *William Faulkner Manuscripts 15: The Hamlet.* 2 vols. James B. Meriwether, Senior Consulting Editor. New York: Garland, 1987.

----------. *William Faulkner's* Wild Palms: *A Study.* Jackson: UP of Mississippi, 1975.

Meeter, Glenn. "Male and Female in *Light in August* and *The Hamlet*: Faulkner's Mythical Method." *Studies in the Novel* 20 (Winter 1988): 404-16.

Meider, Wolfgang. *The Prentice-Hall Encyclopedia of World Proverbs.* Englewood Cliffs, N.J.: Prentice-Hall, 1986.

Meriwether, James B., ed. *Essays Speeches and Public Letters by William Faulkner.* London: Chatto and Windus, 1967.

Meriwether, James B., and Michael Millgate, eds. *Lion in the Garden: Interviews with William Faulkner.* New York: Random House, 1968.

----------. *The Literary Career of William Faulkner: A Bibliographical Study.* Columbia: U of South Carolina P, 1971.

Millgate, Michael. *The Achievement of William Faulkner.* 1966. Athens: U of Georgia, 1988.

Millum, Richard. "The Horns of Dawn: Faulkner and Metaphor." *American Notes and Queries* 11 (May 73): 34.

Milne, Lorus and Margery. *The Audubon Society Field Guide to North American Insects and Spiders.* New York: Knopf, 1980.

Mississippi: A Guide to the Magnolia State. New York: Viking, 1938.

Moreland, Richard C. "Antisemitism, Humor and Rage in William Faulkner's *The Hamlet. Faulkner Journal* 3:1 (Fall 1987): 52-70.

----------. *Faulkner and Modernism.* Madison: U of Wisconsin P, 1990.

Morell, Giliane. "Prisoners of the Inner World: Mother and Daughter in 'Miss Zilphia Gant.'" *Mississippi Quarterly* 28 (Summer 1975): 299-305.

Nicholaisen, Peter. "'The Dark Land Talking the Voiceless Speech': Faulkner and 'Native Soil.'" *Mississippi Quarterly* 45 (Summer 1992): 253-76.

O'Donnell, George Marion. "Faulkner's Mythology." *Faulkner: Four Decades of Criticism.* Ed. Linda Wagner. East Lansing, Mich: Michigan State UP, 1973. 83-93.

Odum, Harold. *Southern Regions of the United States.* Chapel Hill: U of North Carolina P, 1936.

Ohashi, Kenzaburo. "Creation Through Repetition or Self-Parody." *Faulkner Studies in Japan.* Ed. Thomas L. McHaney. Athens: U of Georgia P, 1985. 15-27.

Onoe, Masaji. "Some T. S. Eliot Echoes in Faulkner." *Faulkner Studies in Japan.* Ed. Thomas L. McHaney. Athens: U of Georgia P, 1985. 45-61.

Opie, Iona and Peter. *The Classic Fairy Tales.* New York: Oxford UP, 1974.

Opie, Iona, ed. *A Dictionary of Superstitions.* Oxford: Oxford UP, 1989.

Owsley, Frank L. *Plain Folk of the Old South.* Baton Rouge: Louisiana State UP, 1949.

Parker, Richard. "Two-Way Texan: The Name, Symbols and Function of Faulkner's Buck Hipps." *Notes on Contemporary Literature* 18 (March 1988): 11-12.

Partridge, Eric. *A Dictionary of Slang and Unconventional English.* 8th ed. New York: Macmillan, 1984.

Peterson, Harold L. *Encyclopedia of Firearms.* New York: Dutton, 1964.

Petrides, George A. *A Field Guide to Trees and Shrubs.* 2nd ed. Boston: Houghton Mifflin, 1972.

Pitavy, Francois. "Idiocy and Idealism: A Reflection on the Faulknerian Idiot." *Faulkner and Idealism.* Eds. Michel Gresset and Patrick Samway. Jackson: UP of Mississippi, 1983. 97-111.

Poe, Edgar Allen. "To Helen." *Edgar Allen Poe: Selected Prose, Poetry, and Eureka.* New York: Holt, Rinehart, 1950. 457.

Polk, Noel. "I Taken an Oath of Office Too: Faulkner and the Law." *Fifty Years of Yoknapatawpha: Faulkner and Yoknapatawpha 1979.* Eds. Doreen Fowler and Ann J. Abadie. Jackson: UP of Mississippi, 1980. 159-178.

----------. "Women and the Feminine in *A Fable*." *Faulkner and Women: Faulkner and Yoknapatawpha 1985.* Eds. Doreen Fowler and Ann J. Abadie. Jackson: UP of Mississippi, 1986. 180-204.

Preston, Richard J. *North American Trees.* Ames, Iowa: Iowa State UP, 1948. rpt. 1969.

Prior, Linda. "Theme, Imagery, and Structure in *The Hamlet*." *Mississippi Quarterly* 22 (Summer 1969): 237-56.

Pruvot, Monique. "Le Sacre de la Vache." *Delta* 3 (1976): 105-122.

Raper, Arthur. *Preface to Peasantry: A Tale of Two Black Belt Communities*. Chapel Hill: U of North Carolina P, 1936.

Ragan, David Paul. *Annotations to William Faulkner's* Absalom, Absalom!. New York: Garland, 1991.

Roller, David and Robert W. Twyman, eds. *Encyclopedia of Southern History*. Baton Rouge: Louisiana State UP, 1979.

Ross, Stephen. *Fiction's Inexhaustible Voice*. Athens: U of Georgia P, 1989.

Rossetti, Dante Gabriel. "The Blessed Damozel." *The Collected Works of Dante Gabriel Rossetti*. Ed. William Rossetti. Vol. 1. London: Ellis and Elvey, 1897. 232-36.

Rousselle, Melinda McLeod. *Annotations to William Faulkner's* Sanctuary. New York: Garland, 1989.

Schmitz, Neil. "Forms of Regional Humor." *The Columbia Literary History of the United States*. Ed. Emory Elliot. New York: Columbia UP, 1988. 306-23.

Seigneuret, Jean-Charles. *Dictionary of Literary Themes and Motifs*. Westport, Ct.: Greenwood P, 1988.

Sensibar, Judith. *The Origins of Faulkner's Art*. Austin: U of Texas P, 1984.

Shakespeare, William. *The Complete Signet Classic Shakespeare*. Ed. Sylvan Barnet. New York: Harcourt Brace, 1972.

Shaw, George Bernard. *Man and Superman*. 1903. *Complete Plays with Prefaces*. 6 vols. New York: Dodd, Mead, 1963. III: 483-694.

----------. *The Perfect Wagnerite*. 4th ed. 1923. New York: Dover, 1967.

Shelley, Percy Bysshe. *The Complete Poetical Works of Percy Bysshe Shelley*. Ed. Neville Rogers. 4 vols. Oxford: Clarendon P, 1975.

Showett, H. K. "Faulkner and Scott: Addendum." *Mississippi Quarterly* 22 (Spring 1969): 152-53.

Snell, Susan. *Phil Stone of Oxford: A Vicarious Life*. Athens: U of Georgia P, 1991.

Snyder, Lynn. "Doors, Windows, and Peepholes in *The Hamlet*." *Notes on Mississippi Writers* 21 (1989): 19-30.

Stephen, Leslie and Sidney Lee, eds. *Dictionary of National Biography*. 22 vols. Oxford: Oxford UP, 1967-68.

Stevenson, Burton. *The Macmillan Book of Proverbs, Maxims, and Famous Phrases*. New York: Macmillan, 1968.

Street, James. *Look Away!: A Dixie Notebook*. New York: Viking, 1936.

Swift, Jonathon. *Gulliver's Travels*. New York: Dodd, Mead, 1950.

Swinburne, Algernon Charles. *Poems*. New York: Modern Library. [n.d.].
Symons, Arthur. *The Symbolist Movement in Literature*. New York: Dutton, 1958.
Synge, J. M. *The Playboy of the Western World. The Collected Works of J. M. Synge IV*. Washington: Catholic U of America P, 1982. 51-175.
Taylor, Nancy Dew. *Annotations to William Faulkner's* Go Down Moses. Diss. U of South Carolina, 1990.
Terres, John. *Audubon Society Encyclopedia of North American Birds*. New York: Knopf, 1980.
Thackeray, William Makepeace. *Henry Esmond*. New York: Dodd, Mead, 1945.
Thorpe, Thomas Bangs. *A Repository of Sketches, Including American Character Scenery and Rural Sports*. New York: Appleton, 1854.
Tolstoy, Leo. *Anna Karenina*. 2 vols. Trans. Constance Garnett. New York: Random House, 1939.
Trouard, Dawn. "Eula's Plot: An Irigrarian Reading of Faulkner's Snopes Trilogy." *Mississippi Quarterly* 42 (Summer 1989): 281-97.
Twain, Mark. *Roughing It*. New York: Signet, 1980.
Vance, Rupert. *Human Factors in Cotton Culture: A Study in the Social Geography of the South*. Chapel Hill: U of North Carolina P, 1929.
Walton, Gerald. "A Word List of Southern Farm Terms from Faulkner's *The Hamlet*." *Mississippi Folklore Register* 6 (Summer 1972): 60-75.
Wasson, Ben. *Count No' Count: Flashbacks to Faulkner*. Jackson: U of Mississippi P, 1983.
Watson, James M. *Thinking of Home: William Faulkner's Letters to His Mother and Father 1918-1925*. New York: Norton, 1992.
Watson, Jay. *Forensic Fictions*. Athens: U of Georgia P, 1993.
Weisgerber, Jean. *Faulkner and Dostoievsky*. Athens, Ohio: Ohio UP, 1968.
Wentworth, Harold, ed. *American Dialect Dictionary*. New York: Thomas Y. Crowell, 1944.
Wentworth, Harold and Stuart Berg Flexner, eds. Dictionary of American Slang. New York: Thomas Y. Crowell, 1960.
Weston, Jesse. *From Ritual to Romance*. Garden City: Doubleday, 1957.
Wheeler, Otis. "Some Uses of Folk Humor by Faulkner." *Faulkner: Four Generations of Criticism*. Ed. Linda Wagner. East Lansing, Mich: Michigan State UP, 1973. 68-82.
Williamson, Joel. *William Faulkner and Southern History*. New York: Oxford UP, 1993.

Wilson, Charles Reagan and Ferris, William. *Encyclopedia of Southern Culture*. Chapel Hill: U of North Carolina P, 1989.

Wilson, F. P. *The Oxford Dictionary of English Proverbs*. Third Edition. Oxford: Oxford UP, 1970.

Wittenberg, Judith Bryant. "Faulkner and Women Writers." *Faulkner and Women: Faulkner and Yoknapatawpha, 1985*. Jackson: U P of Mississippi, 1986.

Woodward, C. Vann. *Origins of the New South: 1877-1913*. 1951. Baton Rouge: Louisiana State UP, 1987.

Yonce, Margaret. *Annotations to William Faulkner's* Soldiers' Pay. New York: Garland, 1990.

Young, Stark. *The Pavilion: Of People and Times Remembered, Of Stories and Places*. New York: Scribner's, 1951.

----------. *So Red the Rose*. New York: Scribner's, 1934.

Zola, Emile. *Nana*. Trans. George Holden. New York: Penguin, 1972.